# SIDE by SIDE

## Plus

Book & eText **3**

Life Skills & Test Prep

Career & Academic Readiness

Expanded Reading & Writing

Digital FunZone & Audio

**Steven J. Molinsky** • **Bill Bliss**

Illustrated by **Richard E. Hill**

**Side by Side Plus Book & eText 3**

Pearson Education, 10 Bank Street, White Plains, NY 10606

**Staff credits:** The people who make up the *Side by Side Plus* team, representing content creation, design, manufacturing, marketing, multimedia, project management, publishing, rights management, and testing are Pietro Alongi, Allen Ascher, Rhea Banker, Elizabeth Barker, Lisa Bayrasli, Elizabeth Carlson, Jennifer Castro, Tracey Munz Cataldo, Diane Cipollone, Aerin Csigay, Victoria Denkus, Dave Dickey, Daniel Dwyer, Wanda España, Oliva Fernandez, Warren Fischbach, Pam Fishman, Nancy Flaggman, Patrice Fraccio, Irene Frankel, Aliza Greenblatt, Lester Holmes, Janet Johnston, Caroline Kasterine, Barry Katzen, Ray Keating, Renee Langan, Jaime Lieber, José Antonio Méndez, Julie Molnar, Alison Pei, Pamela Pia, Stuart Radcliffe, Jennifer Raspiller, Kriston Reinmuth, Mary Perrotta Rich, Tania Saiz-Sousa, Katherine Sullivan, Paula Van Ells, Kenneth Volcjak, and Wendy Wolf.

**Contributing authors:** Laura English, Meredith Westfall

**Text composition:** TSI Graphics, Inc.

**Illustrations:** Richard E. Hill

**Photo credits:** Original photography by Paul I. Tañedo. Page 10a Fotosearch RF/Getty Images; p. 10b bahrialtay/Fotolia; p. 10c (top) jiawangkun/Fotolia, (middle) Gary Blakeley/Fotolia, (bottom) Dave Newman/Fotolia; p. 20a (1) svetamart/Fotolia, (2) Monkey Business/Fotolia, (3) Dmitry Ersler/Fotolia, (4) Jose Diez Bey/Shutterstock, (5) steve estvanik/Fotolia, (6) Jamie Wilson/Fotolia; 20c (top right) John Parrot/Stocktrek Images/Getty Images, (middle left) Susan Law Cain/Shutterstock, (middle right) ClassicStock/Alamy, (bottom left) Onur ERSIN/Shutterstock; p. 20d (top) Georgios Kollidas/Shutterstock, (middle) John Parrot/Stocktrek Images/Getty Images, (bottom) Alexander Gardner/Library of Congress (LC-DIG-ppmsca-19215); p. 20e (top) Bain Collection/Library of Congress (LC-USZ62-108038), (middle) Hulton-Deutsch Collection/Corbis; p. 33 (top) epa european pressphoto agency b.v./Alamy, (bottom) Hulton Archive/Getty Images; p. 34 (top left) Karel Miragaya/123RF, (top middle) Dan Himbrechts/Bloomberg/Getty Images, (top right) Reuters/Corbis, (middle left) Rolf Hicker Photography/Alamy, (middle) David R. Frazier Photolibrary, Inc./Alamy, (middle right) Vespasian/Alamy, (bottom) Ned Frisk/Blend Images/Getty Images; p. 36b Tyler Olson/Fotolia; p. 36c Alamy; p. 36d Tetra Images/Alamy; p. 50a (top) DWlabsInc/E+/Getty Images, (bottom) Image Source/Getty Images; p. 50c AVAVA/Shutterstock; p. 65 (top right) Sorbis/Shutterstock, (top middle right) Reuters Photographer/Reuters, (middle right) Bill Varie/Corbis, (bottom left) Ian Lishman/Juice Images/Corbis (bottom middle) LookEngland/Alamy, (bottom right) Susan Steinkamp/Corbis; p. 66 (top left) AP Images, (top middle) blickwinkel/Alamy, (top right) Gordon Wiltsie/National Geographic Image Collection/Glow Images, (middle left) Greatstock Photographic Library/Alamy, (middle) Corbis/Glow Images, (middle right) Tom Williams/Roll Call/Newscom, (bottom) Monkey Business/Fotolia; p. 68b Maridav/Fotolia; p. 68c James Marshall/The Image Works; p. 68d Juanmonino/E+/Getty Images; p. 110c (top) wavebreakmedia/Shutterstock, (bottom) Dorothy Alexander/Alamy; p. 110d (top) Paul Burns/Digital Vision/Getty Images, (bottom) RuslanDashinsky/E+/Getty Images; p. 111 (top) Colorsport/Corbis, (bottom left) AF archive/Alamy, (bottom right) epa european pressphoto agency b.v./Alamy; p. 112 (top left) Ton Koene/SuperStock, (top middle) Eye Ubiquitous/SuperStock, (top right) BPA C Xinhua News Agency/Newscom, (middle left) ITAR-TASS/Newscom, (middle) Corbis Bridge/Alamy, (middle right) AFP/Getty Images/Newscom, (bottom) Jupiterimages/Exactostock/SuperStock; p. 114b ivan kmit/Fotolia; p. 114c KAMBOU SIA/AFP/Getty Images; p. 114d (top) Implementar Films/Alamy, (bottom) Glow Asia RF/Alamy; p. 130b (top left) michaeljung/Fotolia, (top middle left) MediablitzImages/Fotolia, (top middle right) Syda Productions/Fotolia, (top right) Alexandra Karamyshev/Fotolia, (middle left) anmalkov/Fotolia, (middle right) Rubberball/Getty Images, (bottom left) Maria Mitrofanova/Fotolia, (bottom middle left) Elnur/Shutterstock, (bottom middle right) benniephoto/Fotolia, (bottom right) glamour111/Fotolia; p. 144b Ariel Skelley/Brand X/Getty Images; p. 145 Thomas Boehm/Alamy; p. 146 (US) Digital Vision/Photodisc/Getty Images, (Hindu) david pearson/Alamy, (Slovak) Magdalena Rehova/Alamy, (Korean) TOPIC PHOTO AGENCY IN/AGE Fotostock, (Romanian) Caroline Penn/Corbis, (musicians) Massimo Pizzocaro/Alamy, (confetti) kaphotokevm1/Fotolia, (petals) Purestock/Getty Images, (rice) elitravo/Shutterstock, (money) Jonathan Blair/Corbis, (candles) Cleve Bryant/PhotoEdit, Inc, (cake) Jeffrey Banke/Fotolia, (boat) Koichi Kamoshida/AsiaPac/Getty Images, (bouquet) Sergey Nivens/Shutterstock; p. 147 (top left) Stuart Jenner/Shutterstock, (top middle) Glow Images/SuperStock, (top right) ARENA Creative/Shutterstock, (bottom left) Deklofenak/Fotolia, (bottom middle left) Blend Images/Shutterstock, (bottom middle right) Jenkedco/Shutterstock, (bottom right) Mart of Images/Alamy; p. 148b Bob Mahone/The Image Works; p. 148c Frances Roberts/Alamy Stock Photo; p. 148d Andres Rodriguez/Alamy.

The authors gratefully acknowledge the contribution of Tina Carver in the development of the original *Side by Side* program.

Side by Side Plus Book & eText with Audio CD 3: ISBN 13 – 978-0-13-382899-3; ISBN 10 – 0-13-382899-9

Printed in the United States of America
3   18

# CONTENTS

Red type indicates standards-based lessons.

**Red type indicates standards-based lessons.**

Dear Friends,

Welcome to *Side by Side Plus*—a special edition for adult learners that offers an integrated standards-based and grammar-based approach to language learning!

## Flexible Language Proficiency *Plus* Life Skills

The core mission of *Side by Side Plus* is to build students' general language proficiency so they can use English flexibly to meet their varied needs, life circumstances, and goals. We strongly believe that language teachers need to preserve their role as true teachers of language even as we fill our lesson plans with required life-skill content and prepare students for standardized tests. Our program helps you accomplish this through a research-based grammatical sequence and communicative approach in which basic language lessons in each unit lead to standards-based lessons focused on students' life-skill roles in the community, family, school, and at work.

## Keys to Promoting Student Persistence and Success

**STUDENT-CENTERED LEARNING**  The core methodology of *Side by Side Plus* is the guided conversation—a brief, structured dialog that students practice in pairs and then use as a framework to create new conversations. Through this practice, students work together to develop their language skills "side by side." They are not dependent on the teacher for all instruction, and they know how to learn from each other. This student-centered methodology and the text's easy-to-use format enable students to study outside of class with any speaking partner—a family member, a friend or neighbor, a tutor, or a co-worker, even if that person is also an English language learner. If students need to attend class intermittently or "stop out" for a while, they have the skills and text material to continue learning on their own.

**MEANINGFUL INSTRUCTION RELEVANT TO STUDENTS' LIVES**  Throughout the instructional program, civics topics and tasks connect students to their community, personalization questions apply lesson content to students' life situations, and critical-thinking activities build a community of learners who problem-solve together and share solutions.

**EXTENDING LEARNING OUTSIDE THE CLASSROOM**  The magazine-style Gazette sections in *Side by Side Plus* provide motivating material for students to use at home. Feature articles, vocabulary enrichment, and other activities reinforce classroom instruction through high-interest material that

students are motivated to use outside of class. A bonus Audio CD offers entertaining radio program-style recordings of key Gazette activities. (See the inside back cover for a description of other media materials and software designed to extend learning through self-study.)

**SUFFICIENT PRACTICE + FREQUENT ASSESSMENT = SUCCESS**  Students need to experience success as language learners. While other programs "cover" many learning objectives, *Side by Side Plus* offers students carefully-sequenced intensive practice that promotes mastery and the successful application of language skills to daily life. Students can observe their achievement milestones through the program's frequent assessments, including check-up tests and skills checklists in the text and achievement tests in the accompanying workbook.

**THE "FUN FACTOR"**  We believe that language instruction is most powerful when it is joyful. There is magic in the power of humor, fun, games, and music to encourage students to take risks with their emerging language, to "play" with it, and to allow their personalities to shine through as their language skills increase. We incorporate these elements into our program to motivate students to persist in their language learning not only because they need it, but also because they enjoy it.

**MULTILEVEL INSTRUCTION**  *Side by Side Plus* provides exceptional resources to support multilevel instruction. The Teacher's Guide includes step-by-step instructions for preparing below-level and at-level students for each lesson and hundreds of multilevel activities for all students, including those above-level. The accompanying Multilevel Activity & Achievement Test Book and CD-ROM offer an array of reproducible multilevel worksheets and activities.

We hope your students enjoy using *Side by Side Plus*. We are confident that these resources will help them persist and succeed through a language learning experience that is effective . . . relevant to their lives . . . and fun!

*Steven J. Molinsky*
*Bill Bliss*

*Side by Side* has helped over 25 million students worldwide persist and succeed as language learners. Now, in this special edition for adult learners in standards-based programs, *Side by Side Plus* builds students' general language proficiency *and* helps them apply these skills for success meeting the needs of daily life and work.

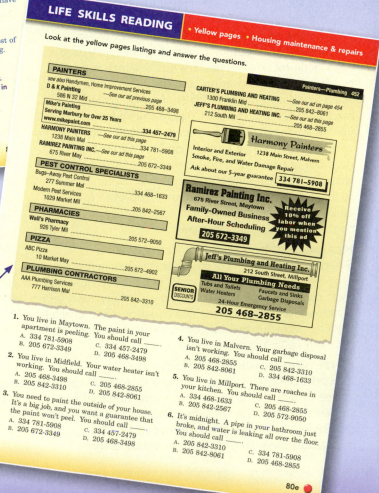

**Standards-based lessons** at the end of every unit apply students' language learning to their life-skill roles in the community, family, school, and at work. Students develop the key competencies included in CASAS, BEST Plus, EFF, SCANS, Model Standards, and other major state and local curriculum frameworks and assessment systems.

**Real-life conversation practice** in authentic life-skill situations gets students talking through interactive pair work. **Extensive photographs and illustrations** provide clear contexts and support vocabulary learning.

**Critical thinking** and **problem-solving activities** help students focus on issues and problems and share ideas, experiences, and solutions.

**Teamwork activities** promote cooperative learning as students work together in pairs, groups, or as a class to share information and complete tasks.

**Realia-based reading activities** include yellow pages listings, maps, job applications, utility bills, workplace messages, medical appointment cards, store sale signs, advertisements, coupons, a health care poster, an accident report, a rental agreement, an apartment building notice, an employee manual, and a medical history form.

**Life skills writing activities** include lists, notes, personal information forms, employment application forms, a cover letter, and a resume.

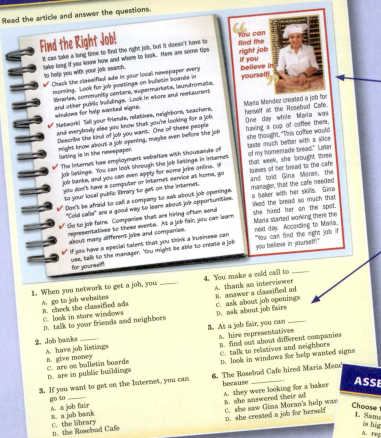

Read the article and answer the questions.

## Find the Right Job!

It can take a long time to find the right job, but it doesn't have to take long if you know how and where to look. Here are some tips to help you with your job search.

✓ Check the classified ads in your local newspaper every morning. Look for job postings on bulletin boards in libraries, community centers, supermarkets, laundromats, and other public buildings. Look in store and restaurant windows for help wanted signs.

✓ Network! Tell your friends, relatives, neighbors, teachers, and everybody else you know that you're looking for a job. Describe the kind of job you want. One of these people might know about a job opening, maybe even before the job listing is in the newspaper.

✓ The Internet has employment websites with thousands of job listings. You can look through the job listings in Internet job banks, and you can even apply for some jobs online. If you don't have a computer or Internet service at home, go to your local public library to get on the Internet.

✓ Don't be afraid to call a company to ask about job opportunities. "Cold calls" are a good way to learn about job opportunities.

✓ Go to job fairs. Companies that are hiring often send representatives to these events. At a job fair, you can learn about many different jobs and companies.

✓ If you have a special talent that you think a business can use, talk to the manager. You might be able to create a job for yourself!

*"You can find the right job if you believe in yourself!"*

Maria Mendez created a job for herself at the Rosebud Cafe. One day while Maria was having a cup of coffee there, she thought, "This coffee would taste much better with a slice of my homemade bread." Later that week, she brought three loaves of her bread to the cafe and told Gina Moran, the manager, that the cafe needed a baker with her skills. Gina liked the bread so much that she hired her on the spot. Maria started working there the next day. According to Maria, "You can find the right job if you believe in yourself!"

1. When you network to get a job, you ——.
   A. go to job websites
   B. check the classified ads
   C. look in store windows
   D. talk to your friends and neighbors

2. Job banks ——.
   A. have job listings
   B. give money
   C. are on bulletin boards
   D. are in public buildings

3. If you want to get on the Internet, you can go to ——.
   A. a job fair
   B. a job bank
   C. the library
   D. the Rosebud Cafe

4. You make a cold call to ——.
   A. thank an interviewer
   B. answer a classified ad
   C. ask about job openings
   D. ask about job fairs

5. At a job fair, you can ——.
   A. hire representatives
   B. find out about different companies
   C. talk to relatives and neighbors
   D. look in windows for help wanted signs

6. The Rosebud Cafe hired Maria Mendez because ——.
   A. they were looking for a baker
   B. she answered their ad
   C. she saw Gina Moran's help wanted [sign]
   D. she created a job for herself

**Narrative reading passages** offer practice with simple magazine articles on topics such as job search strategies, identity theft, small talk at work, and career advancement. **Academic lessons** in school textbook formats prepare students for success in continuing education through subject-matter content including government, history, and health.

**Reading comprehension exercises** in multiple-choice formats help students prepare for the reading section of standardized tests.

**Check-up tests** allow a quick assessment of student achievement and help prepare students for the kinds of test items found on standardized tests.

More complete **Achievement Tests** for each unit, including listening test items, are available as reproducible masters and printable disk files in the Teacher's Guide with Multilevel Activity & Achievement Test Book and CD-ROM. They are also available in the companion Activity & Test Prep Workbook.

**Vocabulary checklists** and **language skill checklists** help students review words they have learned, keep track of the skills they are developing, and identify vocabulary and skills they need to continue to work on. These lists promote student persistence as students assess their own skills and check off all the ways they are succeeding as language learners.

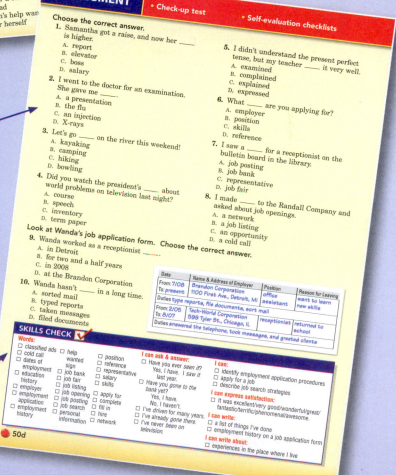

Choose the correct answer.

1. Samantha got a raise, and now her —— is higher.
   A. report
   B. elevator
   C. boss
   D. salary

2. I went to the doctor for an examination. She gave me ——.
   A. a presentation
   B. the flu
   C. an injection
   D. X-rays

3. Let's go —— on the river this weekend!
   A. kayaking
   B. camping
   C. hiking
   D. bowling

4. Did you watch the president's —— about world problems on television last night?
   A. course
   B. speech
   C. inventory
   D. term paper

5. I didn't understand the present perfect tense, but my teacher —— it very well.
   A. examined
   B. complained
   C. explained
   D. expressed

6. What —— are you applying for?
   A. employer
   B. position
   C. skills
   D. reference

7. I saw a —— for a receptionist on the bulletin board in the library.
   A. job posting
   B. job bank
   C. representative
   D. job fair

8. I made —— to the Randall Company and asked about job openings.
   A. a network
   B. a job listing
   C. an opportunity
   D. a cold call

Look at Wanda's job application form. Choose the correct answer.

9. Wanda worked as a receptionist ——.
   A. in Detroit
   B. for two and a half years
   C. in 2008
   D. at the Brandon Corporation

10. Wanda hasn't —— in a long time.
   A. sorted mail
   B. typed reports
   C. taken messages
   D. filed documents

| Date | Name & Address of Employer | Position | Reason for Leaving |
|---|---|---|---|
| From: 7/08 To: present | Brandon Corporation 1100 First Ave., Detroit, MI | office assistant | want to learn new skills |
| Duties: type reports, file documents, sort mail | | | |
| From: 2/05 To: 8/07 | Tech-World Corporation 599 Tyler St., Chicago, IL | receptionist | returned to school |
| Duties: answered the telephone, took messages, and greeted clients | | | |

**SKILLS CHECK** ✓

**Words:**
- ☐ classified ads
- ☐ cold call
- ☐ dates of employment
- ☐ education history
- ☐ employer
- ☐ employment application
- ☐ employment history
- ☐ help wanted sign
- ☐ job bank
- ☐ job fair
- ☐ job listing
- ☐ job opening
- ☐ job posting
- ☐ job search
- ☐ personal information
- ☐ position
- ☐ reference
- ☐ representative
- ☐ salary
- ☐ skills
- ☐ apply for
- ☐ complete
- ☐ fill in
- ☐ hire
- ☐ network

**I can ask & answer:**
- ☐ Have you ever seen it? Yes, I have. I saw it last year.
- ☐ Have you gone to the bank yet? Yes, I have. No, I haven't.
- ☐ I've driven for many years.
- ☐ I've already gone there.
- ☐ I've never been on television.

**I can:**
- ☐ identify employment application procedures
- ☐ apply for a job
- ☐ describe job search strategies

**I can express satisfaction:**
- ☐ It was excellent/very good/wonderful/great/fantastic/terrific/phenomenal/awesome.

**I can write:**
- ☐ a list of things I've done
- ☐ employment history on a job application form

**I can write about:**
- ☐ experiences in the place where I live

50d

vii

# Scope and Sequence

| Unit | Topics & Vocabulary | Grammar | Functional Communication | Listening & Pronunciation | Writing |
|---|---|---|---|---|---|
| **1** | • Describing habitual & ongoing activities<br>• Telling about likes & dislikes<br>• Describing frequency of actions<br>• Telling about personal background & interests<br>• Emergency room check-in<br>• Preventing identity theft<br>• Civics: U.S. government<br>• Reading a social studies textbook lesson | REVIEW:<br>• Simple present tense<br>• Present continuous tense<br>• Subject & object pronouns<br>• Possessive adjectives<br>• Time expressions | • Engaging in small talk about self, family, interests, & leisure activities<br>• Asking for & reacting to information<br>• Giving personal information | • Listening for correct tense & person in information questions<br>• Pronouncing reduced *are* | • Writing about studying English<br>• Writing about yourself, your family, & your interests<br>• Filling out a patient information form<br>• Writing the names of current federal, state, & local government officials |
| **2** | • Reporting past activities<br>• Mishaps<br>• Difficult experiences<br>• Describing a trip<br>• Apologizing for lateness at work<br>• Giving an excuse<br>• Traffic accident report<br>• Civics: U.S. history | REVIEW:<br>• Simple past tense (Regular & irregular verbs)<br>• Past continuous tense | • Asking for & reporting information<br>• Reacting to bad news<br>• Apologizing<br>• Giving excuses | • Listening for correct tense & meaning in information questions<br>• Pronouncing *Did you* | • Writing about a trip you took<br>• Filling out a traffic accident report<br>• Creating a timeline |
| **3** | • Describing future plans & intentions<br>• Telling about the future<br>• Expressing time & duration<br>• Talking on the telephone<br>• Plans for the future<br>• Asking a favor<br>• Calling in sick at work<br>• Calling school to report a child's absence<br>• Writing a note to the teacher<br>• Parent-school communication<br>• Reading a campus map | REVIEW:<br>• Future: Going to<br>• Future: Will<br>• Future continuous tense<br>• Time expressions<br>• Possessive pronouns | • Asking & telling about future plans<br>• Engaging in small talk about weekend plans<br>• Making a telephone call to someone you know<br>• Asking a favor<br>• Asking to borrow an item | • Listening to conversations & making deductions about people's plans<br>• Pronouncing *going to* | • Writing about something you're looking forward to<br>• Writing a note to the teacher to explain a child's absence |
| **Gazette Reading & Writing Workshop** | • Immigration around the world<br>• Ellis Island<br>• Interpreting a chart with population statistics<br>• Culture concept: Immigrant neighborhoods around the world<br>• Interview with an immigrant<br>• Idioms<br>• Education: Community college new student information | • Simple present tense<br>• Simple past tense<br>• Using present tense to express future<br>• Future: Going to<br>• Future: Will<br>• Parts of speech<br>• Combining sentences | • Describing neighborhoods<br>• Describing personal history<br>• Using idiomatic expressions | • Listening to messages on a telephone answering machine | • Writing an e-mail or instant message to tell about what you did last weekend & what you plan to do next weekend<br>• Writing a friendly letter |

## CORRELATION and PLACEMENT KEY

*Side by Side Plus 3* correlates with the following standards-based curriculum levels and assessment system score ranges.

*For correlation keys to other major state and local curriculum frameworks, please visit:*
http://pearseneltusa.com/molinskyandbliss

| | |
|---|---|
| NRS (National Reporting System) Educational Functioning Level | Low Intermediate |
| BEST Plus 2.0 (Basic English Skills Test) | 453–484 (SPL 4) |
| BEST Literacy | 64–67 (SPL 4) |
| CASAS Reading | 201–210 |
| CASAS Listening | 200–209 |
| CASAS Writing | 201–225 |
| TABE CLAS-E Reading & Writing | 483–514 |
| TABE CLAS-E Listening & Speaking | 486–525 |

## LIFE SKILLS, CIVICS, TEST PREPARATION, CURRICULUM STANDARDS AND FRAMEWORKS

| Life Skills, Civics, & Test Preparation | EFF | SCANS/Employment Competencies | CASAS | LAUSD | Florida* |
|---|---|---|---|---|---|
| • Asking & answering personal information questions: name, address, telephone number, social security number, date of birth, place of birth, height, weight, marital status<br>• Providing information about family members<br>• Checking in at an emergency room<br>• Interpreting a narrative reading about identity theft<br>• Civics: Describing three branches of government, their functions, & their elected officials<br>• Identifying current federal, state, & local government officials | • Interact in a way that is friendly<br>• Identify family relationships<br>• Develop & express sense of self<br>• Work together<br>• Keep pace with change<br>• Provide for family members' safety | • Sociability<br>• Self-esteem<br>• Participate as a member of a team | 0.2.1, 0.2.2, 0.2.4, 5.5.2, 5.5.3, 5.5.4, 5.5.8 | 1, 2, 3, 32 | 4.05.01, 4.05.02, 4.05.04, 4.12.03 |
| • Apologizing & giving a reason for being late for work<br>• Critical thinking: Good & bad excuses for being late for work<br>• Interpreting & filling out traffic accident reports<br>• Civics: U.S. history—major events, historical documents, key leaders<br>• Study skill: Creating a history timeline | • Work together<br>• Reflect & evaluate<br>• Understand, interpret, & work with symbolic information | • Self-management: Assess self accurately<br>• Responsibility<br>• Participate as a member of a team<br>• See things in the mind's eye (Interpret a diagram) | 0.1.4, 1.9.7, 5.2.1, 5.2.2 | 4b, 23 | 4.02.02, 4.02.05, 4.12.04, 4.15.03 |
| • Calling in sick at work<br>• Calling school to report a child's absence<br>• Parent-school communication<br>• Interpreting a letter to parents from a school principal<br>• Identifying U.S. school structure & grading system<br>• Describing school expectations for students & parents<br>• Interpreting a campus map to locate classrooms, offices, & other facilities | • Interact in a way that is friendly<br>• Plan: Set a goal<br>• Provide for family members' safety & physical needs<br>• Understand, interpret, & work with symbolic information | • Sociability<br>• Allocate time<br>• Responsibility<br>• Understand an organizational system (high school)<br>• See things in the mind's eye (Interpret a chart & a map) | 0.1.2, 0.1.3, 0.1.4, 0.2.4, 2.5.4, 2.5.5 | 3, 5a, 5b, 10, 11, 12b, 57 | 4.14.01, 4.14.02, 4.15.12 |
| • Interpreting narrative readings about immigration & Ellis Island<br>• Civics: U.S. immigration<br>• Interpreting statistical facts in a table<br>• Interpreting telephone messages on an answering machine | • Respect others & value diversity<br>• Understand, interpret, & work with numerical information<br>• Identify family relationships<br>• Use technology | • Acquire & evaluate information<br>• Work with cultural diversity<br>• Identify goal-relevant activities<br>• Work with technology | 0.2.1, 0.2.3, 2.1.7, 2.7.2, 4.8.7, 7.2.4 | 1, 9, 18, 50 | 4.05.01, 4.06.02, 4.15.09, 4.15.12 |

**EFF:** Equipped for the Future (Content standards, Common activities, & Role maps)
**SCANS:** Secretary's Commission on Achieving Necessary Skills (U.S. Department of Labor)
**CCRS:** College and Career Readiness Standards for Adult Education (U.S. Department of Education)
**CASAS:** Comprehensive Adult Student Assessment System
**LAUSD:** Los Angeles Unified School District (ESL Beginning High content standards)
**Florida:** Adult ESOL Low Intermediate Standardized Syllabi

(*Florida benchmarks 4.15.0, 4.16.0, and 4.17.0 are covered in every unit.)

# Scope and Sequence

| Unit | Topics & Vocabulary | Grammar | Functional Communication | Listening & Pronunciation | Writing |
|---|---|---|---|---|---|
| **4** | • Describing skills<br>• Describing actions that have occurred<br>• Describing actions that haven't occurred yet<br>• Making recommendations<br>• Things to do where you live<br>• Making lists<br>• Employment application procedures<br>• Job application forms<br>• Employment history<br>• Job search strategies | • Present perfect tense | • Expressing ability<br>• Expressing jealousy<br>• Engaging in small talk about experiences, movies, books, videos, and restaurants<br>• Inquiring about & indicating completion of tasks<br>• Expressing satisfaction | • Listening to narratives about tasks accomplished & indicating these tasks on a checklist<br>• Pronouncing contractions with *is* & *has* | • Making a checklist of tasks done at school, at work, or at home<br>• Writing about things you have done & haven't done in the place where you live<br>• Filling out a job application form |
| **5** | • Discussing duration of activity<br>• Medical symptoms & problems<br>• Career advancement<br>• Telling about family members<br>• Job interview<br>• Giving employment history<br>• Cover letters & resumes<br>• Employee manual: Workplace policies & expectations | • Present perfect vs. present tense<br>• Present perfect vs. past tense<br>• Since/For<br>• Time expressions | • Asking for & reporting information<br>• Engaging in small talk about interests & experiences<br>• Reacting to information<br>• Asking for clarification | • Listening for information about time & duration in conversations<br>• Pronouncing reduced *have* & *has* | • Writing a story about your English teacher<br>• Writing about your activities & interests<br>• Writing a cover letter & a simple resume |
| **Gazette**<br>**Reading & Writing Workshop** | • "24/7" work schedules<br>• Culture concept: Unique jobs around the world<br>• Interview with a working couple about their work schedule<br>• Interpreting a bar graph with information about vacation time in different countries<br>• Idioms<br>• Career exploration: Finding the job that is right for you | • Present perfect tense<br>• Simple present tense<br>• Since/For<br>• Common nouns & proper nouns | • Describing people's work schedules<br>• Giving your opinion<br>• Describing vacation time in different countries<br>• Using idiomatic expressions | • Listening to voice-mail messages at work | • Writing an e-mail or instant message to tell about things you have done<br>• The Writing Process |
| **6** | • Discussing duration of activity<br>• Reporting household repair problems<br>• Describing tasks accomplished<br>• Describing experiences<br>• Job interviews<br>• Renting an apartment<br>• Lease information<br>• Apartment rules<br>• Utility bills<br>• Housing maintenance & repairs<br>• Yellow pages | • Present perfect continuous tense<br>• Since/For<br>• Time expressions | • Asking for & reporting information<br>• Expressing surprise<br>• Expressing nervousness<br>• Reassuring someone<br>• Asking about & telling about previous experiences | • Listening for particular forms of verbs in sentences<br>• Listening & making deductions about who is speaking<br>• Pronouncing reduced *for* | • Writing about places where you have lived, worked, & gone to school<br>• Making a list of apartment building rules |
| **7** | • Discussing recreation preferences<br>• Discussing things you dislike doing<br>• Habits<br>• Describing talents & skills<br>• Telling about important decisions<br>• Requests at work<br>• Thanking someone<br>• Borrow & lending<br>• Workplace notes & messages<br>• "Small talk" at work | • Gerunds<br>• Infinitives<br>• Review: Present perfect & present perfect continuous tenses | • Engaging in small talk about leisure activities<br>• Introducing yourself<br>• Attracting someone's attention<br>• Offering & responding to advice<br>• Expressing envy<br>• Expressing appreciation<br>• Sharing news about future plans<br>• Congratulating | • Listening & making deductions about the context of conversations<br>• Pronouncing reduced *to* | • Writing about an important decision<br>• Making a list of topics for small talk |

## LIFE SKILLS, CIVICS, TEST PREPARATION, CURRICULUM STANDARDS AND FRAMEWORKS

| Life Skills, Civics, & Test Preparation | EFF | SCANS/Employment Competencies | CASAS | LAUSD | Florida* |
|---|---|---|---|---|---|
| • Job responsibilities<br>• Following a sequence of employment application procedures<br>• Describing employment history including employer, dates of employment, position, salary, supervisor, & reason for leaving<br>• Identifying sources of job opportunities<br>• Identifying job search strategies | • Interact in a way that is friendly<br>• Create & pursue vision & goals<br>• Work together<br>• Plan: Develop an organized approach of activities & objectives | • Sociability<br>• Self-management: Monitor progress<br>• Decision-making<br>• Allocate time<br>• Understand an organizational system (workplace operations)<br>• Identify goal-relevant activities<br>• Self-management: Set personal goals<br>• Participate as a member of a team<br>• Identify human resources (occupations & work skills) | 0.2.2, 0.2.4, 4.1.2, 4.1.3, 4.1.5, 4.6.1, 4.6.4 | 2, 3, 42, 43, 44, 45, 47b | 4.01.01, 4.01.02, 4.01.04, 4.01.05, 4.01.06 |
| • Describing medical symptoms & problems during an examination<br>• Describing family members<br>• Career advancement<br>• Job interview<br>• Describing work experience<br>• Cover letters & resumes<br>• Interpreting a new employee manual<br>• Identifying workplace policies & expectations | • Identify problems<br>• Identify a strong sense of family<br>• Identify family relationships<br>• Work together<br>• Create & pursue vision & goals<br>• Exercise rights & responsibilities | • Understand an organizational system (workplace)<br>• Participate as a member of a team<br>• Identify human resources (occupations & work skills) | 0.1.6, 0.2.1, 0.2.3, 0.2.4, 4.1.2, 4.1.5, 4.2.1, 4.2.4 | 1, 3, 7, 9, 43, 44, 46 | 4.01.01, 4.01.02, 4.01.03, 4.01.05, 4.01.06, 4.01.07 |
| • Interpreting a narrative reading about work schedules<br>• Describing working parents' activities & responsibilities<br>• Interpreting statistical information in a bar graph<br>• Interpreting voice-mail messages at the workplace | • Keep pace with change<br>• Respect others & value diversity<br>• Identify a strong sense of family<br>• Identify supportive family relationships<br>• Provide for family members' safety & physical needs<br>• Analyze & use information<br>• Understand, interpret, & work with numbers<br>• Use technology | • Work with cultural diversity<br>• Acquire & evaluate information<br>• See things in the mind's eye (Interpret a bar graph)<br>• Work with technology | 0.2.3, 2.1.7, 4.8.7, 6.7.2 | 9, 18, 50 | 4.01.01, 4.01.02, 4.02.01, 4.02.02, 4.06.02, 4.15.09, 4.15.12 |
| • Reporting apartment maintenance & repair problems<br>• Job interview<br>• Job responsibilities<br>• Inquiring about lease information when renting an apartment<br>• Apartment building rules & regulations<br>• Interpreting utility bills<br>• Credit ratings<br>• Interpreting an apartment building notice to tenants<br>• Interpreting yellow pages listings | • Provide for family members' safety & physical needs<br>• Develop & express sense of self<br>• Work together<br>• Manage resources<br>• Analyze & use information | • Allocate time<br>• Identify goal-relevant activities<br>• Self-esteem<br>• Understand a social system (apartment building rules & regulations)<br>• Participate as a member of a team<br>• Acquire & evaluate information | 1.4.2, 1.5.3, 1.8.1, 1.8.2, 4.1.5 | 25, 26, 27, 43 | 4.01.06, 4.05.03, 4.06.04, 4.06.05, 4.08.03, 4.11.07, 4.11.08 |
| • Making & responding to requests at work<br>• Workplace tasks<br>• Borrowing & lending items<br>• Thanking someone<br>• Workplace notes<br>• Workplace e-mail messages<br>• Making small talk at work<br>• Understanding the importance of small talk<br>• Interpreting paycheck & pay stub information | • Interact in a way that is friendly<br>• Advocate & influence<br>• Develop & express sense of self<br>• Interact in a way that is courteous<br>• Create & pursue vision & goals<br>• Work together<br>• Interact in a way that is tactful | • Sociability<br>• Self-esteem<br>• Identify goal-relevant activities<br>• Self-management: Set personal goals<br>• Participate as a member of a team<br>• Understand an organizational system (workplace operations) | 0.1.3, 0.1.4, 0.2.4, 4.6.4 | 3, 4a, 5a, 5b, 5e, 47d | 4.01.02, 4.02.05, 4.02.06 |

# Scope and Sequence

| Unit | Topics & Vocabulary | Grammar | Functional Communication | Listening & Pronunciation | Writing |
|---|---|---|---|---|---|
| **8** | • Discussing things people had done<br>• Discussing preparations for events<br>• Describing consequences of being late<br>• Describing accomplishments<br>• Scheduling medical appointments<br>• Medical appointment cards<br>• Medical history forms<br>• Preventive care recommendations<br>• Public health information<br>• Nutrition: A healthy plate<br>• Reading a health textbook lesson | • Past perfect tense<br>• Past perfect continuous tense | • Asking for & reporting information<br>• Engaging in small talk about leisure activities<br>• Sharing news about someone<br>• Discussing feelings<br>• Sharing experiences | • Listening to questions & choosing the correct response<br>• Pronouncing reduced *had* | • Writing about plans that fell through<br>• Writing about something you accomplished |
| **Gazette**<br>**Reading & Writing Workshop** | • The Jamaican bobsled team<br>• Culture concept: Children & sports training around the world<br>• Interview with an athlete<br>• Interpreting a line graph with number facts<br>• Idioms<br>• Health: Immunizations & vaccines | • Gerunds<br>• Infinitives | • Describing popular sports & children's sports training<br>• Using idiomatic expressions | • Listening to sports broadcasts on the radio | • Writing an e-mail or instant message to tell about a favorite hobby<br>• The Writing Process |
| **9** | • Discussing when things are going to happen<br>• Remembering & forgetting<br>• Discussing obligations<br>• Asking for & giving advice<br>• School assignments<br>• Making plans by telephone<br>• Talking about important people in your life<br>• Shopping for clothing<br>• Identifying bargains<br>• Returning & exchanging defective items<br>• Advertisements<br>• Store coupons | • Two-word verbs: Separable, Inseparable | • Asking for & reporting information about future events<br>• Reminding someone<br>• Remembering & forgetting<br>• Making & responding to invitations<br>• Expressing obligation<br>• Asking for & offering advice | • Listening to determine subject matter of conversations<br>• Pronouncing linked "t" between vowels | • Writing letters to offer advice<br>• Writing about someone you admire |
| **10** | • Coincidences<br>• Asking for & giving reasons<br>• Describing people's backgrounds, interests, & personalities<br>• Looking for a job<br>• Referring people to someone else<br>• Discussing opinions<br>• Describing people's similarities & differences<br>• Requesting help at work<br>• Giving & following a sequence of instructions<br>• Operating equipment<br>• Career advancement<br>• Continuing education<br>• Developing a personal education plan<br>• Career education: Career counselor profile | • Connectors:<br>And . . . too<br>And . . . either<br>So, But, Neither<br>• Correcting run-on sentences | • Engaging in small talk<br>• Giving excuses<br>• Asking for & reporting information<br>• Offering a suggestion<br>• Describing family members | • Listening to determine subject matter of conversations<br>• Pronouncing contrastive stress | • Writing about how you & another person are the same & different<br>• Punctuation<br>• The Writing Process |
| **Gazette**<br>**Reading & Writing Workshop** | • Traditions, customs, modern life, & the ways people meet<br>• Interpreting a bar graph with number facts about social behavior in different countries<br>• Culture concept: Wedding customs & traditions around the world<br>• Interviews with couples about how they met<br>• Idioms | • Two-word verbs: Separable, Inseparable<br>• Simple present tense<br>• Simple past tense | • Describing customs & traditions<br>• Describing how people met<br>• Using idiomatic expressions | • Listening to answering machine messages to make deductions about people's likes & plans | • Writing an e-mail or instant message to tell about a best friend |

| Life Skills, Civics, & Test Preparation | EFF | SCANS/Employment Competencies | CASAS | LAUSD | Florida* |
|---|---|---|---|---|---|
| • Making, confirming, rescheduling, & canceling medical appointments<br>• Interpreting medical appointment cards<br>• Identifying public health clinics & other medical offices offering free or inexpensive medical care<br>• Medical history forms<br>• Preventive care recommendations<br>• Immunizations<br>• Medical screening tests available in the community<br>• Public health information<br>• Nutrition: A healthy plate | • Create & pursue vision & goals<br>• Manage resources<br>• Develop & express sense of self<br>• Provide for family members' safety & physical needs<br>• Identify community needs & resources<br>• Analyze & use information | • Identify goal-relevant activities<br>• Self-management: Set personal goals<br>• Allocate resources<br>• Acquire & evaluate information<br>• See things in the mind's eye (Interpret a chart & a diagram) | 0.2.4, 1.1.1, 1.1.7, 3.1.1, 3.2.1, 3.2.2 | 3, 31, 36, 37, 38, 39, 40, 41 | 4.05.03, 4.07.01, 4.07.03, 4.07.05, 4.07.06, 4.07.07, 4.07.08, 4.07.09 |
| • Interpreting a narrative reading about international sports<br>• Interpreting statistical facts in a line graph<br>• Interpreting sports broadcasts on the radio | • Respect others & value diversity<br>• Analyze & use information<br>• Understand, interpret, & work with numbers | • Work with cultural diversity<br>• Self-management: Set personal goals<br>• Acquire & evaluate information<br>• See things in the mind's eye (Interpret a line graph) | 0.2.1, 0.2.3, 4.8.7, 6.7.1 | 1, 9, 50 | 4.05.01, 4.15.09, 4.15.12 |
| • Family chores & responsibilities<br>• Feedback on performance<br>• Child-rearing<br>• Offering assistance to a customer<br>• Asking for clothing in a store<br>• Describing clothing<br>• Identifying sale prices & bargains<br>• Returning & exchanging defective products<br>• Interpreting store advertisements<br>• Calculating sale prices<br>• Comparing products & prices at different stores<br>• Interpreting food product coupons | • Manage resources<br>• Identify supportive family relationships<br>• Meet family needs & responsibilities<br>• Guide & support others<br>• Work together<br>• Gather, analyze, & use information | • Identify goal-relevant activities<br>• Self-management: Assess self accurately<br>• Responsibility<br>• Participate as a member of a team<br>• Allocate money<br>• Acquire & evaluate information | 1.2.1, 1.2.2, 1.2.3, 1.3.3, 1.3.5, 1.3.9 | 28, 29, 30 | 4.08.02, 4.11.01, 4.11.02, 4.11.04, 4.11.06, 4.11.10, 4.15.12 |
| • Job interview<br>• Requesting & offering help at work<br>• Giving & following a sequence of instructions for operating equipment at work<br>• Identifying skills, education, & positive job evaluations necessary for job retention & promotion<br>• Identifying appropriate behavior, attire, attitudes, & social interactions for job retention & promotion<br>• Identifying programs & classes available in adult & career education | • Interact in a way that is friendly<br>• Develop & express sense of self<br>• Guide & support others<br>• Identify a strong sense of family<br>• Seek & receive assistance<br>• Give direction<br>• Work together<br>• Create & pursue vision & goals<br>• Analyze & use information<br>• Keep pace with change<br>• Plan: Set a goal; Develop an organized approach of activities & objectives | • Sociability<br>• Teach others new skills<br>• Participate as a member of a team<br>• Acquire & evaluate information<br>• Identify goal-relevant activities<br>• Self-management: Set personal goals | 0.1.4, 0.2.1, 0.2.4, 2.5.5, 4.8.2, 7.1.1 | 1, 3, 4b, 13, 47b, 48, 53 | 4.03.01, 4.03.02, 4.03.03, 4.03.04, 4.05.01, 4.05.02, 4.05.04 |
| • Interpreting statistical facts in a bar graph<br>• Interpreting answering machine messages | • Respect others & value diversity<br>• Identify the family system<br>• Analyze & use information<br>• Understand, interpret, & work with numbers<br>• Use technology | • Work with cultural diversity<br>• See things in the mind's eye (Interpret a bar graph)<br>• Work with technology | 0.2.1, 0.2.3, 4.8.7, 6.7.2 | 1, 9, 50 | 4.06.02, 4.15.09, 4.15.12 |

**Review:**
**Simple Present Tense**
**Present Continuous Tense**
**Subject & Object Pronouns**

**Possessive Adjectives**
**Time Expressions**

- **Describing Habitual and Ongoing Activities**
- **Telling About Likes and Dislikes**
- **Describing Frequency of Actions**
- **Telling About Personal Background and Interests**

- **Emergency Room Check-In**
- **Preventing Identity Theft**
- **Civics: U.S. Government**
- **Reading a Social Studies Textbook Lesson**

## VOCABULARY PREVIEW

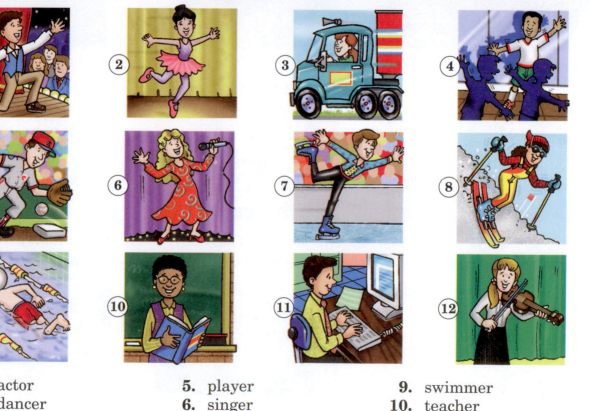

1. actor
2. dancer
3. driver
4. instructor
5. player
6. singer
7. skater
8. skier
9. swimmer
10. teacher
11. typist
12. violinist

# They're Busy

| Am | I |  |
|---|---|---|
| Is | he / she / it | eating? |
| Are | we / you / they | |

| Yes, | I | am. |
|---|---|---|
| | he / she / it | is. |
| | we / you / they | are. |

| (I am) | I'm | |
|---|---|---|
| (He is) | He's | |
| (She is) | She's | |
| (It is) | It's | eating. |
| (We are) | We're | |
| (You are) | You're | |
| (They are) | They're | |

**A.** Are you busy?

**B.** Yes, I am. I'm studying.

**A.** What are you studying?

**B.** I'm studying English.

**1.** Is Alan busy?
*baking • cookies*

**2.** Is Doris busy?
*reading • the newspaper*

**3.** Are your parents busy?
*painting • the kitchen*

**4.** Are you busy?
*writing • a letter*

**5.** Are you and Tom busy?
*cooking • dinner*

**6.** Is Ann busy?
*knitting • a sweater*

**7.** Is your brother busy?
*ironing • his shirts*

**8.** Are Mr. and Mrs. Garcia busy?
*cleaning • their garage*

**9.** Is Beethoven busy?
*composing • a symphony*

# What Are They Doing?

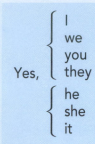

$$
\text{Do} \begin{Bmatrix} \text{I} \\ \text{we} \\ \text{you} \\ \text{they} \end{Bmatrix} \text{eat?} \qquad \text{Does} \begin{Bmatrix} \text{he} \\ \text{she} \\ \text{it} \end{Bmatrix}
$$

$$
\text{Yes,} \begin{Bmatrix} \text{I} \\ \text{we} \\ \text{you} \\ \text{they} \end{Bmatrix} \text{do.} \qquad \begin{Bmatrix} \text{he} \\ \text{she} \\ \text{it} \end{Bmatrix} \text{does.}
$$

$$
\begin{Bmatrix} \text{I} \\ \text{We} \\ \text{You} \\ \text{They} \end{Bmatrix} \text{eat.} \qquad \begin{Bmatrix} \text{He} \\ \text{She} \\ \text{It} \end{Bmatrix} \text{eats.}
$$

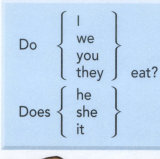

**A.** What are you doing?

**B.** I'm practicing the piano.

**A.** Do you practice the piano very often?

**B.** Yes, I do. I practice the piano whenever I can.

**1.** What's Carol doing?
*watch the news*

**2.** What's Edward doing?
*swim*

**3.** What are you doing?
*study math*

**4.** What are Mr. and Mrs. Park doing?
*exercise*

**5.** What are you and your friend doing?
*play Scrabble*

**6.** What's Mrs. Anderson doing?
*read poetry*

**7.** What's Daniel doing?
*play baseball with his daughter*

**8.** What are you doing?
*chat online with my friends*

**9.**

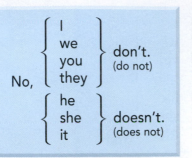

| No, | I / we / you / they | don't. (do not) |
| | he / she / it | doesn't. (does not) |

| I'm not . . . | |
| He / She / It | isn't . . . (is not) |
| We / You / They | aren't . . . (are not) |

**A.** Do you like to ski?

**B.** No, I don't. I'm not a very good skier.

**1.** Does Richard like to sing?

*singer*

**2.** Does Brenda like to swim?

*swimmer*

**3.** Do Mr. and Mrs. Adams like to skate?

*skaters*

**4.** Does Arthur like to dance?

*dancer*

**5.** Do you like to type?

*typist*

**6.** Do you and your friend like to act?

*actors*

**7.** Does your grandmother like to drive?

*driver*

**8.** Do you like to play sports?

*athlete*

**9.** Does Howard like to cook?

*cook*

## PRACTICING

My sisters, my brother, and I are busy this afternoon. We're staying after school, and we're practicing different things.

I'm practicing soccer. I practice soccer every day after school. My soccer coach tells me I'm an excellent soccer player, and my friends tell me I play soccer better than anyone else in the school. I want to be a professional soccer player when I grow up. That's why I practice every day.

My sister Anita is practicing tennis. She practices tennis every day after school. Her tennis coach tells her she's an excellent tennis player, and her friends tell her she plays tennis better than anyone else in the school. Anita wants to be a professional tennis player when she grows up. That's why she practices every day.

My brother Hector is practicing the violin. He practices the violin every day after school. His music teacher tells him he's an excellent violinist, and his friends tell him he plays the violin better than anyone else in the school. Hector wants to be a professional violinist when he grows up. That's why he practices every day.

My sisters Jenny and Vanessa are practicing ballet. They practice ballet every day after school. Their ballet instructor tells them they're excellent ballet dancers, and their friends tell them they dance better than anyone else in the school. Jenny and Vanessa want to be professional ballet dancers when they grow up. That's why they practice every day.

### Q & A

You're talking with the person who told the story on page 5. Using this model, create dialogs based on the story.

**A.** *What's your sister Anita* doing?
**B.** *She's* practicing *tennis*.
**A.** *Does she* practice very often?
**B.** Yes, *she does*. *She practices* every day after school.
**A.** *Is she a* good *tennis player*?
**B.** Yes, *she is*. *Her tennis instructor* says *she's* excellent, and *her* friends tell *her she plays tennis* better than anyone else in the school.

## LISTENING

Listen and choose the correct answer.

1. a. I practice football.
   b. I'm practicing football.

2. a. Yes, I am.
   b. Yes, I do.

3. a. Yes, I am.
   b. Yes, I do.

4. a. She reads the newspaper.
   b. She's reading the newspaper.

5. a. My husband cooks.
   b. My husband is cooking.

6. a. No, they aren't.
   b. No, they don't.

7. a. Yes, when he grows up.
   b. Yes, when she grows up.

8. a. Yes, we do.
   b. Yes, you do.

9. a. Yes, they are.
   b. Yes, we are.

10. a. He's playing soccer.
    b. He wants to be a soccer player.

## IN YOUR OWN WORDS

### FOR WRITING AND DISCUSSION

**Tell about studying English.**

Do you go to English class? Where?
When do you go to class?
What's your teacher's name?

When do you practice English?
How do you practice?
Who do you practice with?

# How Often?

| | | |
|---|---|---|
| I | my | me |
| he | his | him |
| she | her | her |
| it | its | it |
| we | our | us |
| you | your | you |
| they | their | them |

*possessive adjective pronouns*

*under the weather – Enfermo*
*↳ Im not feeling well*
*Idiom*

### Time Expressions

| every day/week/weekend/month/year | once a | |
|---|---|---|
| every morning/afternoon/evening/night | twice a | day/week/month/year |
| every Sunday/Monday/Tuesday/. . . | three times a | |
| every Sunday morning/afternoon/evening/night | | |
| every January/February/March/. . . | all the time | |

*sh*

*ain'ts*
*↳ Bad*
*I'am not*

**A.** Who are you calling?

**B.** **I'm** calling **my** sister in San Francisco.

**A.** How often do you call **her**?

**B.** I call **her** every Sunday evening.

*One aueck →weekly*
*↳*
*Better answer*

**A.** What are George and Herman talking about?

**B.** **They're** talking about **their** grandchildren.

**A.** How often do they talk about **them**?

**B.** They talk about **them** all the time.

*several*
*more than two*

1. Who is Mr. Tanaka calling?
*son in New York*

2. Who is Mrs. Kramer writing to?
*daughter in the army*

3. What are the students talking about?
*teachers*

4. Who is Lenny arguing with?
*landlord*

5. Who is Martha sending an e-mail to?
*granddaughter in Orlando*

6. Who is Mr. Crabapple shouting at?
*employees*

7. What are your parents complaining about?
*telephone bill*

8. What is George watching?
*favorite TV talk show*

9. Who is Little Red Riding Hood visiting?
*grandmother*

10.

## How to Say It!

### Asking for and Reacting to Information

**A.** Tell me, *where are you from?*

**B.** *I'm from Madagascar.*

**A.** { Oh.
Really?
Oh, really?
That's interesting.

Practice the interactions on this page, using expressions for asking for and reacting to information.

## INTERACTIONS *Sharing Opinions*

**Talking about yourself:**

Where are you from?
Where do you live now?

What do you do?
Where do you work/study?

**Talking about family:**

Are you married?
Are you single?

Who are the people in your family?*
What are their names?
Where do they live?

**Talking about interests:**

What do you like to do
in your free time?

How often do you watch TV?
listen to music? go to movies?
play sports?

Practice conversations with other students. Get to know each other as you talk about yourselves, your families, and your interests.

\* wife, husband, mother, father, daughter, son, sister, brother, grandmother, grandfather, granddaughter, grandson, aunt, uncle, cousin

**SIDE** *by* **SIDE**
**JOURNAL**

Write in your journal about yourself, your family, and your interests.

| Listen. Then say it. | Say it. Then listen. |
|---|---|
| Who **are** you calling? | Who **are** you writing to? |
| What **are** they talking about? | What **are** they complaining about? |
| Where **are** you from? | Where **are** they studying? |
| What **are** you doing? | What **are** their names? |

## GRAMMAR FOCUS

### PRESENT CONTINUOUS TENSE

| (I am) | I'm | |
|---|---|---|
| (He is) (She is) (It is) | He's She's It's | eating. |
| (We are) (You are) (They are) | We're You're They're | |

| Am | I | |
|---|---|---|
| Is | he she it | eating? |
| Are | we you they | |

### TO BE: SHORT ANSWERS

| | I | am. |
|---|---|---|
| Yes, | he she it | is. |
| | we you they | are. |

| | I'm | not. |
|---|---|---|
| No, | he she it | isn't. |
| | we you they | aren't. |

### SIMPLE PRESENT TENSE

| I We You They | eat. |
|---|---|
| He She It | eats. |

| Do | I we you they | eat? |
|---|---|---|
| Does | he she it | |

| Yes, | I we you they | do. |
|---|---|---|
| | he she it | does. |

| No, | I we you they | don't. |
|---|---|---|
| | he she it | doesn't. |

| Subject Pronouns | Possessive Adjectives | Object Pronouns |
|---|---|---|
| I | my | me |
| he | his | him |
| she | her | her |
| it | its | it |
| we | our | us |
| you | your | you |
| they | their | them |

**Choose the correct answer.**

1. Mark is busy. ( He irons  (He's ironing) ) his pants and shirts this morning.
2. My daughter ( (chats)  is chatting ) online with her friends every day.
3. ( (We)  We're ) watch ( are  (our) ) favorite TV program every afternoon.
4. A. What ( (are)  our ) Ann and Rita ( do  (doing) )?
   B. ( (They're)  Their ) talking about ( they're  (their) ) grandchildren.
5. Why ( (are)  do ) your neighbors ( argue  (arguing) ) with the landlord today?
6. ( Is  (Does) ) your son ( (practice)  practicing ) the piano every day?
7. ( I'm calling  (I call) ) my cousins in Denver once a month.
8. A. ( (Is)  Does ) your wife working today?
   B. No, she ( is  (isn't) ). She ( isn't  (doesn't) ) work on Saturday.

## 1  CONVERSATION  GIVING PERSONAL INFORMATION

Look at the patient information form. Practice the conversation with a classmate.

### Patient Information Form

NAME  <u>Rita</u>                          <u>Sanchez</u>
       First                          Last

ADDRESS  <u>84 Central Avenue</u>                    <u>14G</u>
      Number   Street                    Apartment
      <u>Los Angeles</u>                  <u>CA</u>  <u>90034</u>
      City                        State  Zip Code

TELEPHONE  <u>(213) 628-1367</u>      SSN  <u>236-84-7915</u>

DATE OF BIRTH  <u>4/16/91</u>   PLACE OF BIRTH  <u>Mexico City</u>

HEIGHT:  <u>5</u> feet  <u>3</u> inches     WEIGHT:  <u>162</u> pounds

MARITAL STATUS (check):

___ Single  ✓ Married  ___ Divorced  ___ Widowed

FAMILY MEMBERS IN HOUSEHOLD (closest relatives):
Relationship:        Name:

<u>husband</u>        <u>Roberto Sanchez</u>

<u>daughter</u>       <u>Jessica Sanchez</u>

_____        _____

**A.** What's your name?

**B.** _____.

**A.** What's your address?

**B.** _____.

**A.** Home telephone number?

**B.** _____.

**A.** Your social security number?

**B.** _____.

**A.** What's your date of birth?

**B.** _____.

**A.** And your place of birth?

**B.** _____.

**A.** What's your height?

**B.** _____.

**A.** And your weight?

**B.** _____.

**A.** What's your marital status?

**B.** _____.

**A.** What family members live in your household?

**B.** _____.

## 2  TEAMWORK  CHECKING IN AT AN EMERGENCY ROOM

Work with a classmate. You're checking in at an emergency room. Fill out the form and practice the conversation above. (Use any information you wish.)

### Patient Information Form

NAME _____          _____
    First                                    Last

ADDRESS _____
    Number    Street              Apartment  City              State  Zip Code

TELEPHONE _____  SSN _____  DATE OF BIRTH _____  PLACE OF BIRTH _____

HEIGHT: ____ feet ____ inches     WEIGHT: _____ pounds

FAMILY MEMBERS IN HOUSEHOLD (closest relatives):

MARITAL STATUS (check):
___ Single  ___ Married  ___ Divorced  ___ Widowed

Relationship:        Name:                      Relationship:        Name:

_____        _____        _____        _____

_____        _____        _____        _____

**Read the article and answer the questions.**

## Identity Theft

Every year nine million people are victims of identity theft. This common crime occurs when someone steals your personal information—for example, your social security number, your credit card and bank account numbers, or your driver's license. With this information, a thief can buy things with your credit card, withdraw money from your bank accounts, or open new credit card accounts in your name. A person can even buy a car with your credit information.

There are many ways thieves can get your personal information. Of course, they can steal your wallet or break into your house. They can also steal documents from your mailbox or from your trash. If you use your credit card at a restaurant or a store, they can steal your receipt, which has your credit card number and your signature. Some identity thieves get jobs in businesses so that they can steal information about customers and employees. Sometimes thieves bribe employees; they pay them for this information. They also use the telephone and the Internet to get your personal information.

Here are some things you can do to prevent identity theft. Carry only the forms of identification and the credit cards you need. Don't carry your Social Security card. Shred documents that have your personal information, such as pay stubs and account statements, before you throw them in the trash. (You can buy an inexpensive shredder that cuts these documents into very small pieces.) Get your mail from your mailbox every day. If you're going to be away from your home for several days, have a friend get your mail or ask the post office to hold it until your return. When you get money from a cash machine or pay with a credit card, put the receipt in your wallet. Don't throw it in the trash. Check your credit card and bank account statements each month to make sure that nobody else is using them. If a statement doesn't arrive when it should, call the company.

If you do all these things and you are still a victim of identity theft, report the crime to your credit card companies and the police. Close your credit card and bank accounts immediately and open new ones with new account numbers.

1. When someone steals your identity, that person steals your _____.
   A. car
   B. personal information
   C. mailbox
   D. cash

2. According to this article, you shouldn't _____.
   A. get money from a cash machine
   B. put credit card receipts in your wallet
   C. carry your Social Security card
   D. get your mail every day

3. According to this article, you should shred your _____.
   A. credit cards
   B. mail
   C. Social Security card
   D. account statements

4. You shouldn't throw your credit card receipt in the trash because _____.
   A. it has your Social Security number
   B. it has your bank account number
   C. it has your credit card number
   D. you need it to buy things

5. You should _____ every month to see if somebody is using your credit card.
   A. check your credit card statement
   B. call the Federal Trade Commission
   C. call the police
   D. get a new password

6. We can infer that an identity thief isn't going to steal your _____.
   A. passport
   B. tax information
   C. checkbook
   D. dictionary

10b

## The Three Branches of Government

The United States government has three *branches* (parts)—the legislative branch, the executive branch, and the judicial branch.

The legislative branch, also called Congress, makes the laws of the United States and has the power to declare war. It has two parts—the Senate and the House of Representatives. There are one hundred senators, two from each state, and there are 435 representatives. The number of representatives from a state depends on how many people live there. States with very few people, such as Alaska and Wyoming, have only one representative, while states with large populations have more representatives. (California, for example, has 53.) Senators serve a six-year term. Representatives serve a two-year term.

The executive branch enforces the laws. The President, the Vice President, and the Cabinet are all part of this branch of government. The President is the chief executive of the United States and the Commander-in-Chief of the armed forces. When the President signs the bills that Congress writes, they become law. The members of the Cabinet give the President advice. The President appoints them.

Voters elect the President and the Vice President together for a four-year term. They must be thirty-five years old or more and natural-born citizens—they cannot come from another country. If the President dies, the Vice President becomes President. The President can serve two four-year terms.

The Supreme Court and other federal courts belong to the judicial branch of government. They *interpret* (explain) the law. The Supreme Court, the highest court in the land, is the last court to hear cases. Its decisions are final. The nine judges on the court are called Supreme Court justices. They serve for life. When a Supreme Court justice retires or dies, the President appoints a new justice. The Senate must approve this person.

Do you recognize each of these buildings? Who works there?

### Did You Understand?

1. The _____ is part of the executive branch.
   A. Supreme Court
   B. Senate
   C. Cabinet
   D. House of Representatives

2. _____ serves a two-year term.
   A. The President
   B. The Vice President
   C. A senator
   D. A representative

3. _____ writes the bills that become laws.
   A. The Supreme Court
   B. The Cabinet
   C. Congress
   D. The President

4. The President does NOT _____.
   A. appoint Supreme Court justices
   B. change the Supreme Court's decisions
   C. appoint Cabinet members
   D. sign bills

5. In the United States, we do NOT elect _____.
   A. the Vice President
   B. our representatives
   C. our senators
   D. Supreme Court justices

6. Nevada has 3 representatives. We can infer that _____.
   A. more people live in Nevada than in Alaska
   B. Nevada has 3 senators
   C. Nevada is bigger than Alaska
   D. Wyoming's population is larger than Nevada's

### CIVICS TODAY   Write your answers. Then discuss with the class.

Who is the President of the United States? Who is the Vice President?

Who is your representative in Congress? Who are your senators?

Who is the governor of your state? Who is the mayor or city manager of your city?

**Choose the correct answer.**

1. My grandmother is knitting _____.
   A. cookies
   B. dinner
   C. a sweater
   D. her car

2. Roger is very talented. He composes _____.
   A. paintings
   B. music
   C. the violin
   D. computers

3. I'm ironing _____.
   A. my bicycle
   B. my son
   C. the kitchen
   D. these pants

4. My daughter _____ soccer every day after school.
   A. practices
   B. exercises
   C. acts
   D. goes

5. Marisa plays several sports. She's a very good _____.
   A. artist
   B. actress
   C. athlete
   D. driver

6. My height is _____.
   A. 2/19/79
   B. single
   C. 173 pounds
   D. 5 feet 4 inches

7. Unfortunately, identify theft is a common _____.
   A. crime
   B. document
   C. receipt
   D. information

8. If you don't want anyone to steal your identity, you should _____ your pay stubs.
   A. steal
   B. shred
   C. bribe
   D. report

9. There are three _____ of U.S. government.
   A. courts
   B. citizens
   C. bills
   D. branches

10. The executive branch of the government _____.
    A. makes the laws
    B. explains the laws
    C. enforces the laws
    D. writes the laws

## SKILLS CHECK ✔

**Words:**

| | | |
|---|---|---|
| ☐ act | ☐ live | ☐ work |
| ☐ argue | ☐ paint | ☐ write |
| ☐ bake | ☐ play | |
| ☐ call | ☐ practice | ☐ actor |
| ☐ chat | ☐ read | ☐ dancer |
| ☐ clean | ☐ send | ☐ driver |
| ☐ complain | ☐ shout | ☐ instructor |
| ☐ compose | ☐ sing | ☐ player |
| ☐ cook | ☐ ski | ☐ singer |
| ☐ dance | ☐ skate | ☐ skater |
| ☐ do | ☐ study | ☐ skier |
| ☐ drive | ☐ swim | ☐ swimmer |
| ☐ exercise | ☐ talk | ☐ teacher |
| ☐ go | ☐ type | ☐ typist |
| ☐ iron | ☐ visit | ☐ violinist |
| ☐ knit | ☐ watch | |

**I can ask & answer:**

☐ Are you *busy*?
  Yes, I am.
  No, I'm not.

☐ Do you *work*?
  Yes, I do.
  No, I don't.

☐ What are you *cleaning*?
  I'm *cleaning the floor*.

☐ I *work* very often.

**I can ask for and react to information:**

☐ Tell me, _____.
  Oh./Really?/Oh, really?/That's Interesting.

**I can:**

☐ give personal information
☐ check in at an emergency room
☐ fill out a patient information form
☐ describe ways to prevent identity theft
☐ describe the three branches of government
☐ name federal, state, & local government officials

**I can write about:**

☐ myself, my family, and my interests

# 2

## Review:
### Simple Past Tense (Regular and Irregular Verbs)
### Past Continuous Tense

- **Reporting Past Activities**
- **Mishaps**
- **Difficult Experiences**
- **Describing a Trip**

- **Apologizing for Lateness at Work**
- **Giving an Excuse**
- **Traffic Accident Report**
- **Civics: U.S. History**

## VOCABULARY PREVIEW

| | | |
|---|---|---|
| 1. break – broke | 6. go – went | 11. sing – sang |
| 2. buy – bought | 7. hurt – hurt | 12. speak – spoke |
| 3. cut – cut | 8. lose – lost | 13. swim – swam |
| 4. eat – ate | 9. meet – met | 14. teach – taught |
| 5. fall – fell | 10. ride – rode | 15. write – wrote |

# Did They Sleep Well Last Night?

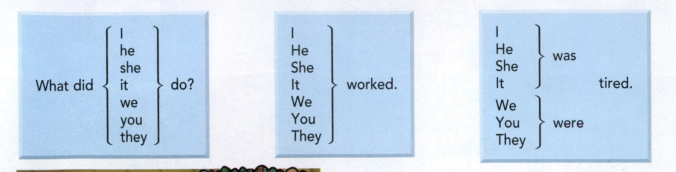

What did { I he she it we you they } do?

I He She It We You They } worked.

I He She It We } was tired.
We You They } were

A. Did Emma sleep well last night?

B. Yes, she did.  She was VERY tired.

A. Why?  What did she do yesterday?

B. She worked in her garden all day.

1. *you*
   *study English*

2. *Rick*
   *paint his apartment*

3. *you and your brother*
   *wash windows*

4. *Ms. Taylor*
   *teach*

5. *Henry*
   *deliver pizzas*

6. *Sarah*
   *write letters*

7. *Matthew*
   *ride his bicycle*

8. *the president*
   *meet important people*

9.

# Did Robert Shout at His Dog?

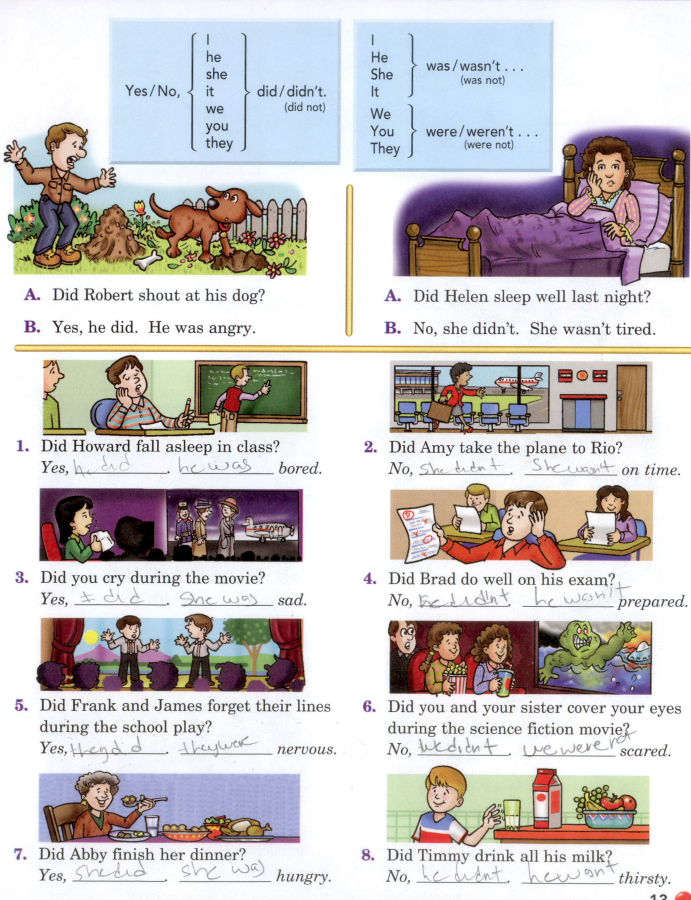

Yes / No, { I / he / she / it / we / you / they } did / didn't. (did not)

I / He / She / It } was / wasn't . . . (was not)

We / You / They } were / weren't . . . (were not)

**A.** Did Robert shout at his dog?

**B.** Yes, he did. He was angry.

**A.** Did Helen sleep well last night?

**B.** No, she didn't. She wasn't tired.

**1.** Did Howard fall asleep in class?
Yes, _he did_. _he was_ bored.

**2.** Did Amy take the plane to Rio?
No, _she didn't_. _She wasn't_ on time.

**3.** Did you cry during the movie?
Yes, _I did_. _She was_ sad.

**4.** Did Brad do well on his exam?
No, _he didn't_. _he wasn't_ prepared.

**5.** Did Frank and James forget their lines during the school play?
Yes, _they did_. _they were_ nervous.

**6.** Did you and your sister cover your eyes during the science fiction movie?
No, _we didn't_. _we weren't_ scared.

**7.** Did Abby finish her dinner?
Yes, _she did_. _she was_ hungry.

**8.** Did Timmy drink all his milk?
No, _he didn't_. _he wasn't_ thirsty.

# How Did Marty Break His Leg?

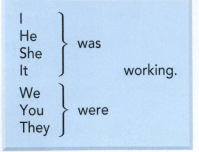

| I | | |
|---|---|---|
| He | was | |
| She | | working. |
| It | | |
| We | | |
| You | were | |
| They | | |

**A.** How did Marty break his leg?

**B.** He broke it while he was snowboarding.

**A.** That's too bad!

**1.** How did Greta sprain her ankle?
*play volleyball*

**2.** How did Larry lose his wallet?
*hike in the woods*

**3.** How did Brian cut himself?
*shave*

**4.** How did Mr. and Mrs. Harper burn themselves?
*prepare dinner*

**5.** How did Stella rip her pants?
*do her daily exercises* ~~ripped~~

**6.** How did your grandfather trip and fall?
*get off a bus*

**7.** How did Peter poke himself in the eye?
*talk on his cell phone*

**8.** How did Marilyn cut herself?
*chop onions*

**9.** How did Timothy get a black eye?
*fight with the kid across the street*

**10.** How did Presto the Magician hurt himself?
*practice a new magic trick*

## How to Say It!

### Reacting to Bad News

That's too bad! | That's a shame! | What a shame! | What a pity! | I'm sorry to hear that.

Practice the conversations in this lesson again. React to the bad news in different ways.

## DIFFICULT EXPERIENCES

Ms. Henderson usually teaches very well, but she didn't teach very well this morning. In fact, she taught very badly. While she was teaching, the school principal was sitting at the back of the room and watching her. It was a very difficult experience for Ms. Henderson. She realized she wasn't teaching very well, but she couldn't do anything about it. She was too nervous.

Stuart usually types very well, but he didn't type very well today. In fact, he typed very badly. While he was typing, his supervisor was standing behind him and looking over his shoulder. It was a difficult experience for Stuart. He realized he wasn't typing very well, but he couldn't do anything about it. He was too upset.

The Baxter Boys usually sing very well, but they didn't sing very well last night. In fact, they sang very badly. While they were singing, their parents were sitting in the audience and waving at them. It was a difficult experience for the Baxter Boys. They realized they weren't singing very well, but they couldn't do anything about it. They were too embarrassed.

The president usually speaks very well, but he didn't speak very well this afternoon. In fact, he spoke very badly. While he was speaking, several demonstrators were standing at the back of the room and shouting at him. It was a difficult experience for the president. He realized he wasn't speaking very well, but he couldn't do anything about it. He was too angry.

## Q & A

Ms. Henderson, Stuart, the Baxter Boys, and the president are talking with friends about their difficult experiences. Using this model, create dialogs based on the story on page 16.

**A.** You know . . . I didn't *teach* very well *this morning*.
**B.** You didn't?
**A.** No. In fact, I *taught* very badly.
**B.** That's strange. You usually *teach* VERY well. What happened?
**A.** While I was *teaching, the school principal was sitting at the back of the room and watching me.*
**B.** Oh. I bet that was a very difficult experience for you.
**A.** It was. I *was* very *nervous*.

## MATCH

We often use colorful expressions to describe how we feel. Try to match the following expressions with the feelings they describe.

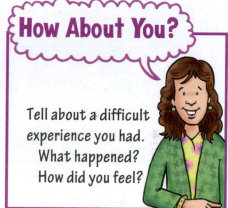

> **How About You?**
>
> Tell about a difficult experience you had. What happened? How did you feel?

___f___ **1.** "My stomach is growling."          a. angry
___c___ **2.** "I can't keep my eyes open."          b. embarrassed
___h___ **3.** "I'm jumping for joy!"          c. tired
___a___ **4.** "I'm seeing red!"          d. nervous
___g___ **5.** "I'm feeling blue."          e. scared
___d___ **6.** "I'm on pins and needles!" *          f. hungry
___e___ **7.** "I'm shaking like a leaf!"          g. sad
___b___ **8.** "I'm ashamed to look at them straight in the eye."          h. happy

## LISTENING

Listen and choose the correct answer.

**1.** a. Yes, I did. ⟵(circled)
   b. Yes, I was.

**2.** a. Yes, they did.
   b. Yes, they were. ⟵(circled)

**3.** a. He played soccer.
   b. He was playing soccer. ⟵(circled)

**4.** a. No. I wasn't hungry. ⟵(circled)
   b. Yes. I wasn't hungry.

**5.** a. He lost his wallet.
   b. He was jogging in the park. ⟵(circled)

**6.** a. She was nervous.
   b. She was looking over my shoulder. ⟵(circled)

**7.** a. Yes. I was prepared. ⟵(circled)
   b. No. I was prepared.

**8.** a. I cut myself. ⟵(circled)
   b. I was too upset.

# Tell Me About Your Vacation

Tell me about your vacation.

It was very nice.

1. **A.** Did you go to Paris?
   **B.** No, _____we didn't_____.
   **A.** Where _____did you go_____?
   **B.** _____We went_____ to Rome.

2. **A.** Did you get there by boat?
   **B.** No, ___we didn't___.
   **A.** How ___did you get by___?
   **B.** ___we got___ by plane.

3. **A.** Did you stay in a big hotel?
   **B.** No, ___I didn't___.
   **A.** What kind of ___hotel did you stay___?
   **B.** ___I stayed in___ a small hotel.

4. **A.** Did you eat in fancy restaurants?
   **B.** No, ___we didn't___.
   **A.** Where ___did you eat___?
   **B.** ___we ate in a___ cheap restaurants.

Where is the post office?

5. **A.** Did you speak Italian?
   **B.** No, ___I didn't___.
   **A.** What language ___did you speak___?
   **B.** ___I spoke___ English.

6. **A.** Did you take many pictures?
   **B.** No, ___I didn't___.
   **A.** How many ___pictures did you take___?
   **B.** ___I took___ just a few pictures.

**7. A.** Did you buy any clothing?
 **B.** No, _we didn't_.
 **A.** What _did you buy_?
 **B.** _we bought_ souvenirs.

**8. A.** Did you swim in the Mediterranean?
 **B.** No, _we didn't_.
 **A.** Where _did you swim_?
 **B.** _we swam_ in the pool at our hotel.

**9. A.** Did you see the Colosseum?
 **B.** No, _we didn't_.
 **A.** What _did you see_?
 **B.** _we saw_ the Vatican.

**10. A.** Did you get around the city by taxi?
 **B.** No, _we didn't_.
 **A.** How _did you get around_?
 **B.** _we got_ by bus.

**11. A.** Did you meet a lot of Italians?
 **B.** No, _we didn't_.
 **A.** Who _did you met_?
 **B.** _we met_ a lot of other tourists.

**12. A.** Did you come home by plane?
 **B.** No, _we didn't_.
 **A.** How _did you come_?
 **B.** _we come_ by boat.

**SIDE by SIDE JOURNAL**

Write in your journal about a trip you took. Where did you go? How did you get there? Where did you stay? What did you do there? How long were you there? Did you have a good time?

*(If you have some photographs of your trip, bring them to class and talk about them with other students.)*

**Listen. Then say it.**

Did you go to Madrid?

Did you speak Spanish?

Where did you stay?

What did you do?

**Say it. Then listen.**

Did you meet a lot of people?

Did you have a good time?

How did you get there?

When did you get home?

## GRAMMAR FOCUS

SIMPLE PAST TENSE

| What did | I he she it we you they | do? |
|---|---|---|

| I He She It We You They | worked. |
|---|---|

| Did | I he she it we you they | fall asleep? |
|---|---|---|

| Yes, | I he she it we you they | did. |
|---|---|---|

| No, | I he she it we you they | didn't. |
|---|---|---|

| I He She It | was | tired. |
|---|---|---|
| We You They | were | |

| I He She It | wasn't | tired. |
|---|---|---|
| We You They | weren't | |

PAST CONTINUOUS TENSE

| I He She It | was | working. |
|---|---|---|
| We You They | were | |

**Choose the correct answer.**

1. A. What ( do you did ( did you do )) last weekend?
   B. We (( went   were going )) to the beach.

2. A. Did you ( ate ( eat )) all your dinner?
   B. No, we ( did ( didn't )). We ( wasn't ( weren't )) very hungry.

3. A. How (( did they burn )   they burned ) themselves?
   B. They ( were baking ( were baked )) cookies.

4. A. Did you (( sleep )   slept ) well last night?
   B. Yes, I (( did )   didn't ). I ( were ( was )) very tired.

5. A. (( Did he took )   Did he take ) the bus?
   B. No, he ( wasn't ( didn't )). He ( take ( took )) the train.

6. A. ( How ( How did )) your grandmother (( fall )   fell )?
   B. She ( was falling ( fell )) while ( was she ( she was )) getting off a bus.

● 20

## 1 CONVERSATION   APOLOGIZING FOR BEING LATE

Practice conversations between an employee and a supervisor.  Apologize for being late for work.

**A.** I'm sorry I'm late for work.

**B.** What happened?

**A.** <u>I woke up late</u>

**B.** Oh.  That's too bad.

**1.** I had a flat tire.

**2.** I missed the bus.

**3.** My car broke down.

**4.** The trains were running late.

**5.** Traffic was terrible. There was a bad accident.

**6.** My daughter woke up with a high fever.  I had to take her to the doctor.

## 2 TEAMWORK   CRITICAL THINKING

Work with a classmate.  What are some good excuses and bad excuses for being late for work?  Make two lists.  Practice new conversations with the good excuses. Then discuss your lists with your classmates.

| Good Excuses | Bad Excuses |
|---|---|
| I had a flat tire. | I met an old friend on the street. |
| I woke up late | I forgot my jacket at home and I needed to returned |
| I had a Terrible headache | I brought my husband to his job, his car broke down. |

Look at the traffic accident report and answer the questions.

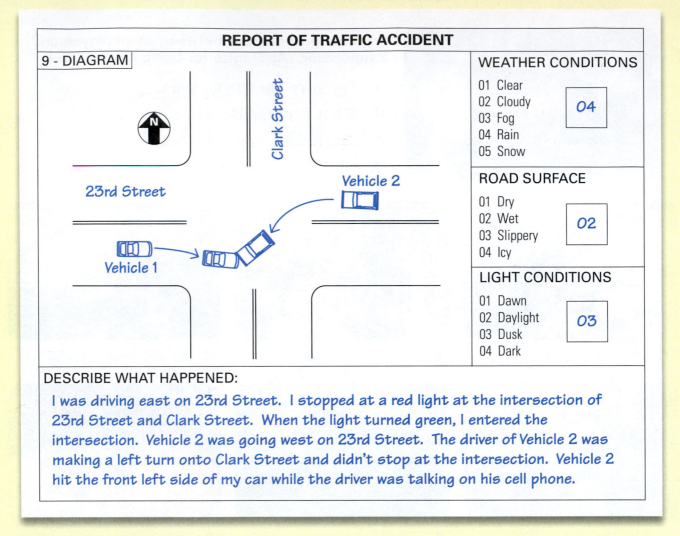

**REPORT OF TRAFFIC ACCIDENT**

9 - DIAGRAM

Clark Street

23rd Street

Vehicle 2

Vehicle 1

| WEATHER CONDITIONS | |
|---|---|
| 01 Clear | |
| 02 Cloudy | |
| 03 Fog | 04 |
| 04 Rain | |
| 05 Snow | |

| ROAD SURFACE | |
|---|---|
| 01 Dry | |
| 02 Wet | 02 |
| 03 Slippery | |
| 04 Icy | |

| LIGHT CONDITIONS | |
|---|---|
| 01 Dawn | |
| 02 Daylight | 03 |
| 03 Dusk | |
| 04 Dark | |

DESCRIBE WHAT HAPPENED:

I was driving east on 23rd Street. I stopped at a red light at the intersection of 23rd Street and Clark Street. When the light turned green, I entered the intersection. Vehicle 2 was going west on 23rd Street. The driver of Vehicle 2 was making a left turn onto Clark Street and didn't stop at the intersection. Vehicle 2 hit the front left side of my car while the driver was talking on his cell phone.

1. The driver of Vehicle 1 was _____.
   A. driving north
   B. driving west
   C. driving east
   D. making a turn

2. The driver of Vehicle 2 _____.
   A. was making a right turn
   B. hit the front right side of Vehicle 1
   C. was driving east
   D. was talking on a cell phone

3. The road was _____ when the accident occurred.
   A. dry
   B. wet
   C. slippery
   D. icy

4. The driver of Vehicle 2 was turning _____.
   A. left onto 23rd Street
   B. right onto 23rd Street
   C. left onto Clark Street
   D. right onto Clark Street

5. _____ when the accident occurred.
   A. The traffic light was green
   B. It was foggy
   C. It was snowing
   D. It was dark

6. The accident occurred at 6:30 P.M. We can infer that *dusk* means _____.
   A. it was bright
   B. it was sunny
   C. it was starting to get light
   D. it was starting to get dark

**Read about the history of the United States and complete the sentences with these words.**

| began | described | ended | fought | lost | met | needed | sent | signed | wrote |

### THE REVOLUTIONARY WAR

The Revolutionary War _____ [1] in 1775 and _____ [2] in 1783. The American colonies and England _____ [3] for eight years because the colonies wanted to be independent from England. The English soldiers had more experience than the Americans, but England _____ [4] the war.

### THE DECLARATION OF INDEPENDENCE

In 1776, representatives from the thirteen colonies _____ [5] at Independence Hall in Philadelphia. At the meeting, they decided to declare their independence. Thomas Jefferson was a great writer. He _____ [6] the Declaration of Independence. This document says that the government must do what the people say and that all people have important rights.

### JULY 4, 1776

On July 4, 1776, representatives of all thirteen colonies _____ [7] the Declaration of Independence. John Hancock's signature is famous because it is larger than all the others. Today July 4th, Independence Day, is an important national holiday.

### THE CONSTITUTION

After the Revolutionary War, each state had its own laws. The central government was very weak. The thirteen states _____ [8] a strong central government. In 1787, they _____ [9] representatives to Philadelphia to write a Constitution for the new country. The Constitution _____ [10] the powers of the national and state governments. It is the highest law in the United States.

| became | began | bought | fought | grew | led | lost | met | served | signed | thought | was |
|---|---|---|---|---|---|---|---|---|---|---|---|

## GEORGE WASHINGTON

Americans call George Washington "the father of our country." He was the leader of the Colonial Army during the Revolutionary War, and he was the leader of the representatives who _____ [1] in Philadelphia in 1787 to write the Constitution. In 1789, George Washington _____ [2] the first president of the United States. He _____ [3] two terms.

## THE CIVIL WAR

The Civil War was a war between the states in the North and the states in the South. It _____ [4] in 1861 and ended in 1865. In the South, there were big farms called plantations where people _____ [5] cotton. The workers on these plantations were slaves—people from Africa who had no rights or freedoms. The plantation owners _____ [6] and sold them like furniture. People in the Northern states _____ [7] slavery was wrong and wanted to free the slaves. In 1861, eleven Southern states formed the Confederacy and _____ [8] against the Northern states (the Union). The Southern states _____ [9] the war.

## ABRAHAM LINCOLN

Abraham Lincoln _____ [10] the sixteenth president. He _____ [11] the Northern states during the Civil War and kept the nation together. In 1863, he _____ [12] the Emancipation Proclamation, a document that freed the slaves. Five days after the Civil War ended, a man killed Lincoln. Americans remember Abraham Lincoln and George Washington on Presidents' Day, a national holiday on the third Monday in February.

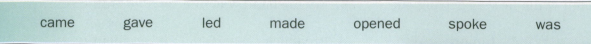

| came | gave | led | made | opened | spoke | was | worked |

## IMMIGRATION

In the 1800s, many factories _____ [1] in American cities. These factories needed workers. Immigrants from many different countries _____ [2] to the United States and _____ [3] in the factories. In the 1900s, the government _____ [4] laws to stop immigration from many countries. The Immigration Act of 1965 changed this. It _____ [5] people from any country the right to apply to come to the United States.

## THE CIVIL RIGHTS MOVEMENT

During the 1950s and 1960s, the civil rights movement worked to end discrimination against Blacks in the United States. Martin Luther King, Jr., the most famous civil rights leader, _____ [6] protests and demonstrations. He _____ [7] a great speaker. Hundreds of thousands of people heard him when he _____ [8] at the March on Washington in 1963. Americans remember Martin Luther King, Jr., on a national holiday on the third Monday in January.

## HISTORY QUIZ

1. When did the Revolutionary War begin?
2. Who wrote the Declaration of Independence?
3. When is Independence Day?
4. What is the highest law in the United States?
5. Who is called "the father of our country"?
6. Who fought in the Civil War?
7. What document freed the slaves?
8. Who was the president during the Civil War?
9. What law made immigration easier?
10. Who was the most famous civil rights leader?

## TEAMWORK  U.S. HISTORY TIMELINE

Timelines are charts that show dates and events. Work with a classmate. Think about eight important events in U.S. history that occurred between 1770 and 1870. Make a timeline like the one below, and write each event and its year on the timeline.

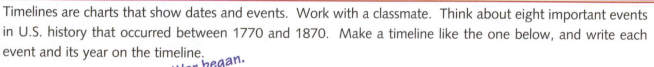

The Revolutionary War began.

1770  1775  1780  1790  1800  1810  1820  1830  1840  1850  1860  1870

**Choose the correct answer.**

1. He _____ and fell while he was getting out of a taxi.
   A. ripped          C. taught
   B. tripped         D. took

2. I sprained my _____ while I was jogging through the park.
   A. ankle           C. pants
   B. uncle           D. wallet

3. I'm really upset. I _____ my cell phone.
   A. met             C. hiked
   B. slept           D. lost

4. I fell asleep during the class because I was _____.
   A. prepared        C. bored
   B. scared          D. embarrassed

5. We _____ the city by taxi.
   A. got             C. took
   B. got around      D. went

6. My husband was in a terrible traffic _____.
   A. light           C. report
   B. vehicle         D. accident

7. When the light turned green, the car _____ the intersection.
   A. hit             C. turned
   B. entered         D. stopped

8. It was a long war. The two sides _____ against each other for five years.
   A. led             C. fought
   B. lost            D. declared

9. Americans remember Martin Luther King, Jr., on a national holiday in _____ every year.
   A. January         C. July
   B. February        D. September

10. I believe that all people should have the same _____.
    A. rights         C. signature
    B. discrimination D. immigration

## SKILLS CHECK ✔

**Words:**

□ burn
□ chop
□ cover
□ cry
□ deliver
□ finish
□ growl
□ hike
□ jump
□ look
□ paint
□ play
□ poke
□ practice
□ prepare
□ realize
□ rip
□ shave
□ shout
□ snowboard
□ sprain
□ stay
□ study
□ talk

□ trip
□ type
□ wash
□ watch
□ wave
□ work

□ become – became
□ begin – began
□ break – broke
□ buy – bought
□ come – came
□ cut – cut
□ do – did
□ drink – drank
□ eat – ate
□ fall – fell
□ feel – felt
□ fight – fought
□ forget – forgot
□ get – got
□ give – gave
□ go – went
□ grow – grew

□ have – had
□ hurt – hurt
□ keep – kept
□ lead – led
□ lose – lost
□ make – made
□ meet – met
□ ride – rode
□ see – saw
□ send – sent
□ shake – shook
□ sing – sang
□ sit – sat
□ sleep – slept
□ speak – spoke
□ stand – stood
□ swim – swam
□ take – took
□ teach – taught
□ tell – told
□ think – thought
□ wake – woke
□ write – wrote

**I can ask & answer:**

□ Did you *work*?
   Yes, I did. / No, I didn't.
   What did you do?
   I *worked*.

□ I was/wasn't *on time*.
□ We were/weren't *on time*.

□ I was *working*.
□ We were *working*.

□ Who/What/Where/How/How many/What kind of . . .
   did _____?

**I can react to bad news:**

□ That's too bad!/That's a shame!/What a shame!/
   What a pity!/I'm sorry to hear that.

**I can:**

□ apologize for being late for work
□ evaluate good and bad excuses for being late for work
□ interpret a traffic accident report
□ identify important events and people in U.S. history
□ create a history timeline

**I can write about:**

□ a trip I took

## 3

**Review:**
**Future: Going to**
**Future: Will**
**Future Continuous Tense**

**Time Expressions**
**Possessive Pronouns**

- **Describing Future Plans and Intentions**
- **Telling About the Future Expressing Time and Duration**
- **Talking on the Telephone**
- **Asking a Favor**

- **Calling in Sick at Work**
- **Calling School to Report a Child's Absence**
- **Writing a Note to the Teacher**
- **Parent-School Communication**
- **Reading a Campus Map**

## VOCABULARY PREVIEW

1. yesterday morning
2. this morning
3. tomorrow morning
4. yesterday afternoon
5. this afternoon
6. tomorrow afternoon
7. yesterday evening
8. this evening
9. tomorrow evening
10. last night
11. tonight
12. tomorrow night

# What Are They Going to Do?

What
am I
is { he / she / it }
are { we / you / they }
going to do?

(I am) I'm
(He is) He's
(She is) She's
(It is) It's
(We are) We're
(You are) You're
(They are) They're
} going to read.

## Time Expressions

yesterday
this  } morning / afternoon / evening
tomorrow

last night
tonight
tomorrow night

last { week / month / year / Sunday / Monday / ...
this { spring / summer / ...
next { January / February / ...

**A.** Are you going to buy a donut this morning?

**B.** No, I'm not.  I bought a donut YESTERDAY morning.

**A.** What are you going to buy?

**B.** I'm going to buy a muffin.

1. Is Mr. Hopper going to have cake for dessert tonight?

   *ice cream*

3. Are you and your family going to go to Europe this summer?

   *Hawaii*

5. Are your parents going to watch the movie on Channel 4 this Friday night?

   *the news program on Channel 7*

7. Is the chef going to make onion soup today?

   *pea soup*

9. Are you and your brother going to play cards this afternoon?

   *chess*

2. Is Valerie going to sing folk songs this evening?

   *Broadway show tunes*

4. Is Gary going to wear his gray suit today?

   *his blue suit*

6. Is Elizabeth going to go out with Jonathan this Saturday evening?

   *Bob*

8. Is your sister going to take biology this semester?

   *astronomy*

10. Are you going to be Superman this Halloween?

    *Batman*

# READING

## PLANS FOR THE WEEKEND

It's Friday afternoon, and all the employees at the Liberty Insurance Company are thinking about their plans for the weekend. Milton is going to work in his garden. Diane is going to go hiking in the mountains. Carmen and Tom are going to play tennis. Jack is going to go water-skiing. Kate is going to build a tree house for her children. And Ray and his family are going to have a picnic.

Unfortunately, the employees at the Liberty Insurance Company are going to be very disappointed. According to the radio, it's going to "rain cats and dogs" all weekend.

## ✔ READING CHECK-UP

### Q & A

The employees at the Liberty Insurance Company are talking with each other. Using this model, create dialogs based on the story.

**A.** Tell me, *Milton*, what are you going to do this weekend?
**B.** I'm going to *work in my garden*. How about you, *Diane*? What are YOU going to do?
**A.** I'm going to *go hiking in the mountains*.
**B.** Well, have a nice weekend.
**A.** You, too.

**How About You?**

What are you going to do this weekend? What's the weather forecast?

# LISTENING

Listen to the conversation and choose the answer that is true.

1. a. He's going to wear his gray suit.
   b. He's going to wear his brown suit.

2. a. They're going to have dinner at home.
   b. They're going to have dinner at a restaurant.

3. a. They're going to watch Channel 5.
   b. They're going to watch Channel 9.

4. a. He's going to call a mechanic.
   b. He's going to call an electrician.

5. a. She's going to go to the supermarket tomorrow.
   b. She's going to work in her garden tomorrow.

6. a. They're going to buy the computer.
   b. They aren't going to buy the computer.

# Will Ms. Martinez Return Soon?

| (I will) | I'll | |
|---|---|---|
| (He will) | He'll | |
| (She will) | She'll | |
| (It will) | It'll | work. |
| (We will) | We'll | |
| (You will) | You'll | |
| (They will) | They'll | |

| I | |
|---|---|
| He | |
| She | |
| It | won't work. |
| We | (will not) |
| You | |
| They | |

**A.** Will Ms. Martinez return soon?

**B.** Yes, she will. She'll return in a little while.

**A.** Will your sister return soon?

**B.** No, she won't. She won't return for a long time.

**1.** Will the play begin soon?

*Yes, _____. _____ at 7:30.*

**2.** Will the concert begin soon?

*No, _____. _____ until 8:00.*

**3.** Will Ken and Kim see each other again soon?

*Yes, _____. _____ this Saturday night.*

**4.** Will Larry and Lisa see each other again soon?

*No, _____. _____ until next year.*

**5.** Will the train arrive soon?

*Yes, _____. _____ in a few minutes.*

**6.** Will Flight 216 arrive soon?

*No, _____. _____ for several hours.*

**7.** Will David get out of the hospital soon?

*Yes, _____. _____ in a few days.*

**8.** Will Ralph get out of jail soon?

*No, _____. _____ for a few years.*

# Will You Be Home This Evening?

I'll
He'll
She'll
It'll
We'll
You'll
They'll
} be working.

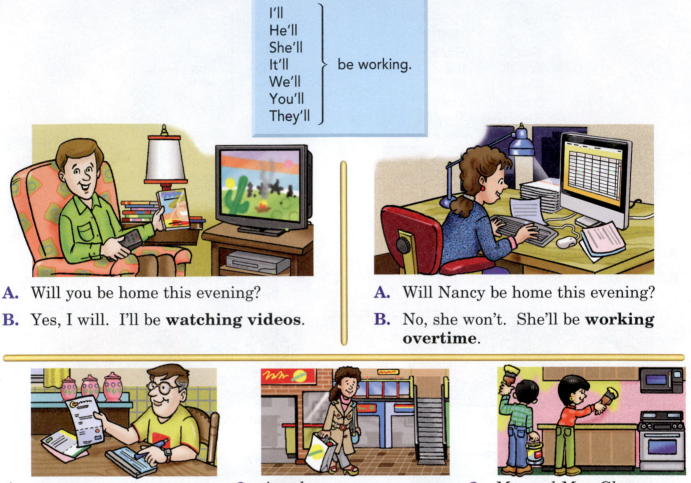

**A.** Will you be home this evening?

**B.** Yes, I will. I'll be **watching videos**.

**A.** Will Nancy be home this evening?

**B.** No, she won't. She'll be **working overtime**.

**1.** *you*
*pay bills*

**2.** *Angela*
*shop at the mall*

**3.** *Mr. and Mrs. Chen*
*paint their kitchen*

**4.** *your sister*
*attend a meeting*

**5.** *you and your family*
*ice skate*

**6.** *Vincent*
*browse the web*

**7.** *you*
*do research at the library*

**8.** *Tess*
*fill out her income tax form*

**9.** *Mr. and Mrs. Silva*
*work out at their health club*

# Can You Call Back a Little Later?

Hi, _____. This is _____. Can you talk for a minute?

I'm sorry. I can't talk right now. I'm _____ing. Can you call back a little later?

Sure. How much longer will you be _____ing?

I'll probably be _____ing for another _____ minutes.

Fine. I'll call you in _____ minutes.

Speak to you soon.

Good-bye.

**Create conversations based on the model above.**

1. *do homework*

2. *iron*

3. *wash my windows*

4. *have dinner*

5. *give the kids a bath*

6.

# Could You Do Me a Favor?

| I | me | mine |
|---|---|---|
| he | him | his |
| she | her | hers |
| it | it | — |
| we | us | ours |
| you | you | yours |
| they | them | theirs |

Joe

**A.** Could you do me a favor?

**B.** Sure. What is it?

**A.** I have to fix a flat tire, and I don't have a jack. Could I possibly borrow yours?

**B.** I'm sorry. I'm afraid I don't have one.

**A.** Oh. Do you know anybody who does?

**B.** Yes. You should call Joe. I'm sure he'll be happy to lend you his.

**A.** Thanks. I'll call him right away.

**A.** Could you do me a favor?

**B.** Sure. What is it?

**A.** I have to _____, and I don't have a _____. Could I possibly borrow yours?

**B.** I'm sorry. I'm afraid I don't have one.

**A.** Oh. Do you know anybody who does?

**B.** Yes. You should call _____. I'm sure _____'ll be happy to lend you _____ (his/hers/theirs).

**A.** Thanks. I'll call _____ (him/her/them) right away.

**1.** *fix my front steps*
*hammer*

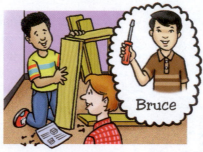

**2.** *assemble my new*
*bookshelf*
*screwdriver*

**3.** *write a composition*
*dictionary*

**4.** *adjust my satellite dish*
*ladder*

**5.** *go to a wedding*
*tuxedo*

**6.**

---

## How to Say It!

### Asking for a Favor

**A.** 
- Could you do me a favor?
- Could you possibly do me a favor?
- Could you do a favor for me?
- Could I ask you a favor?

**B.** Sure. What is it?

**Practice the conversations in this lesson again. Ask for a favor in different ways.**

## SAYING GOOD-BYE

Mr. and Mrs. Karpov are at the Moscow airport. They're saying good-bye to their son Sasha and his family. It's a very emotional day. In a few minutes, Sasha and his family will get on a plane and fly to Canada. They won't be coming back. They're leaving Russia permanently, and Mr. and Mrs. Karpov won't be seeing them for a long, long time.

Sasha and his family are excited about their plans for the future. They're going to stay with his wife's relatives in Toronto. Sasha will work in the family's restaurant. His wife, Marina, will take any job she can find during the day, and she'll study English at night. The children will begin school in September.

Mr. and Mrs. Karpov are both happy and sad. They're happy because they know that their son will have a good life in his new home. However, they're sad because they know they're going to be very lonely. Their apartment will be quiet and empty, and they won't see their grandchildren grow up.

Some day Mr. and Mrs. Karpov will visit Toronto, or perhaps they'll even move there. But until then, they're going to miss their family very much. As you can imagine, it's very difficult for them to say good-bye.

## ✔ READING CHECK-UP

### TRUE OR FALSE?

1. Sasha and his family will be leaving Russia for a few minutes.
2. Marina's relatives live in Toronto.
3. Mr. Karpov is happy, and Mrs. Karpov is sad.
4. Mr. and Mrs. Karpov might move to Toronto.
5. Mr. and Mrs. Karpov are sad because they'll be at the Moscow airport until they visit Toronto or move there.

## How About You?

- Tell about an emotional day in your life when you had to say good-bye.

- Tell about YOUR plans for the future.

Jerry is looking forward to this weekend. He isn't going to think about work. He's going to read a few magazines, work on his car, and relax at home with his family.

Amanda is looking forward to her birthday. Her sister is going to have a party for her, and all her co-workers and friends are going to be there.

Mr. and Mrs. Cook are looking forward to their summer vacation. They're going to go camping. They're going to hike several miles every day, take a lot of pictures, and forget about all their problems at home.

Mr. and Mrs. Lee are looking forward to their retirement. They're going to get up late every morning, visit friends every afternoon, and enjoy quiet evenings at home together.

What are YOU looking forward to? A birthday? a holiday? a day off? Talk about it with other students in your class.

**SIDE by SIDE JOURNAL**

Write in your journal about something you're looking forward to: What are you looking forward to? When is it going to happen? What are you going to do?

going to = gonna

**Listen.  Then say it.**

Are you going to buy bread today?

What are you going to eat?

I'm going to go camping.

**Say it.  Then listen.**

Is she going to watch TV?

What's he going to wear?

They're going to make dinner.

## GRAMMAR FOCUS

### FUTURE: GOING TO

| What | am | I | going to do? |
|---|---|---|---|
| | is | he she it | |
| | are | we you they | |

| (I am) | I'm | going to read. |
|---|---|---|
| (He is) | He's | |
| (She is) | She's | |
| (It is) | It's | |
| (We are) | We're | |
| (You are) | You're | |
| (They are) | They're | |

### POSSESSIVE PRONOUNS

mine
his
hers
—
ours
yours
theirs

### FUTURE: WILL

| (I will) | I'll | work. |
|---|---|---|
| (He will) | He'll | |
| (She will) | She'll | |
| (It will) | It'll | |
| (We will) | We'll | |
| (You will) | You'll | |
| (They will) | They'll | |

| I | won't work. |
|---|---|
| He | |
| She | |
| It | |
| We | |
| You | |
| They | |

### FUTURE CONTINUOUS TENSE

| (I will) | I'll | be working. |
|---|---|---|
| (He will) | He'll | |
| (She will) | She'll | |
| (It will) | It'll | |
| (We will) | We'll | |
| (You will) | You'll | |
| (They will) | They'll | |

**Complete the sentences.**

1. A. What _____ you _____ _____ buy?
   B. _____ _____ _____ buy a new suit.

2. A. _____ Ms. Romero be back soon?
   B. Yes, _____ _____. _____ _____ back in an hour.

3. A. I don't have a ladder.  Can I possibly borrow yours?
   B. I can't find _____.  You should ask Mr. King. I'm sure _____ be happy to lend you _____.

4. A. Are you and your wife _____ _____ go to Canada for your vacation?
   B. No.  I think _____ probably _____ to Mexico.

5. A. _____ the flight from Dallas arrive soon?
   B. No, _____ _____. _____ _____ _____ until after midnight.

6. A. _____ your parents be home this evening?
   B. Yes, _____ _____. _____ _____ watching their favorite TV program.

# LIFE SKILLS

- Calling in sick at work
- Writing a note to the teacher
- Calling school to report a child's absence

## 1 CONVERSATION  CALLING IN SICK AT WORK

**Practice with a classmate.**

**A.** Hello. This is ____(first & last name)____.
I won't be able to come to work today.
_____

**B.** I'm sorry to hear that.

**A.** If I feel better tomorrow, I'll come to work.

**B.** Okay. Thank you for calling.

**1.** I have a bad stomachache.

**2.** I hurt my back.

**3.** I have a high fever.

**4.**

## 2 CONVERSATION  CALLING SCHOOL TO REPORT A CHILD'S ABSENCE

**Practice with a classmate. Leave a message on the school voice-mail system.**

**A.** This is the school attendance line. After the tone, please give your name, your child's name, and the reason for your child's absence. Thank you.

**B.** Hello. This is ____(first & last name)____.
My daughter/son ____(child's first name)____ won't be in school today.
_____
Thank you.

 **1.** He has a bad cold.

 **2.** She has a bad toothache.

 **3.** She has a bad rash.

**4.**

## 3 CLOZE READING & WRITING  A NOTE TO THE TEACHER

**Complete the note.**

going to
She'll
She's
will
won't

January 26

Dear Ms. Carter,

My daughter Yolanda _____ [1] be absent from school tomorrow. _____ [2] be in the hospital. She also _____ [3] be in school the next day. _____ [4] _____ [5] return to school next Monday.

Sincerely,
Anna Garcia

**Your child will be absent from school tomorrow. Write a note to tell the teacher.**

**JHS** **Jefferson High School**
**360 Grant Avenue, Pineland FL 33945**

Dear Parents:

In a few weeks, your children will be entering our high school as our new ninth grade class. The next four years will be very exciting. Your children will be with us through their freshman, sophomore, junior, and senior years. This letter contains some important information for you.

Students at Jefferson High School must come to school every day unless they are sick, they have a medical or dental appointment, or they have another very good reason. Children who are absent very often cannot learn. Furthermore, education is *compulsory* for children between the ages of 6 and 16—they have to attend school.

If you know that your children are going to be absent, call the school's attendance line at 239-0922 on or before the day of the absence and leave a message explaining the reason for the absence. Although we want our students to be in school every day, they should not come to school if they have a high fever or if they might give an illness to another student.

| Grade | Percent | Meaning |
|-------|-----------|------------------|
| A | 90% – 100% | excellent |
| B | 80% – 89% | above average |
| C | 70% – 79% | satisfactory |
| D | 60% – 69% | needs improvement |
| F | 0 – 59% | unsatisfactory |

Students bring home report cards four times a year. The chart to the right explains the grades that you will see on these report cards. We are proud that a large number of students at Jefferson High School are honor roll students who receive grades of A or B in all their classes.

Homework is an important part of learning. It teaches students how to work independently and to manage their time. Your children will have about two hours of homework each day. Please make sure they have time to do their homework.

"Latch-key children" who come home to an empty house after school often get into trouble because there is nobody at home to supervise them. If your children attend an after-school program, you won't have to worry about their safety. Your children can participate in many interesting after-school activities. These include theater, photography, art, and sports.

We hope you attend school events and parent-teacher association meetings during the school year. If you have time, you can also volunteer to help at the school. We also hope to see you at our open house on October 26th, where you will have the opportunity to visit the school and meet your children's teachers.

Sincerely,

*Eva Fernandez*
Eva Fernandez, Principal

1. This letter is for the parents of _____.
   A. all students at this school
   B. students entering the ninth grade
   C. students with poor attendance
   D. honor students

2. Parents should NOT _____.
   A. supervise their children
   B. visit the school
   C. keep sick children at home
   D. send sick children to school

3. We can infer that the third year of high school is the _____ year.
   A. freshman
   B. sophomore
   C. junior
   D. senior

4. Honor students _____.
   A. need improvement
   B. get unsatisfactory grades
   C. are below average
   D. get high grades

5. According to this letter, homework teaches students to _____.
   A. work on their own
   B. work for freedom
   C. work with others
   D. work until late at night

6. The open house is _____.
   A. a parent-teacher association meeting
   B. a time to visit and meet the teachers
   C. at the principal's house
   D. for latch-key children

Look at the map of Clarksdale Community College and answer the questions.

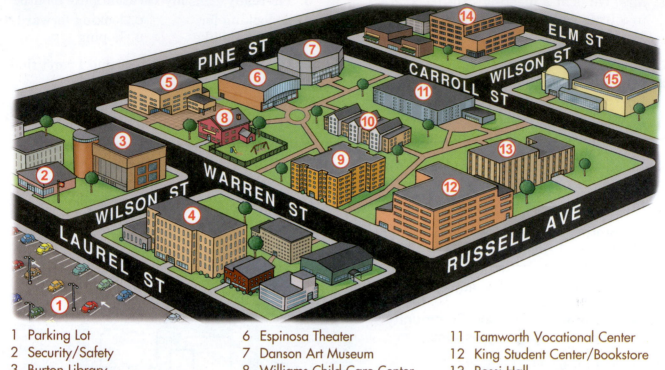

1  Parking Lot
2  Security/Safety
3  Burton Library
4  Baker Administration Building
5  Patterson Music Building

6  Espinosa Theater
7  Danson Art Museum
8  Williams Child-Care Center
9  Carter Hall
10  Lopez Hall

11  Tamworth Vocational Center
12  King Student Center/Bookstore
13  Rossi Hall
14  Fletcher Science Center
15  Rivera Gym

1. Carter Hall is on _____.
   A. Pine Street
   B. Warren Street
   C. Russell Avenue
   D. Wilson Street

2. Espinosa Theater is _____.
   A. across from Rossi Hall
   B. around the corner from the student center
   C. between the music building and the museum
   D. next to the vocational center

3. When you go from the student center to the gym, you pass _____.
   A. Danson Art Museum
   B. Patterson Music Building
   C. Fletcher Science Center
   D. Rossi Hall

4. You can buy books for your courses at _____.
   A. Baker Administration Building
   B. King Student Center
   C. Burton Library
   D. Carter Hall

5. The basketball court is in _____.
   A. Building 5
   B. Building 11
   C. Building 12
   D. Building 15

6. Susan is learning how to be a welder in _____.
   A. Building 2
   B. Building 4
   C. Building 11
   D. Building 14

7. The chemistry labs are in the building _____.
   A. on Elm Street
   B. on Laurel Street
   C. on Russell Avenue
   D. on Warren Street

8. Someone stole Amy's wallet. She should go to the building _____.
   A. on Pine Street
   B. on Warren Street
   C. on Laurel Street
   D. on Elm Street

# ASSESSMENT
- **Check-up test**
- **Self-evaluation checklists**

**Choose the correct answer.**

1. Mrs. Wu is at a meeting. She'll _____ in a little while.
   - A. return
   - B. receive
   - C. require
   - D. realize

2. My wife and I will be _____ our income tax returns tonight.
   - A. writing
   - B. paying
   - C. filling out
   - D. working out

3. I'll be happy to _____ you my screwdriver.
   - A. take
   - B. browse
   - C. borrow
   - D. lend

4. My brother and I will be _____ a wedding in Cleveland this weekend.
   - A. arriving
   - B. attending
   - C. assembling
   - D. adjusting

5. I'm really _____ my vacation next month.
   - A. looking for
   - B. looking like
   - C. looking forward to
   - D. hoping

6. Oh, no! I have a flat tire, and I can't find my _____.
   - A. lock
   - B. ladder
   - C. hammer
   - D. jack

7. My daughter is a _____ in high school. She'll be going to college next year.
   - A. sophomore
   - B. senior
   - C. junior
   - D. freshman

8. This afternoon's meeting is _____ for all employees.
   - A. compulsory
   - B. capable
   - C. independent
   - D. absent

**Look at the map of Fairview Community College and answer the questions.**

9. Davis Library is _____.
   - A. next to the science center
   - B. across from the gym
   - C. next to the theater
   - D. between Ramirez Hall and De Costa Hall

10. To go from the parking lot to the theater, you pass _____.
    - A. De Costa Hall
    - B. the library
    - C. the student center
    - D. Ramirez Hall

1 Ramirez Hall
2 Davis Library
3 De Costa Hall
4 Grant Administration Building
5 Henderson Theater
6 Jenkins Student Center
7 Chang Science Center
8 Delgado Gym
9 Parking Lot

## SKILLS CHECK ✓

**Words:**
- ☐ adjust
- ☐ assemble
- ☐ attend
- ☐ borrow
- ☐ browse
- ☐ call back
- ☐ come back
- ☐ do research
- ☐ fill out
- ☐ get out
- ☐ give *the kids* a bath
- ☐ go water-skiing
- ☐ hike
- ☐ ice skate
- ☐ imagine
- ☐ lend
- ☐ look forward to
- ☐ pay bills
- ☐ relax
- ☐ return
- ☐ stay with
- ☐ work on
- ☐ work out

**I can ask & answer:**
- ☐ What are you going to *do*? I'm going to *read*.
- ☐ Will you *be home this evening*? Yes, I will. / No, I won't.
- ☐ I'll *work*.
- ☐ I won't *work*.
- ☐ I'll be *working*.
- ☐ How much longer will you be *ironing*?
- ☐ I'll be *ironing* for *another 10 minutes*.

**I can:**
- ☐ call in sick at work
- ☐ call school to report a child's absence
- ☐ interpret a high school grading system
- ☐ describe school procedures
- ☐ identify parent responsibilities
- ☐ interpret a college campus map

**I can ask a favor:**
- ☐ Could you do me a favor?
- ☐ Could you possibly do me a favor?
- ☐ Could you do a favor for me?
- ☐ Could I ask you a favor?

**I can write:**
- ☐ a note to my child's teacher

**I can write about:**
- ☐ something I'm looking forward to

● **32d**

Feature Article
Fact File
Around the World
Interview
We've Got Mail!

**SIDE** *by* **SIDE** Gazette

Global Exchange
Listening
Fun with Idioms
What Are They
Saying?

Volume 3　　　　　　　　　　　　　　　　　　　　　　　　　Number 1

# Immigration Around the World

### Where do immigrants move, and why?

More than 145 million immigrants live outside their native countries. Immigrants move to other countries for different reasons. Some people move because of war, political or economic problems, or natural disasters such as earthquakes and floods. Some immigrants move to be with family members, to marry, or to find better living conditions.

Where are immigrants moving from? And what countries are they moving to? One of the largest immigration flows is from Latin America and Asia to the United States. Another immigrant flow is from Eastern Europe, the former Soviet republics, and North Africa to Western Europe. Many immigrants also move from Africa and Asia to the Middle East. In countries such as Saudi Arabia, 90% of the total population is now foreign born.

When immigrants arrive in a new country, they often live in urban neighborhoods. As a result of immigration, many city neighborhoods change. Immigrants open new stores, restaurants, and other businesses. For example, the historic Esquilino neighborhood in Rome is now the home of a large number of Chinese immigrants. There are also

*Immigrants arriving in their new country*

many new immigrants from Albania, Moldova, Bulgaria, and Ukraine. In some schools in Athens, 50% of the children are foreign born. Los Angeles and New York are two cities in the United States with very large immigrant populations. In Los Angeles, 37% of the population is foreign born, and children in the public schools speak 82 different languages. In New York, 40% of the population is foreign born, and children speak 140 different languages in the schools.

## Ellis Island

Ellis Island was an immigration center on an island in the harbor of New York City. Between 1892 and 1954, 12 million immigrants passed through Ellis Island. At Ellis Island, immigration officials checked immigrants' documents, gave them medical examinations, and decided if the immigrants could stay in the United States. Most immigrants came from Italy, Russia, Hungary, Austria, Austria-Hungary, Germany, England, and Ireland. More than 40% of all Americans today have a present or past relative who came through Ellis Island.

*Ellis Island registration hall*

## FACT FILE

### Countries with Large Numbers of Immigrants

| Country | Immigrant Population (in millions) |
|---|---|
| United States | 28.4 |
| Germany | 7.5 |
| Saudi Arabia | 6 |
| Canada | 4.9 |
| Australia | 4.4 |
| France | 4.3 |

# Immigrant Neighborhoods

**T**here are many interesting immigrant neighborhoods around the world. In these neighborhoods, immigrants can often speak their native languages, buy products from their countries, and eat in restaurants that serve their favorite foods.

a Cuban neighborhood in Miami, Florida

Vietnamese immigrants in Sydney, Australia

Turkish immigrants in Berlin, Germany

Chinatown in Toronto, Canada

Japanese immigrants in Sao Paulo, Brazil

a Russian neighborhood in Brooklyn, New York

**What are different immigrant neighborhoods you know?**

# Interview

*A Side by Side Gazette reporter recently visited Mr. Tran Nguyen, a Vietnamese immigrant in Australia. Mr. Nguyen lives and works in a Vietnamese and Chinese neighborhood in the suburbs of Melbourne.*

**Q: When did you immigrate to Australia, and why?**

**A:** Well, my brother left Vietnam in 1983 and came here to Australia. Seven years later, his wife and children joined him. I came here three years ago with my wife and children to be with my brother and his family.

**Q: Do you work?**

**A:** Yes. I work seven days a week in my brother's restaurant, and I go to English classes at night.

**Q: What did you do in Vietnam?**

**A:** I was a teacher. I taught mathematics. I want to be a teacher here someday, but first I want to send my children to college.

**Q: What do you miss most about Vietnam?**

**A:** I miss my community and my friends. In Vietnam, people took care of each other. It's not the same here. Everyone here works very hard. People are very busy. They don't have much time to spend with friends.

**Q: What do you like about your life here?**

**A:** We have many opportunities. My wife and I both have good jobs, and my son and daughter will go to college someday. I think we will have a very good future here, and we're very grateful.

## We've Got Mail!

Dear Side by Side,

I have a question about tenses in English. Sometimes I hear people use the present tense when they are talking about the future. For example, I was watching a TV program in English yesterday, and I heard a man say, "I'm flying to London tomorrow. My plane leaves at 9:30." But if a man is talking about tomorrow, shouldn't he use the future tense? I think the correct way to say this is: "I'm going to fly to London tomorrow. My plane will leave at 9:30." Did the man on the TV program make a mistake?

Sincerely,

"Tense About the Future"

Dear "Tense About the Future,"

Your question is a very good one. No, the man on the TV program didn't make a mistake. We often use the present tense to talk about events in the future or about definite plans that we have. For example, you can say:

My brother's wedding is next Saturday.
I'm having a party tomorrow.
They're going to the beach this weekend.
The plumber is coming tomorrow morning.

We can also use the present tense to talk about future events that happen at a definite time or on a regular schedule. For example, you can say:

The movie begins at 7:30 tonight.
The office opens tomorrow morning at 9 A.M.
The train arrives at 6:15.
The store closes tonight at 10 P.M.

So, you don't need to be "tense" about the future! You can use both the present and the future tenses to talk about future time.

We hope this answers your question. Thanks for your letter, and good luck with your English!

Sincerely,

*Side by Side*

---

### Global Exchange

**NickyG:** Hi. It's Sunday night here, and I just finished my biology homework. Before I turn off my computer, I want to tell you about my weekend. It was really great. I went camping with some of my friends. We left early Saturday morning and drove to the mountains. We hiked for several hours to a beautiful lake. We went swimming, we cooked over a campfire, and we slept outside. We told stories and sang songs until after midnight. In the morning, we made a big breakfast, we swam again, and then we packed up our things, hiked back to the car, and came home. How about you? How was your weekend? Write back soon. Okay?

**Smile9:** Hi. It's Monday morning here. I'm sitting in the computer lab at my school, and your message just arrived! I'm happy to hear from you again. My weekend wasn't as exciting as yours. I have final exams in all my courses this week, so I stayed home and studied all weekend. But I'm really looking forward to next weekend. Our family is going to travel to the place where my parents grew up. We're having a big family reunion on Saturday. All my relatives will be there. We don't see them very often, so it will be a very special time. I'll tell you about it when I return. Oh. Here comes my teacher! I've got to go! Talk to you soon.

Send a message to a keypal. Tell about what you did last weekend. Tell about your plans for next weekend.

---

### LISTENING

*You have five messages!*

## You Have Five Messages!

| | | | | |
|---|---|---|---|---|
| _e_ | ❶ | Sarah | **a.** | will be visiting his parents. |
| ____ | ❷ | Bob | **b.** | will be studying. |
| ____ | ❸ | Paula | **c.** | will be attending a wedding. |
| ____ | ❹ | Joe | **d.** | will go to the party. |
| ____ | ❺ | Carla | **e.** | will be taking her uncle to the hospital. |

---

# FUN with IDIOMS

## Do You Know These Expressions?

_e_ **1.** It's raining cats and dogs!

____ **2.** What's cooking?

____ **3.** I'm tied up right now.

____ **4.** I'll give you a ring tomorrow.

____ **5.** The English test was a piece of cake!

____ **6.** The English test was no picnic!

**a.** I'll call you.

**b.** It was difficult.

**c.** It was easy.

**d.** What's new?

**e.** It's raining very hard.

**f.** I'm busy.

## What Are They Saying?

## Parts of Speech

A **noun** names a person, place, thing, or idea.
A **pronoun** takes the place of a noun.
A **verb** names an action.
An **adjective** describes a noun or a pronoun.
An **adverb** describes a verb, an adjective, or another adverb.
A **preposition** relates a noun or pronoun to another word.

## Combining Sentences

Sometimes two sentences repeat some information. You can combine sentences to make one better sentence.

| | | |
|---|---|---|
| **Nouns** | I turned on the <u>computer</u>. <br> I turned on the <u>printer</u>. | I turned on the <u>computer</u> and the <u>printer</u>. |
| **Pronouns** | <u>She</u> will return soon. <br> <u>I</u> will return soon. | <u>She</u> and <u>I</u> will return soon. |
| **Verbs** | We <u>swam</u> yesterday. <br> We <u>played tennis</u> yesterday. | We <u>swam</u> and <u>played tennis</u> yesterday. |
| **Adjectives** | I was <u>tired</u> yesterday. <br> I was <u>angry</u> yesterday. | I was <u>tired</u> and <u>angry</u> yesterday. |
| **Adverbs** | You type <u>quickly</u>. <br> You type <u>accurately</u>. | You type <u>quickly</u> and <u>accurately</u>. |
| **Prepositions** | I cleaned <u>inside</u> the house. <br> I cleaned <u>outside</u> the house. | I cleaned <u>inside</u> and <u>outside</u> the house. |

## Practice the conversation with a classmate.

My son has a headache.
My son has an earache.

**A.** Can you combine these two sentences?

**B.** Yes. *My son has a headache and an earache.*

**A.** What did you combine?

**B.** I combined the **nouns** *headache* and *earache*.

## Combine the sentences. Then practice new conversations about them.

1. The test was long.
   The test was difficult.

2. I always drive slowly.
   I always drive carefully.

3. He worked late last night.
   I worked late last night.

4. Parents attended the meeting.
   Students attended the meeting.

5. We put the boxes on the table.
   We put the boxes under the table.

6. I'll wash the dishes tonight.
   I'll dry the dishes tonight.

## West Community College
### NEW STUDENT INFORMATION

Welcome to West Community College! We understand that new students have many questions, so here is some important information for your first days at the college.

### First Steps

**1. Get a student photo ID card.** You will need a student photo identification card to make appointments with counselors, take assessment tests, borrow books from the library, and get a parking permit. To get your free student photo ID card, go to Room 121 in the Student Activities Center. The office is open Monday–Thursday 8:00 A.M. to 6:00 P.M. and Friday 8:00 A.M. to 4:00 P.M.

**2. Get a parking permit.** If you drive and want to park your car in Parking Lot A, B, or C, you will need a parking permit and sticker. Go to the Parking Office, Room 103, in the Student Activities Center. Bring your student photo ID card, your driver's license, and your car's license plate number. After you get your parking permit, you will need to buy a parking sticker. The fee for the sticker is $30 per semester, including the summer term, or $50 for a full year.

**3. Sign up for assessment tests.** All new students must take English and math assessment tests. These tests help us place you in the appropriate English or math class. You cannot register for any classes until you take the tests. Sign up for the assessment tests in the Assessment Office, Room 101, in Williams Hall. The Assessment Office is open Monday–Friday 8:00 A.M. to 4:00 P.M. and Saturday 8:00 A.M. to 11:30 A.M. You can also sign up online. Go to the West Community College website and click on "New Students" and "Assessment Tests."

**4. Take your assessment tests.** Please be at the Student Academic Assistance Office 15 minutes before your test appointment time. The Student Academic Assistance Office is in Murphy Hall, Room 212. You need to take two one-hour tests—an English test and a math test. The office will send your test scores to the Advising Office within 24 hours. They will also send your test scores to your online West Community College account. Sign in to check your test scores.

**5. Register for classes at the Advising Office.** You must have your assessment test scores before you register for classes. To register, go to the Advising Office on the second floor of Williams Hall, Room 205. You can come in any time to meet with an advisor. You and your advisor will discuss your assessment tests, your study plans, and your classes. Your advisor will help you register for classes and plan your schedule for the year.

After you complete these steps, you are ready to begin classes! Congratulations, and welcome to West Community College!

### Important Campus Services

Here are the most important places on campus. For more information, visit our website.

**Student Activities Center:** The center is really the heart of the college. It's a great place to relax and meet with classmates. The center has a cafeteria, two coffee shops, a pizza shop, and several meeting rooms. There is also an Activities Office, where you can find out about campus music, theater, and sports events. There is a large game room in the basement. Campus clubs and organizations have meetings in the Activities Center. There are more than 30 clubs and student groups. In addition, there is a Community Service Office, where you can find out about opportunities to volunteer, and the Campus Employment Office, where you can get information about jobs available on campus and in the community.

**Advising Office:** The Advising Office staff helps students in a variety of ways. First, an advisor can help you select courses and plan your schedule. In addition, an advisor can refer you to the many resources available in the office. For example, there is a Study Smart program to help students improve their study skills. Students can sign up for a free one-month course. An advisor can also give information about the Student Academic Assistance program. This program includes the Writing Center, the Math Center, and the Science Tutoring Center. Whenever you are having trouble with your studies, advisors are available to help you find ways to improve your skills.

**Bookstore:** At the bookstore, you can buy textbooks, rent textbooks, and buy software and computers at low prices. We also have a textbook buyback program every Monday morning until noon. Bring in your used textbooks, and you can receive money for them. You can also shop online. Just go to the West Community College website. Hours: Monday–Thursday 7:30 A.M. to 6:30 P.M., Friday 7:30 A.M. to 4:30 P.M., and Saturday 8:00 A.M. to 3:00 P.M.

**Library:** In addition to our library's large collection of books and journals, it has free Internet, laptops you can borrow, a computer lab, e-books, and an online website. Your student photo ID is your library card. New students should take the one-hour orientation class. It is every Wednesday at noon. Library hours: Monday–Thursday 8:00 A.M. to 8:00 P.M., Friday 8:00 A.M. to 6:00 P.M., and Saturday and Sunday 12 noon to 6:00 P.M.

**Health Center:** Health services are only for West Community College students. You must call or come into the Health Center to make an appointment. Most appointments are $10.00. You must pay by cash, check, or credit card when you come in for your appointment. Free health services include flu shots, first-aid care, blood pressure check, pregnancy tests, counseling to stop smoking, and educational brochures. Mental health services are also available. Our counselors can help you discuss problems and find assistance. There is individual and group counseling. Hours: Monday–Thursday 8:00 A.M. to 8:30 P.M. and Friday 8:00 A.M. to 4:30 P.M.

**Career Center:** The Career Center is on the second floor of Williams Hall. You can meet with a career counselor to discuss your future plans. There is a career library with books, videos, and job resources. We  also offer classes on how to find a job, write a resume and cover letter, and prepare for an interview. Call or go online to make an appointment. Hours: Monday–Thursday 8:00 A.M. to 6:30 P.M. and Friday 8:00 A.M. to 4:30 P.M.

**Financial Aid Office:** West Community College aims to provide an excellent education for all students. About 50% of our students receive financial aid while they attend college. Financial aid can be a loan, a scholarship, a special grant, or on-campus employment. Almost 75% of our students work while they go to school. Financial aid counselors will help you put together the financial aid that you need. They will also help you apply for Federal Student Aid. No appointment is necessary. Hours: Monday–Thursday 8:00 A.M. to 6:30 P.M. and Friday 8:00 A.M. to 4:30 P.M.

1. New students must take assessment tests before they _____.
   - (A) register for classes
   - (B) receive a parking permit
   - (C) get a student identification card
   - (D) open an online West Community College account

2. Each assessment test takes _____.
   - (A) 15 minutes
   - (B) one hour
   - (C) two hours
   - (D) four hours

3. New students can meet with an advisor in _____.
   - (A) the Assessment Office
   - (B) the Student Activity Center
   - (C) Murphy Hall, Room 212
   - (D) Williams Hall, Room 205

4. The Student Academic Assistance program gives students _____.
   - (A) photo ID cards
   - (B) software and computers
   - (C) information about student activities and clubs
   - (D) help with their classes and with study skills

5. For information about how to pay for college courses, students go to the _____.
   - (A) Financial Aid Office
   - (B) Advising Office
   - (C) Career Center
   - (D) Campus Employment Office

6. The _____ is open the most hours per week.
   - (A) bookstore
   - (B) health center
   - (C) library
   - (D) career center

7. In a *textbook buyback program*, the bookstore _____.
   - (A) sells used books
   - (B) returns used books
   - (C) buys used books from students
   - (D) buys used books from companies

8. *Mental health services* help students with their _____.
   - (A) interview skills
   - (B) emotional problems
   - (C) nutritional health
   - (D) test-taking skills

## Think & Share

1. Why is it important for the college to have a Student Academic Assistance program? Why do students sometimes need additional help?
2. In your opinion, are there enough campus services at West Community College? Should there be more? If so, what other services do you think the college should have, and why?

Write a friendly letter to your classmates. Introduce yourself. Tell about your family. Tell about where you are from. Describe how and why you moved to your new home. Tell about when and where you studied English before. Tell about what else you are doing now. Describe what you want to do in the future. Also tell about any interesting hobbies or interests you have.

**heading** —
Your street address
Your city, state  Zip Code
Today's date:  Month day, year

Dear Classmates, —— **salutation**

**body**

[In the first paragraph, tell about yourself and your family. Where are you from?  Which family members live with you or near you?  Which family members live in another place?  Indent the first line of each paragraph.]

[In the second paragraph, describe life back home before you left.  What was your life like back home?  Why did you leave?]

[In the third paragraph, tell about your journey.  How did you leave?  When?  Where did you go first?  Where else did you go after that?  Describe any interesting or important information about your journey.]

[In the fourth paragraph, tell about schools you went to and jobs you had before you moved here.  What did you study?  Did you study English before?  Where?  What work did you do?  Where did you work?]

[In the fifth paragraph, tell about what you are doing now in addition to studying English.  Are you working?  Are you studying something else?  Also tell about your plans for the future.  What do you want to do?]

[In the sixth paragraph, tell about any hobbies or interests you have, or share anything else that you want your classmates to know about you.]

[In the seventh paragraph, tell your classmates how you feel about your English class, and thank them for reading your letter.]

**closing** —— Sincerely,

**signature** —— *Your signature*

Friendly letters are personal.  You can write or type a friendly letter.  This type of letter has five parts:

The **heading** shows your address and the date.  In the address, use a comma between the city and state.  In the date, use a comma between the day and the year.

The **salutation** is the greeting.  Capitalize the first word of the salutation and the person's name.  Use a comma after the person's name.

The **body** contains the content of the letter.  Indent each paragraph.

The **closing** comes at the end of the letter.  Capitalize only the first word in the closing.  Use a comma after the closing.

The **signature** shows your name.  Don't print your name.  Write your signature.

# Present Perfect Tense

**4**

- **Describing Skills**
- **Describing Actions That Have Occurred**
- **Describing Actions That Haven't Occurred Yet**
- **Making Recommendations**

- **Things To Do Where You Live**
- **Making Lists**
- **Employment Application Procedures**
- **Job Application Forms**
- **Employment History**
- **Job Search Strategies**

## VOCABULARY PREVIEW

**Things to Do Today**

1 ☐ go to the bank

2 ☐ do the laundry

3 ☐ get a haircut

4 ☐ write to Grandma

5 ☐ take the dog for a walk

6 ☐ give the dog a bath

7 ☐ speak to the landlord

8 ☐ drive the kids to their dance lesson

9 ☐ eat lunch

10 ☐ ride my exercise bike

11 ☐ swim

12 ☐ see a movie

**Things I've Done Today:** I've . . .

- ☑ **1.** gone to the bank
- ☑ **2.** done the laundry
- ☑ **3.** gotten a haircut
- ☑ **4.** written to Grandma
- ☑ **5.** taken the dog for a walk
- ☑ **6.** given the dog a bath
- ☑ **7.** spoken to the landlord
- ☑ **8.** driven the kids to their dance lesson
- ☑ **9.** eaten lunch
- ☑ **10.** ridden my exercise bike
- ☑ **11.** swum
- ☑ **12.** seen a movie

# I've Driven Trucks for Many Years

**A.** Do you know how to **drive** trucks?

**B.** Yes. I've **driven** trucks for many years.

**1.** *write reports*
   *written*

**2.** *fly airplanes*
   *flown*

**3.** *take X-rays*
   *taken*

**4.** *speak Swahili*
   *spoken*

**5.** *eat with chopsticks*
   *eaten*

**6.** *give injections*
   *given*

**7.** *draw cartoons*
   *drawn*

**8.** *do yoga*
   *done*

**9.** *ride horses*
   *ridden*

# I've Never Eaten Lunch with the Boss

**A.** I'm going to **eat** lunch with the boss tomorrow.

**B.** I'm jealous. I've never **eaten** lunch with the boss.

**1.** *fly in a helicopter*
*flown*

**2.** *see a Broadway show*
*seen*

**3.** *go on a cruise*
*gone*

**4.** *sing at the White House*
*sung*

**5.** *swim at the Ritz Hotel*
*swum*

**6.** *get a raise*
*gotten*

**7.** *be on television*
*been*

**8.** *take a ride in a hot-air*
*balloon*
*taken*

**9.** *ride in a limousine*
*ridden*

# Have You Ever Seen a Rainbow?

see
saw
seen

see a rainbow

**A.** Have you ever **seen** a rainbow?

**B.** Yes, I have.  I **saw** a rainbow last year.

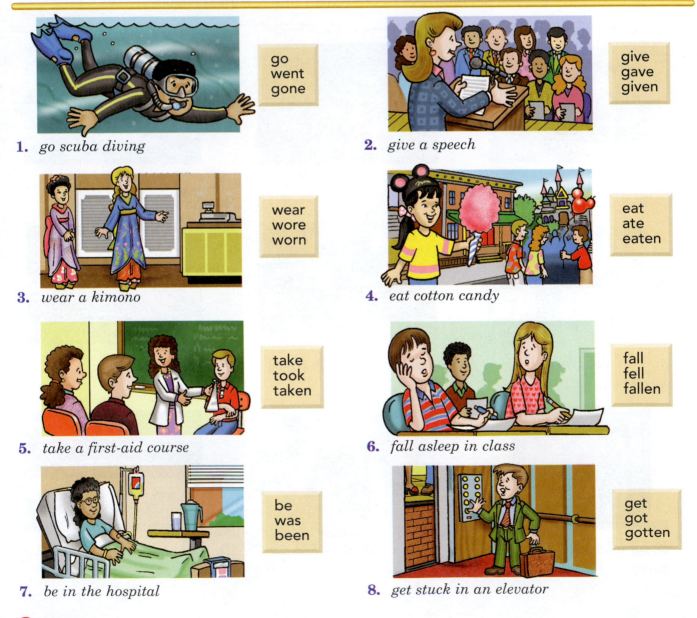

go
went
gone

**1.** *go scuba diving*

give
gave
given

**2.** *give a speech*

wear
wore
worn

**3.** *wear a kimono*

eat
ate
eaten

**4.** *eat cotton candy*

take
took
taken

**5.** *take a first-aid course*

fall
fell
fallen

**6.** *fall asleep in class*

be
was
been

**7.** *be in the hospital*

get
got
gotten

**8.** *get stuck in an elevator*

# Have You Written the Report Yet?

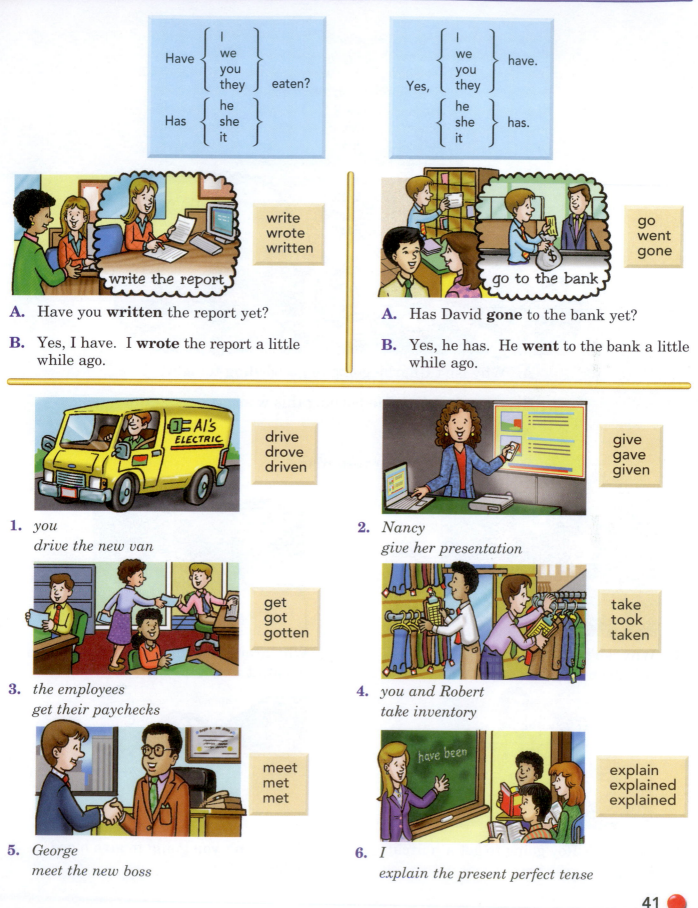

Have { I / we / you / they } eaten?

Has { he / she / it }

Yes, { I / we / you / they } have.

{ he / she / it } has.

write
wrote
written

**write the report**

**A.** Have you **written** the report yet?

**B.** Yes, I have. I **wrote** the report a little while ago.

go
went
gone

**go to the bank**

**A.** Has David **gone** to the bank yet?

**B.** Yes, he has. He **went** to the bank a little while ago.

drive
drove
driven

**1.** *you*
*drive the new van*

give
gave
given

**2.** *Nancy*
*give her presentation*

get
got
gotten

**3.** *the employees*
*get their paychecks*

take
took
taken

**4.** *you and Robert*
*take inventory*

meet
met
met

**5.** *George*
*meet the new boss*

have been

explain
explained
explained

**6.** *I*
*explain the present perfect tense*

# He's Already Gone Bowling This Week

| | | |
|---|---|---|
| (I have) | I've | |
| (We have) | We've | |
| (You have) | You've | |
| (They have) | They've | eaten. |
| (He has) | He's | |
| (She has) | She's | |
| (It has) | It's | |

go
went
gone

**A.** Why isn't Charlie going to **go** bowling tonight?

**B.** He's already **gone** bowling this week.

**A.** Really? When?

**B.** He **went** bowling yesterday.

see
saw
seen

**1.** Why isn't Vicky going to see a movie this evening?

eat
ate
eaten

**2.** Why aren't Mr. and Mrs. Kendall going to eat at a restaurant tonight?

get
got
gotten

**3.** Why isn't Roy going to get a haircut today?

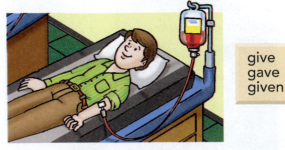

give
gave
given

**4.** Why aren't you going to give blood today?

take
took
taken

**5.** Why isn't Shirley going to take her children to the zoo this afternoon?

wear
wore
worn

**6.** Why isn't Fred going to wear his purple tie today?

drive
drove
driven

**7.** Why aren't you and your family going to drive to the mountains today?

write
wrote
written

**8.** Why isn't Julie going to write to her best friend today?

do
did
done

**9.** Why isn't Gary going to do his laundry today?

swim
swam
swum

**10.** Why aren't your parents going to swim at the health club today?

buy
bought
bought

**11.** Why aren't you going to buy bananas today?

have
had
had

**12.** Why aren't Mr. and Mrs. Davis going to have spaghetti for dinner tonight?

wash
washed
washed

**13.** Why isn't Jim going to wash his car this morning?

play
played
played

**14.** Why isn't your grandmother going to play Bingo today?

# READING

me
Maggie
Mark   Betty   Mike   nobody

## WE CAN'T DECIDE

My friends and I can't decide what to do tonight. I don't want to see a movie. I've already seen a movie this week. Maggie doesn't want to go bowling. She has already gone bowling this week. Mark doesn't want to eat at a restaurant. He has already eaten at a restaurant this week. Betty and Mike don't want to play cards. They have already played cards this week. And NOBODY wants to go dancing. We have all gone dancing this week.

It's already 9 P.M., and we still haven't decided what we're going to do tonight.

# ROLE PLAY

You and other students are the people in the story above. Create a role play based on the situation. Use these lines to start your conversation.

**A.** Look! It's already 9 P.M., and we still haven't decided what we're going to do tonight. Does anybody have any ideas?
**B.** I don't know.
**C.** Do you want to see a movie?
**D.** No, not me. I've already . . .
**E.** Does anybody want to . . . ?
**F.** I don't. I've already . . .
**G.** I have an idea. Let's . . .
**H.** No, I don't want to do that. I've already . . .

# COMPLETE THE STORY

Fill in the correct words to complete the story.

Alvin has a very bad cold. He has been sick all week. He has tried very hard to get rid of his cold, but nothing he has done has helped. At the beginning of the week, he went to a clinic and saw a doctor. He followed the doctor's advice all week. He stayed home, took aspirin, drank* orange juice, ate chicken soup, and rested in bed.

At this point, Alvin is extremely frustrated. Even though he has _____ ¹ to a clinic and _____ ² a doctor, _____ ³ home, _____ ⁴ aspirin, _____ ⁵ orange juice, _____ ⁶ chicken soup, and _____ ⁷ in bed, he STILL has a very bad cold. Nothing he has _____ ⁸ has helped.

\* drink – drank – drunk

 **44**

# They Haven't Had the Time

I
We
You
They
} haven't
(have not)

He
She
It
} hasn't
(has not)

eaten.*

**A.** Do you like to **swim**?

**B.** Yes, but I haven't **swum** in a long time.

**A.** Why not?

**B.** I haven't had the time.

**A.** Does Rita like to **draw**?

**B.** Yes, but she hasn't **drawn** in a long time.

**A.** Why not?

**B.** She hasn't had the time.

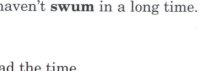

**1.** Do you like to ride your bicycle?

**2.** Does Arthur like to write poetry?

**3.** Does Kathy like to go kayaking?

**4.** Do you and your brother like to play Monopoly?

**5.** Does Laura like to make her own clothes?

**6.** Do you like to see your old friends?

**7.** Do Mr. and Mrs. Bell like to take dance lessons?

**8.** Does Grandpa like to do magic tricks?

**9.**

* In the present perfect tense, the word after **have** or **has** is a past participle. Some past participles are the same as the past tense (for example, **played**, **washed**, **made**). Other past participles are different from the past tense (for example, **swum**, **drawn**, **ridden**). We will tell you when the past participles are different. A list of these words is in the Appendix at the end of the book.

# Has Timmy Gone to Bed Yet?

| Have | I / we / you / they | eaten? |
|---|---|---|
| Has | he / she / it | |

| No, | I / we / you / they | haven't. |
|---|---|---|
| | he / she / it | hasn't. |

**A.** Has Timmy gone to bed yet?

**B.** No, he hasn't. He has to go to bed now.

**1.** *Amanda*
*do her homework*

**2.** *you*
*take your medicine*

**3.** *James*
*get up*

**4.** *Debbie and Danny*
*leave for school*

**5.** *Jennifer*
*call her supervisor*

**6.** *you*
*write your term paper*

**7.** *you and your sister*
*feed the dog*

**8.** *you*
*speak to your landlord*

**9.** *Harry*
*pay his electric bill*

### WORKING OVERTIME

I'm an employee of the Goodwell Computer Company. This is a typical Friday afternoon at our office. All the employees are working overtime. We haven't gone home because we haven't finished our work yet. Friday is always a very busy day.

The secretary still hasn't typed two important letters. The bookkeeper hasn't written all the paychecks. The office clerks haven't delivered all the mail. And the boss still hasn't spoken to three important people who are waiting to see her.

As for me, I'm the custodian, and I haven't finished my work yet either. I still haven't cleaned all the offices because my co-workers haven't gone home yet! I'm not really surprised. Friday is always a very busy day at our office.

## ✔ READING *CHECK-UP*

### Q & A

The custodian at the Goodwell Computer Company is talking with the employees on a typical Friday afternoon. Using this model, create dialogs based on the story.

**A.** I see you haven't gone home yet.
**B.** No, I haven't. I still haven't *typed two important letters*.
**A.** Well, have a good weekend.
**B.** You, too.

### WHAT'S THE WORD?

1. **A.** Have you (see) _____ the letter from the Lexon Company?
   **B.** Yes. I _____ it on your desk.

2. **A.** Have you (eat) _____ lunch yet?
   **B.** Yes. I _____ a few minutes ago.

3. **A.** Has the bookkeeper (go) _____ to the bank yet?
   **B.** Yes, she _____. She _____ there this morning.

4. **A.** Have you (speak) _____ to the boss about your vacation?
   **B.** Yes, I _____. I _____ to her about it yesterday.

5. **A.** Have you (make) _____ plans for my trip to Chicago yet?
   **B.** Yes. I _____ them yesterday.

6. **A.** Has anybody (read) _____ today's *New York Times*?
   **B.** Yes. I _____ it on my way to work.

7. **A.** Has the office clerk (take) _____ the mail to the post office yet?
   **B.** No, he _____. He _____ it to the mail room, but _____ _____ _____ it to the post office yet.

8. **A.** Has John (finish) _____ his work?
   **B.** Yes, he _____. He's already (go) _____ home.

# Have You Seen Any Good Movies Recently?

A. Have you seen any good movies recently?

B. Yes, I have.  I saw a very good movie last week.

A. Really?  What movie did you see?

B. I saw *The Wedding Dancer*.

A. Oh.  How was it?

B. It was excellent.  It's one of the best movies I've ever seen.

---

A. Have you _____ any good _____s recently?

B. Yes, I have.  I _____ a very good _____ last week.

A. Really?  What _____ did you _____?

B. I _____ "_____."

A. Oh.  How was it?

B. It was excellent.  It's one of the best _____s I've ever _____.

**1.** *read • book*

**2.** *rent • video*

**3.** *go to • restaurant*

## How to Say It!

**Expressing Satisfaction**

A. How was it?

B.
It **was** excellent.
It was very good.
It was wonderful.
It was great.
It was fantastic.
It was terrific.
It was phenomenal.
It was awesome.

**Practice the conversations in this lesson again.  Express satisfaction in different ways.**

## READING

### LINDA LIKES NEW YORK

Linda has lived in New York for a long time.  She has done a lot of things in New York.  She has gone to the top of the Empire State Building, she has visited the Statue of Liberty, she has taken a tour of the United Nations, and she has seen several Broadway shows.

However, there are a lot of things she hasn't done yet.  She hasn't gone to any museums, she hasn't seen Ellis Island, and she hasn't been in Times Square on New Year's Eve.

Linda likes New York.  She has done a lot of things, and there are still a lot more things to do.

## LISTENING

Linda is on vacation in San Francisco.  This is her list of things to do.  Check the things on the list Linda has already done.

Alan is a secretary in a very busy office.  This is his list of things to do before 5 P.M. on Friday.  Check the things on the list Alan has already done.

It's Saturday, and Judy and Paul Johnson are doing lots of things around the house.  This is the list of things they have to do today.  Check the things on the list they've already done.

___ see the Golden Gate Bridge
___ visit Golden Gate Park
___ take a tour of Alcatraz prison
___ go to Chinatown
___ ride a cable car
___ eat at Fisherman's Wharf
___ buy souvenirs

___ call Mrs. Porter
___ type the letter to the Mervis Company
___ take the mail to the post office
___ go to the bank
___ send an e-mail to the company's office in Denver
___ speak to the boss about my salary

___ do the laundry
___ wash the kitchen windows
___ pay the bills
___ give the dog a bath
___ clean the garage
___ fix the bathroom sink
___ repair the fence
___ vacuum the living room rug

Make a List!

Make a list of things you usually do at school, at work, or at home.  Then check the things you've already done this week.  Share your list with other students.  Tell about what you've done and what you haven't done.

| he is = he's | she is = she's |
|---|---|
| he has = he's | she has = she's |

**Listen.  Then say it.**

**He is** a good painter.

**He has** painted for a long time.

**She is** a good teacher.

**She has** taught for a long time.

**Say it.  Then listen.**

**He is** a taxi driver.

**He has** driven a taxi for a long time.

**She is** an actress.

**She has** acted for a long time.

SIDE by SIDE JOURNAL

Think about your experiences in the place where you live.  What have you done?  What haven't you done yet?  Write about it in your journal.

## GRAMMAR FOCUS

### PRESENT PERFECT TENSE

| (I have) | I've | |
|---|---|---|
| (We have) | We've | |
| (You have) | You've | |
| (They have) | They've | eaten. |
| (He has) | He's | |
| (She has) | She's | |
| (It has) | It's | |

| I | | |
|---|---|---|
| We | haven't | |
| You | | |
| They | | eaten. |
| He | | |
| She | hasn't | |
| It | | |

| Have | I we you they | eaten? |
|---|---|---|
| Has | he she it | |

| Yes, | I we you they | have. |
|---|---|---|
| | he she it | has. |

| No, | I we you they | haven't. |
|---|---|---|
| | he she it | hasn't. |

### IRREGULAR VERBS

be – was/were – been
do – did – done
draw – drew – drawn
drink – drank – drunk
drive – drove – driven
eat – ate – eaten
fall – fell – fallen
fly – flew – flown
get – got – gotten
give – gave – given
go – went – gone
ride – rode – ridden
see – saw – seen
sing – sang – sung
speak – spoke – spoken
swim – swam – swum
take – took – taken
wear – wore – worn
write – wrote – written

**Complete the sentences with the correct forms of these verbs.**

| be | draw | go | ride | see | sing | take | wear |
|---|---|---|---|---|---|---|---|

**1.** I love to draw. _____ _____ for many years.

**2.** _____ you ever _____ a rainbow?

**3.** My parents _____ never _____ dance lessons.

**4.** _____ already _____ that song.  We _____ it a little while ago.

**5.** My grandson _____ _____ his bicycle in a long time.

**6.** _____ you ever _____ on TV?  Yes, I _____.

**7.** Joe _____ already _____ that tie this week. He _____ it yesterday.

**8.** _____ Marta _____ to sleep yet?  Yes, _____ _____. She _____ to sleep an hour ago.

## 1 READING  HOW TO FILL OUT AN EMPLOYMENT APPLICATION

It's important to fill out an employment application form completely and correctly.  Read the suggestions for completing this company's form.

### Steps for Completing Your Job Application Form

1. Fill in all your personal information.
2. State the position you are applying for.
3. Complete your education history, including high school, college, and vocational school.
4. List your current and former jobs.
5. Write your dates of employment for each position.
6. Write each employer's name and address.
7. Give the reason for leaving each position.
8. Give the names and addresses of three references.
9. Describe your skills, including languages you speak.
10. Check the application to make sure all information is correct and complete.

## 2 CONVERSATION  APPLYING FOR A JOB

Practice with a classmate.  Ask about all the steps for completing a job application form.

A. Have you completed your application form?

B. Yes, I have.

A. Have you <u>filled in all your personal information</u>?**1**

B. Yes, I have.

A. Have you _____?**2**

B. Yes, I have.

A. Have you _____?**3–10**

B. Yes, I have.

## 3 TEAMWORK  APPLICATION FORMS

Find job application forms in the community and bring them to class.  Fill out a form.  Then exchange forms with a classmate and check each other's work. As a class, compare all the different application forms that students find.

**Look at the job application form and answer the questions.**

| NAME | Lessard | Daniel | Louis | DATE | 9/01/16 |
|---|---|---|---|---|---|
| | Last | First | Middle | SOCIAL SECURITY NUMBER | 749-10-2792 |

ADDRESS  895 North West 15th Street  Miami, FL  33132          TELEPHONE NUMBER  (305) 579-3457

**EMPLOYMENT HISTORY (LIST MOST RECENT OR PRESENT EXPERIENCE FIRST)**

| Date | Name & Address of Employer | Position | Salary | Name of Supervisor | Reason for Leaving |
|---|---|---|---|---|---|
| From: 3/16 To: present | Miami Family Physicians 9952 Center Ave., Miami, FL | medical assistant | $29,000/yr | Dr. Omar Hasan | want to learn new skills |
| Duties schedule appointments, measure height and weight, take blood pressure, do lab tests, change dressings | | | | | |
| From: 1/13 To: 2/16 | High Street Medical Associates 1750 High St., Miami, FL | medical assistant | $26,500/yr | Dr. Susan McCann | left for a better job |
| Duties filed medical records, greeted patients, measured their height and weight, and took their blood pressure | | | | | |
| From: 5/09 To: 5/11 | Diamond Health Club 1900 Grand St., Miami, FL | office assistant | $25,500/yr | Debby Lewis | returned to school |
| Duties answered the telephone, sorted mail, filed information, and typed memos | | | | | |
| From: 3/08 To: 4/09 | CompuTech Corporation 1273 Washington Ave., Miami, FL | receptionist | $25,000/yr | Nina Marino | company closed |
| Duties greeted clients, answered the telephone, and took messages | | | | | |
| From: 1/04 To: 2/08 | Dependable Hardware 632 Shore Blvd., Tampa, FL | salesperson | $10.00/hr | Fernando Nuñez | moved to Miami |
| Duties recommended tools and other hardware to customers, took inventory, and operated a cash register | | | | | |
| From: 3/03 To: 12/03 | Buy Low Supermarket 468 West Orange Ave., Tampa, FL | cashier | $7.50/hr | Jeff Carson | left for a better job |
| Duties operated a cash register | | | | | |

1. Daniel worked as _____ for two years.
   A. an office assistant
   B. a receptionist
   C. a salesperson
   D. a cashier

2. After CompuTech Corporation closed, Daniel _____.
   A. returned to school
   B. moved to Miami
   C. answered the telephone and sorted mail
   D. recommended tools and other hardware

3. Daniel is filling out this application on September 1, 2016.  He has worked at Miami Family Physicians for _____.
   A. half a year
   B. a year
   C. a year and a half
   D. nine months

4. Daniel hasn't _____ in a long time.
   A. taken blood pressure
   B. changed dressings
   C. operated a cash register
   D. done lab tests

5. Daniel has _____ in two different jobs.
   A. taken inventory
   B. answered the telephone
   C. scheduled appointments
   D. typed memos

6. We can infer that Daniel attended school _____.
   A. in 2008 and 2009
   B. in 2009 and 2010
   C. in 2010 and 2011
   D. in 2011 and 2012

Read the article and answer the questions.

## Find the Right Job!

It can take a long time to find the right job, but it doesn't have to take long if you know how and where to look. Here are some tips to help you with your job search.

✓ Check the classified ads in your local newspaper every morning. Look for job postings on bulletin boards in libraries, community centers, supermarkets, laundromats, and other public buildings. Look in store and restaurant windows for help wanted signs.

✓ Network! Tell your friends, relatives, neighbors, teachers, and everybody else you know that you're looking for a job. Describe the kind of job you want. One of these people might know about a job opening, maybe even before the job listing is in the newspaper.

✓ The Internet has employment websites with thousands of job listings. You can look through the job listings in Internet job banks, and you can even apply for some jobs online. If you don't have a computer or Internet service at home, go to your local public library to get on the Internet.

✓ Don't be afraid to call a company to ask about job openings. "Cold calls" are a good way to learn about job opportunities.

✓ Go to job fairs. Companies that are hiring often send representatives to these events. At a job fair, you can learn about many different jobs and companies.

✓ If you have a special talent that you think a business can use, talk to the manager. You might be able to create a job for yourself!

> "You can find the right job if you believe in yourself!"

Maria Mendez created a job for herself at the Rosebud Cafe. One day while Maria was having a cup of coffee there, she thought, "This coffee would taste much better with a slice of my homemade bread." Later that week, she brought three loaves of her bread to the cafe and told Gina Moran, the manager, that the cafe needed a baker with her skills. Gina liked the bread so much that she hired her on the spot. Maria started working there the next day. According to Maria, "You can find the right job if you believe in yourself!"

1. When you network to get a job, you _____.
   A. go to job websites
   B. check the classified ads
   C. look in store windows
   D. talk to your friends and neighbors

2. Job banks _____.
   A. have job listings
   B. give money
   C. are on bulletin boards
   D. are in public buildings

3. If you want to get on the Internet, you can go to _____.
   A. a job fair
   B. a job bank
   C. the library
   D. the Rosebud Cafe

4. You make a cold call to _____.
   A. thank an interviewer
   B. answer a classified ad
   C. ask about job openings
   D. ask about job fairs

5. At a job fair, you can _____.
   A. hire representatives
   B. find out about different companies
   C. talk to relatives and neighbors
   D. look in windows for help wanted signs

6. The Rosebud Cafe hired Maria Mendez because _____.
   A. they were looking for a baker
   B. she answered their ad
   C. she saw Gina Moran's help wanted sign
   D. she created a job for herself

## Choose the correct answer.

1. Samantha got a raise, and now her _____ is higher.
   A. report
   B. elevator
   C. boss
   D. salary

2. I went to the doctor for an examination. She gave me _____.
   A. a presentation
   B. the flu
   C. an injection
   D. X-rays

3. Let's go _____ on the river this weekend!
   A. kayaking
   B. camping
   C. hiking
   D. bowling

4. Did you watch the president's _____ about world problems on television last night?
   A. course
   B. speech
   C. inventory
   D. term paper

5. I didn't understand the present perfect tense, but my teacher _____ it very well.
   A. examined
   B. complained
   C. explained
   D. expressed

6. What _____ are you applying for?
   A. employer
   B. position
   C. skills
   D. reference

7. I saw a _____ for a receptionist on the bulletin board in the library.
   A. job posting
   B. job bank
   C. representative
   D. job fair

8. I made _____ to the Randall Company and asked about job openings.
   A. a network
   B. a job listing
   C. an opportunity
   D. a cold call

## Look at Wanda's job application form.  Choose the correct answer.

9. Wanda worked as a receptionist _____.
   A. in Detroit
   B. for two and a half years
   C. in 2008
   D. at the Brandon Corporation

10. Wanda hasn't _____ in a long time.
    A. sorted mail
    B. typed reports
    C. taken messages
    D. filed documents

| Date | Name & Address of Employer | Position | Reason for Leaving |
|---|---|---|---|
| From: 7/16 To: present | Brandon Corporation 1100 First Ave., Detroit, MI | office assistant | want to learn new skills |
| Duties type reports, file documents, sort mail | | | |
| From: 2/13 To: 8/15 | Tech-World Corporation 599 Tyler St., Chicago, IL | receptionist | returned to school |
| Duties answered the telephone, took messages, and greeted clients | | | |

## SKILLS CHECK ✔

**Words:**
- ☐ classified ads
- ☐ cold call
- ☐ dates of employment
- ☐ education history
- ☐ employer
- ☐ employment application
- ☐ employment history

- ☐ help wanted sign
- ☐ job bank
- ☐ job fair
- ☐ job listing
- ☐ job opening
- ☐ job posting
- ☐ job search
- ☐ personal information

- ☐ position
- ☐ reference
- ☐ representative
- ☐ salary
- ☐ skills

- ☐ apply for
- ☐ complete
- ☐ fill in
- ☐ hire
- ☐ network

**I can ask & answer:**
- ☐ Have you ever *seen it*? Yes, I have. I *saw it* last year.
- ☐ Have you *gone to the bank* yet? Yes, I have. No, I haven't.
- ☐ I've *driven* for many years.
- ☐ I've already *gone there*.
- ☐ I've never *been on television*.

**I can:**
- ☐ identify employment application procedures
- ☐ apply for a job
- ☐ describe job search strategies

**I can express satisfaction:**
- ☐ It was excellent/very good/wonderful/great/ fantastic/terrific/phenomenal/awesome.

**I can write:**
- ☐ a list of things I've done
- ☐ employment history on a job application form

**I can write about:**
- ☐ experiences in the place where I live

# Present Perfect vs. Present Tense
# Present Perfect vs. Past Tense
# Since/For

- Discussing Duration of Activity
- Medical Symptoms and Problems
- Career Advancement
- Telling About Family Members
- Job Interview

- Giving Employment History
- Cover Letters and Resumes
- Employee Manual: Workplace Policies and Expectations

## VOCABULARY PREVIEW

1. astronaut
2. cashier
3. clerk
4. computer programmer
5. doctor/physician
6. guidance counselor
7. guitarist
8. journalist
9. manager
10. musician
11. police officer
12. president
13. salesperson
14. taxi driver
15. vice president

# How Long?

| for | since |
|-----|-------|
| three hours | three o'clock |
| two days | yesterday afternoon |
| a week | last week |
| a long time | 2000 |
| • | • |
| • | • |
| • | • |

**A.** How long have you known* each other?

**B.** We've known each other **for three years**.

*know – knew – known

**A.** How long have you been sick?

**B.** I've been sick **since last Friday**.

**1.** How long have Tom and Janet known each other?

*two years*

**2.** How long have Mr. and Mrs. Garcia been married?

*1995*

**3.** How long have you had a stomachache?
*ten o'clock this morning*

**4.** How long has Melanie had the measles?
*five days*

**5.** How long has Ms. Bennett been a guidance counselor?
*nineteen years*

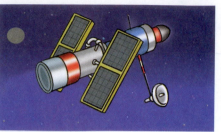

**6.** How long have there been satellites in space?
*1957*

**7.** How long have you owned this car?
*three and a half years*

**8.** How long has Bob owned his own house?
*1999*

**9.** How long have you been interested in astronomy?
*many years*

**10.** How long has Glen been interested in photography?
*a long time*

**11.** How long have you been here?
*1979*

**12.** How long has your son had blue hair?
*a week*

## A VERY DEDICATED DOCTOR

Dr. Fernando's waiting room is very full today. A lot of people are waiting to see him, and they're hoping that the doctor can help them. George's neck has been stiff for more than a week. Martha has had a bad headache since yesterday, and Lenny has felt dizzy since early this morning. Carol has had a high fever for two days, Bob's knee has been swollen for three weeks, Bill's arm has been black and blue since last weekend, and Tommy and Julie have had little red spots all over their bodies for the past twenty-four hours.

Dr. Fernando has been in the office since early this morning. He has already seen a lot of patients, and he will certainly see many more before the day is over. Dr. Fernando's patients don't know it, but he also isn't feeling well. He has had a pain in his back since last Thursday, but he hasn't taken any time to stay at home and rest. He has had a lot of patients this week, and he's a very dedicated doctor.

## ✔ READING CHECK-UP

### Q & A

Dr. Fernando's patients are talking to him about their problems. Using this model, create dialogs based on the story.

**A.** So how are you feeling today, *George*?
**B.** Not very well, Dr. Fernando.
**A.** What seems to be the problem?
**B.** *My neck is stiff.*
**A.** I see. Tell me, how long *has your neck been stiff?*
**B.** *For more than a week.*

### CHOOSE

1. They've known each other since _____.
   a. 2000
   b. three years

2. I've been interested in astronomy for _____.
   a. last year
   b. one year

3. She has been a doctor for _____.
   a. two years ago
   b. two years

4. He has had a toothache since _____.
   a. yesterday
   b. two days

5. We've been here for _____.
   a. one hour
   b. one o'clock

6. There have been two robberies in our neighborhood since _____.
   a. one month
   b. last month

7. My grandparents have owned this house for _____.
   a. a long time
   b. many years ago

8. They've been in love since _____.
   a. last spring
   b. three months

### CHOOSE

1. My right arm has been very _____.
   a. dizzy
   b. stiff

2. My son has a high _____.
   a. fever
   b. pain

3. Tell me, how long has your knee been _____?
   a. nauseous
   b. swollen

4. Ted's leg has been black and _____.
   a. blue
   b. red

5. Dr. Fernando, there are several patients in the _____.
   a. past 24 hours
   b. waiting room

6. Look! I have spots all over my _____!
   a. measles
   b. body

# Since I Was a Little Girl

**A.** Do you know how to ski?

**B.** Yes. I've known how to ski **since I was a little girl**.

**A.** Are you two engaged?

**B.** Yes. We've been engaged **since we finished college**.

**1.** Does your sister Jennifer play the cello?

*since she was eight years old*

**2.** Is your friend Michael a professional musician?

*since he graduated from music school*

**3.** Do you have a personal computer?
*since I started high school*

**4.** Are you interested in modern art?
*since I read about Picasso*

**5.** Is Paul interested in Russian history?
*since he visited Moscow*

**6.** Does Timmy know how to count to ten?
*since he was two years old*

**7.** Do you like jazz?
*since I was a teenager*

**8.** Do you own your own business?
*since I got out of the army*

**9.** Do you know Mr. Wilson?
*since I was a little boy*

**10.** Do you have termites?
*since we bought the house*

**11.** Are you afraid of boats?
*since I saw "Titanic"*

**12.** Do your children know about "the birds and the bees"?*
*since they were nine years old*

*the facts of life

# Have You Always Taught History?

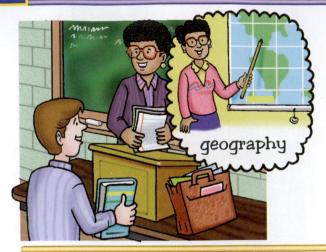

**A.** Have you always taught history?

**B.** No. **I've taught** history for the past three years. Before that, **I taught** geography.

**A.** Has Victor always been a taxi driver?

**B.** No. **He's been** a taxi driver since he immigrated to this country. Before that, **he was** an engineer.

1. Have you always liked classical music?
   *the past five years*

2. Has Carlos always been the store manager?
   *last January*

3. Has Kimberly always had short hair?
   *she started her new job*

4. Has your son always wanted to be an astronaut?
   *the past five or six years*

**5.** Has Ron always spoken with a southern accent?

*he moved to Georgia*

**6.** Have you and your wife always had a dog?

*the last six months*

**7.** Have you always drunk skim milk?

*I went on a diet*

**8.** Has Carol always owned a sports car?

*she won the lottery*

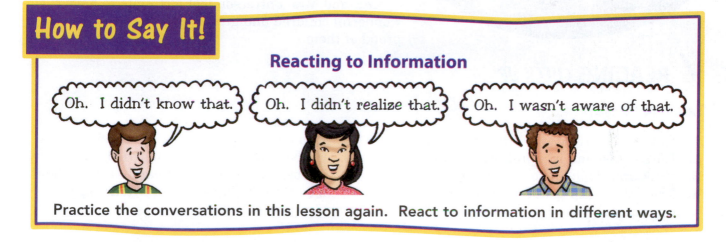

## How to Say It!

### Reacting to Information

Oh. I didn't know that.

Oh. I didn't realize that.

Oh. I wasn't aware of that.

Practice the conversations in this lesson again. React to information in different ways.

## How About You?

What is your present address? How long have you lived there?
What was your last address? How long did you live there?

Who is the leader of your country? How long has he/she been the leader?
Who was the last leader of your country? How long was he/she the leader?

Who is your English teacher now? How long has he/she been your teacher?
Who was your last English teacher? How long was he/she your teacher?

# READING

## A WONDERFUL FAMILY

Mr. and Mrs. Patterson are very proud of their family. Their daughter, Ruth, is a very successful engineer. She has been an engineer since she finished college. Her husband's name is Pablo. They have been happily married for thirty-five years. Pablo is a professional guitarist. He has known how to play the guitar since he was four years old.

Ruth and Pablo have two children. Their son, David, is a computer programmer. He has been interested in computers since he was a teenager. Their daughter, Rita, is a physician. She has been a physician since she finished medical school in 1997.

Mr. and Mrs. Patterson also have a son, Herbert. Herbert is single. He has been a bachelor all his life. He's a famous journalist. They haven't seen him since he moved to Singapore several years ago.

Mr. and Mrs. Patterson feel fortunate to have such wonderful children and grandchildren. They're very proud of them.

## ✔ READING CHECK-UP

### TRUE OR FALSE?

1. Ruth got married thirty-five years ago.
2. Ruth's husband is a professional violinist.
3. Ruth and Pablo have two teenagers.
4. The Pattersons' grandson is interested in computers.
5. Rita has been in medical school since 1997.
6. Herbert has never been married.
7. Herbert hasn't seen his parents since they moved to Singapore several years ago.

# LISTENING

Listen to the conversation and choose the answer that is true.

1. a. She doesn't have a backache now.
   b. She still has a backache.

2. a. His father is an engineer.
   b. His father isn't an engineer.

3. a. Her knee isn't swollen now.
   b. Her knee is still swollen.

4. a. He isn't a teenager.
   b. He's a teenager.

5. a. She has lived in Tokyo for five years.
   b. She lived in Tokyo for five years.

6. a. Roger lives in Cairo.
   b. Roger has lived in Cairo.

7. a. Amy went home two days ago.
   b. Amy hasn't been home for two days.

8. a. He has lived in Toronto for three years.
   b. He lived in Toronto for three years.

## WORKING THEIR WAY UP TO THE TOP

Louis is very successful. For the past six years, he has been the manager of the Big Value Supermarket on Grant Street. Louis has worked very hard to get where he is today. First, he was a clerk for two years. Then, he was a cashier for three years. After that, he was an assistant manager for five years. Finally, six years ago, he became the manager of the store. Everybody at the Big Value Supermarket is very proud of Louis. He started at the bottom, and he has worked his way up to the top.

Kate is very successful. For the past two years, she has been the president of the Marcy Company. Kate has worked very hard to get where she is today. She started her career at the Marcy Department Store in Dallas, Texas. First, she was a salesperson for three years. Then, she was the manager of the Women's Clothing Department for ten years. Then, she was the store manager for eight years. After that, she moved to New York and became a vice president. Finally, two years ago, she became the president. Everybody at the Marcy Company is very proud of Kate. She started at the bottom, and she has worked her way up to the top.

## ✔ READING CHECK-UP

### TRUE, FALSE, OR MAYBE?

Answer True, False, or Maybe (if the answer isn't in the story).

1. Louis started as a cashier at the Big Value Supermarket.
2. He has worked there for sixteen years.
3. All employees at the Big Value Supermarket start at the bottom.
4. Kate has been the manager of the Women's Clothing Department in Dallas for ten years.
5. The Women's Clothing Department was on the bottom floor of the store.
6. Kate hasn't been a vice president for two years.

*My English Teacher*

# Writing

**Write a story about your English teacher.**

How long have you known him/her?
How long has he/she been an English teacher?
What did he/she do before that? How long?

Where does he/she live?
How long has he/she lived there?
Has he/she lived anywhere else? Where? How long?

Besides teaching English, what is your English teacher interested in?
How long has he/she been interested in that?

**A.**  George!

**B.**  Tony!  I can't believe it's you!  I haven't seen you in years.

**A.**  That's right, George.  It's been a long time.  How have you been?

**B.**  Fine.  And how about YOU?

**A.**  Everything's fine with me, too.

**B.**  Tell me, Tony, do you still live on Main Street?

**A.**  No.  I haven't lived on Main Street for several years.  I live on River Road now.
And how about YOU?  Do you still live on Central Avenue?

**B.**  No.  I haven't lived on Central Avenue since 1995.  I live on Park Boulevard now.

**A.**  Tell me, George, are you still a barber?

**B.**  No.  I haven't been a barber for several years.  I'm a computer programmer now.
And how about YOU?  Are you still a painter?

**A.**  No.  I haven't been a painter for a long time.  I'm a carpenter now.

**B.**  Tell me, Tony, do you still play the saxophone?

**A.**  No.  I haven't played the saxophone for many years.  And how about YOU?
Do you still go fishing on Saturday mornings?

**B.**  No.  I haven't gone fishing on Saturday mornings since I got married.

**A.**  Well, George, I'm afraid I have to go now.  We should get together soon.

**B.**  Good idea, Tony.  It's been a long time.

Pretend that it's ten years from now. You're walking along the street and suddenly you meet a student who was in your English class. Try this conversation. Remember, you haven't seen this person for ten years.

**A.** _____!

**B.** _____! I can't believe it's you! I haven't seen you in years.

**A.** That's right, _____. It's been a long time. How have you been?

**B.** Fine. And how about YOU?

**A.** Everything's fine with me, too.

**B.** Tell me, _____, do you still live on _____?

**A.** No. I haven't lived on _____ (for/since) _____. I live on _____ now. And how about YOU? Do you still live on _____?

**B.** No. I haven't lived on _____ (for/since) _____. I live on _____ now.

**A.** Tell me, _____, are you still (a/an) _____?

**B.** No. I haven't been (a/an) _____ (for/since) _____. I'm (a/an) _____ now. And how about YOU? Are you still (a/an) _____?

**A.** No. I haven't been (a/an) _____ (for/since) _____. I'm (a/an) _____ now.

**B.** Tell me, _____, do you still _____?

**A.** No. I haven't _____ (for/since) _____. And how about YOU? Do you still _____?

**B.** No. I haven't _____ (for/since) _____.

**A.** Well, _____, I'm afraid I have to go now. We should get together soon.

**B.** Good idea, _____. It's been a long time.

**Listen.  Then say it.**

How long have you been sick?

How long has Ms. Bennett been a teacher?

Bob has been the manager for six months.

**Say it.  Then listen.**

How long have you known each other?

How long has Mr. Perkins had a stomachache?

Kate has been the president for the past two years.

Write in your journal about your activities and interests. What sport or musical instrument do you play?  How long have you known how to play it?  Why do you like it?  What other things are you interested in?  How long have you been interested in those things?  Why do you like them?

## GRAMMAR FOCUS

SINCE/FOR

|  |  |  |
|---|---|---|
| We've known each other | since | three o'clock. yesterday afternoon. last week. 2000. we were in high school. |
|  | for | three hours. two days. a week. a long time. |

PRESENT PERFECT VS. PRESENT TENSE

I **know** how to ski.

I'**ve known** how to ski since I was a little girl.

PRESENT PERFECT VS. PAST TENSE

Victor **was** an engineer.

He'**s been** a taxi driver since he immigrated.

**Choose the correct word.**

1. My wife and I ( knew    have known ) each other ( since    for ) 1989.

2. My daughter ( is sick    has been sick ) ( since    for ) several days.

3. How long ( have you had    do you have ) a stomachache?

4. ( Are you    Have you been ) interested in photography now?

5. ( We've owned    We own ) our own business ( since    for ) several years.

6. ( She's had    She had ) a cat ( since    for ) last year. Before that, ( she's had    she had ) a dog.

7. Alexander ( was    has been ) a taxi driver ( since    for ) he came to this country. Before that, ( he was    he's been ) an engineer.

8. I ( didn't see    haven't seen ) you in a long time. How ( are    have ) you been?

9. I ( haven't lived    didn't live ) on Oak Street for many years. ( I've lived    I live ) on Pine Street now.

### 1 CONVERSATION DESCRIBING WORK EXPERIENCE

Look at the job application forms. Practice conversations with your classmates.

**A.** Where do you work now?

**B.** I work at _____(employer)_____.

**A.** How long have you worked there?

**B.** I've worked there since _(month)_ _(year)_.

**A.** Where did you work before that?

**B.** I worked at _____(employer)_____.

**A.** How long did you work there?

**B.** I worked there for _(number of years/months)_.

1.

| DATE | EMPLOYER |
|---|---|
| From: 6/15 To: present | Zenith Computer Company |
| From: 5/13 To: 5/15 | Carter Insurance |

2.

| DATE | EMPLOYER |
|---|---|
| From: 1/16 To: present | The Hamilton Hotel |
| From: 12/14 To: 12/15 | The Bayside Inn |

3.

| DATE | EMPLOYER |
|---|---|
| From: 9/14 To: present | Save-Mart Department Store |
| From: 1/14 To: 8/14 | Super Price Discount Store |

Now practice conversations using your own employment information.
(If you aren't working now, talk about going to school.)

### 2 CONVERSATION ASKING FOR CLARIFICATION

**A.** Have you ever been _____?

**B.** I'm sorry. I don't understand what "_____" means.

**A.** Have you ever been _____?

**B.** I understand. No, I haven't.

**Practice with a classmate.**

**1.** terminated
fired from a job

**2.** incarcerated
in jail

**TEAMWORK** Work with a classmate. What are other questions people have asked you that you didn't understand? Make a list. Then share as a class. Discuss what each question means.

**Read the cover letter and resume and answer the questions.**

568 East 34th Street
Sunrise, FL 33304

January 15, 2017

Ms. Monica Jordan
Seaside Restaurant Company
1200 Marine Avenue
Seaside, FL 33308

Dear Ms. Jordan:

I would like to apply for the position of manager of the Seaside Restaurant. I saw your advertisement in the Sunrise Times. As you can see from my resume, I have the experience and skills to manage a successful restaurant. Under my management, the Garden Restaurant has become the most popular family restaurant in the Sunrise area. The number of people we serve has grown from 200 to 300 customers each night.

I look forward to hearing from you to arrange an interview.

Sincerely,

*Linda Palermo*
Linda Palermo

---

**Linda Palermo**   Tel 954-589-4312
568 East 34th Street, Sunrise, FL 33304

**Work Experience:**

2014–present **Manager**, The Garden Restaurant, Sunrise, FL
Hire, train, and supervise a staff of 15 dining room and kitchen workers. Order supplies. Plan menus. Handle customer complaints.

2010–2013 **Chef**, Ocean House, Miami, FL
Prepared fish, seafood, and vegetable dishes. Created exciting new recipes.

2008–2009 **Prep Cook**, Health Food Markets, North Miami, FL
Worked as part of a kitchen team to prepare takeout food. Peeled, sliced, and chopped ingredients. Kept kitchen area clean.

2007–2008 **Deli Counter Clerk**, Health Foods Markets, North Miami, FL
Weighed and packaged food. Made sandwiches. Prepared salad plates. Recommended food. Gave excellent customer service.

---

1. Linda has been the manager of a restaurant _____.
   A. for one year
   B. since 2010
   C. since 2014
   D. since she left Health Foods Market

2. Linda was _____ for four years.
   A. a deli counter clerk
   B. a chef
   C. a prep cook
   D. a manager

3. Linda worked at Health Food Markets _____.
   A. for one year
   B. for two years
   C. for three years
   D. for five years

4. In her present job, Linda does NOT _____.
   A. prepare food
   B. hire cooks and prep cooks
   C. supervise waiters and waitresses
   D. listen to customers when they complain

5. Linda learned about this job from _____.
   A. a friend
   B. the Internet
   C. a help wanted sign
   D. the newspaper

6. Before Linda became manager, the Garden Restaurant _____.
   A. was the most popular restaurant in Sunrise
   B. had 200 customers every night
   C. had 300 customers every night
   D. had more than 200 customers every night

**WRITING** You're applying for a job. Write a cover letter and a resume.

Read the manual for new employees and answer the questions.

## The Brayburn Company

**Hours of Work**—Full-time employees work a 40-hour week—8:00 AM to 5:00 PM, Monday to Friday. Full-time employees get a one-hour lunch break and two fifteen-minute breaks each day.

**Time Clocks and Time Sheets**—Employees either punch a time clock (with a time card) or fill out a time sheet to record the hours they work. If you use the time clock, you must punch in when you start work, punch out for lunch, punch in when you return to work, and punch out at the end of the day. Never punch in for another worker. If you use a time sheet, you must fill out the form each day to record the hours you have worked. At the end of each week, all employees must sign their time cards or time sheets and get their supervisors' signatures. Time cards and time sheets are due in the payroll office every Monday at 9:00 AM.

**Payment Schedule**—Employees get paid each week on Friday. You can either receive your paycheck from your supervisor at 4 PM on Friday or sign up for direct deposit. When you sign up for direct deposit, we deposit your pay into your bank account each Friday.

**Sick Time**—Full-time employees get one paid sick day each month for a total of twelve sick days a year. Employees can take unused sick days from previous years when necessary.

**Vacation Time**—Full-time employees get two weeks of vacation with pay during each of their first ten years of employment. After ten years, they get three weeks of vacation per year. Employees cannot save up their vacation days to use in future years.

**Absence and Tardiness**—It's important to have good attendance and to be on time. Use sick leave as little as possible (for medical reasons only), but stay home when you have a fever and can infect others. If you can't come to work, call your supervisor no later than one hour after your work shift starts. Employees who are often absent or late can lose their jobs.

1. Full-time employees at the Brayburn Company do NOT _____.
   - A. work five days a week
   - B. work forty hours a week
   - C. have a thirty-minute lunch break
   - D. get paid once a week

2. Workers punch out when they _____.
   - A. go to lunch
   - B. arrive at work
   - C. return to work
   - D. receive their paychecks

3. When you sign up for direct deposit of your paycheck, _____.
   - A. you receive your paycheck at 4 PM
   - B. you save up your vacation days
   - C. your supervisor signs your paycheck
   - D. you don't get your paycheck at work

4. Lee has worked for fifteen months. She has taken nine sick days. She hasn't used _____.
   - A. three sick days
   - B. six sick days
   - C. twelve sick days
   - D. fifteen sick days

5. It's Don's eleventh year at work. He can _____.
   - A. take one week of vacation this year
   - B. take two weeks of vacation this year
   - C. take three weeks of vacation this year
   - D. take four weeks of vacation this year

6. If your work shift starts at 8:00 AM and you're going to miss work, _____.
   - A. call your supervisor before 8:00 AM
   - B. call your supervisor before 9:00 AM
   - C. call your supervisor before 10:00 AM
   - D. ask another worker to punch in for you

**Choose the correct answer.**

1. Ahmed called his doctor because he felt _____.
   - A. engaged
   - B. busy
   - C. dizzy
   - D. full

2. We're upset because our house has _____.
   - A. termites
   - B. satellites
   - C. measles
   - D. a high fever

3. When did your parents immigrate to this _____?
   - A. store
   - B. business
   - C. house
   - D. country

4. Someday I want to _____ my own business.
   - A. know
   - B. own
   - C. count
   - D. wait for

5. Ben comes to work early and leaves very late. He's a very dedicated _____.
   - A. store manager
   - B. teenager
   - C. patient
   - D. bachelor

6. Dolores is a professional _____. She plays the cello.
   - A. physician
   - B. musician
   - C. engineer
   - D. journalist

7. I've decided to sign up for _____.
   - A. a sick day
   - B. a timesheet
   - C. my supervisor's signature
   - D. direct deposit of my paycheck

8. All of our employees get _____ with pay.
   - A. good attendance
   - B. a time clock
   - C. two weeks of vacation
   - D. signatures

**Look at Michael Rivera's work experience. Choose the correct answer.**

9. Michael has _____ since 2016.
   - A. waited on customers
   - B. trained sales clerks
   - C. inspected items
   - D. hired sales clerks

10. Michael hasn't _____ for many years.
   - A. worked in Philadelphia
   - B. unpacked boxes
   - C. managed a store
   - D. supervised employees

| Work Experience: | |
|---|---|
| 2016–present | **Store Manager**, Regency Department Store, Philadelphia, PA. Manage the store. Hire and supervise a staff of 75 employees. |
| 2012–2015 | **Assistant Manager**, Regency Department Store, Philadelphia, PA. Helped the store manager. Trained sales clerks. |
| 2006–2011 | **Sales Clerk**, Wilkins Department Store, Atlanta, GA. Waited on customers. Used a cash register. |
| 2004–2005 | **Stock Clerk**, Wilkins Department Store, Atlanta, GA. Unpacked boxes. Inspected items. Put prices on items. |

## SKILLS CHECK ✓

**Words:**
- ☐ astronaut
- ☐ barber
- ☐ carpenter
- ☐ cashier
- ☐ clerk
- ☐ computer programmer
- ☐ doctor/physician
- ☐ engineer
- ☐ guidance counselor
- ☐ guitarist
- ☐ journalist
- ☐ manager
- ☐ musician
- ☐ painter
- ☐ police officer
- ☐ president
- ☐ salesperson
- ☐ taxi driver
- ☐ vice president

- ☐ black and blue
- ☐ dizzy
- ☐ fever
- ☐ measles
- ☐ pain
- ☐ patient
- ☐ stiff
- ☐ swollen

- ☐ absence
- ☐ attendance
- ☐ direct deposit
- ☐ lunch break
- ☐ paycheck
- ☐ payment schedule
- ☐ payroll office
- ☐ shift
- ☐ sick day
- ☐ tardiness
- ☐ time clock
- ☐ time sheet
- ☐ punch in
- ☐ punch out

**I can ask & answer:**
- ☐ How long have you *been here*? I've *been here* for *two years*. I've *been here* since *2005*.
- ☐ I've been *the manager* for *two years*/since *2007*. Before that, I was *a cashier*.
- ☐ Where do you work now?
- ☐ How long have you worked there?
- ☐ Where did you work before that?
- ☐ How long did you work there?

**I can:**
- ☐ describe my work experience
- ☐ ask for clarification
- ☐ interpret a new employee manual
- ☐ describe workplace rules and policies

**I can react to information:**
- ☐ Oh. I didn't know that.
- ☐ Oh. I didn't realize that.
- ☐ Oh. I wasn't aware of that.

**I can write:**
- ☐ a cover letter
- ☐ a simple resume

**I can write about:**
- ☐ my English teacher
- ☐ my activities and interests

Feature Article
Fact File
Around the World
Interview
We've Got Mail!

**SIDE** by **SIDE** **Gazette**

Global Exchange
Listening
Fun with Idioms
What Are They Saying?

Volume 3        Number 2

# "24/7"
# 24 Hours a Day/7 Days a Week

### Work schedules are changing all over the world

*A sign of the times*

More and more companies around the world are operating twenty-four hours a day, seven days a week. Many of these companies do business with companies in other time zones around the world. Other companies sell products to customers worldwide. In an age of instant communication by telephone, by fax, and over the Internet, many businesses must stay open all the time to serve their customers. International banks, computer companies, manufacturing companies, and businesses that sell their products over the World Wide Web are examples of such companies.

Employees of these "24/7" companies have seen changes in their work schedules in recent years. About twenty percent of employees don't work on a traditional "9 to 5" daytime schedule anymore. Their companies have switched them to other shifts, such as 3:00 P.M. to 11:00 P.M., or 11:00 P.M. to 7:00 A.M. In the past, many factory workers, doctors and nurses, police, firefighters, and others had these shifts, but now many office workers have also started to work during these hours.

*The night shift*

Many local businesses have adjusted their hours to serve the employees of these companies. More and more supermarkets are open 24 hours a day. Restaurants and coffee shops close later and open earlier. And businesses such as photocopy centers, health clubs, laundromats, and even some child-care centers are always open.

*Describe the work schedules of people you know. Are there any "24/7" businesses in your area? What's your opinion about these businesses and their employees' work schedules?*

*A typical night at the office*

*A health club that's open 24 hours a day*

*A coffee shop that never closes*

*Late-night shopper at the supermarket*

## Unique Jobs

**S**ome jobs are unique. They exist only in certain countries.

a subway pusher in Japan

a tulip farmer in Holland

a reindeer herder in Siberia

a safari guide in Africa

a coffee plantation worker in Colombia

a dog day-care worker in California

What unique jobs do you know? In what countries do these jobs exist?

# Interview

*Mr. and Mrs. Roberto Souza have two children, ages two and four. Mr. Souza works the day shift at a manufacturing company, and Mrs. Souza works at night in an office. Their lives are certainly busy!*

**Q:** **Mr. Souza, can you describe your typical day?**

**A:** I get up at 5:30 A.M. I take a shower, eat breakfast, and make my lunch. Sometimes I do some laundry before I go to work. I leave the house at 6:30 A.M.

**Q:** **Is anyone in your house awake when you leave?**

**A:** No. Everyone is still asleep. I work from 7:00 A.M. until 3:00 P.M. After work, I pick up my kids at their grandmother's apartment. Usually we go food shopping and then we go home to make dinner. My wife has already left for work. I play with the kids, we eat dinner, and then I put the kids to bed. I'm normally asleep by 10:00 P.M.

**Q:** **And Mrs. Souza, what about your day?**

**A:** The kids and I get up at 7:00. We eat breakfast, and then they play while I do some housework. Sometimes we go to the park or we visit family or friends. Other times we go shopping. I take the kids to my mother's apartment at 2:00 P.M., and I'm at work by 3:00 P.M. I come home at 11:30 P.M. That's my day!

**Q:** **It sounds exhausting! When do you have time to see your husband?**

**A:** Sometimes he waits for me to come home, but usually he has already gone to bed. Believe it or not, we really see each other only on the weekends.

**Q:** **Mr. Souza, what's the most difficult thing about your work schedule?**

**A:** Communication. We leave each other notes and messages about bills, shopping, doctor's appointments, and everything else.

**Q:** **And tell me, Mrs. Souza, is there anything good about these work schedules?**

**A:** Yes. The children are always with a parent or a grandparent. They don't have to go to daycare, which is expensive. We know these schedules won't last forever. When the children are both in school, maybe we can each have a daytime job. I hope so!

## FACT FILE

### Vacation Time in Different Countries

Employees in different countries have different amounts of vacation time. What's the typical amount of vacation time employees receive in different countries you know? How do people usually spend their vacation time?

**Weeks per Year**

| | | | | | |
|---|---|---|---|---|---|
| Australia | Germany | Denmark | Sweden | Japan | USA |

## LISTENING

Hi Sam . . .

### Office Voice Mail

Has Sam . . .

|  |  | Yes | No |
|---|---|---|---|
| 1 | written a note to Mrs. Wilson? | ___ | ___ |
| 2 | called Mr. Chen? | ___ | ___ |
| 3 | sent an e-mail about the meeting? | ___ | ___ |
| 4 | spoken to the custodian? | ___ | ___ |
| 5 | made a list of the employees? | ___ | ___ |
| 6 | given the list to Ms. Baxter? | ___ | ___ |
| 7 | taken the package to the post office? | ___ | ___ |

# FUN with IDIOMS

My new co-worker is a real peach.

She's the top banana in our company.

He's a real ham at office parties.

He's a couch potato.

She's a smart cookie.

He wants to ask for a raise, but he's chicken.

## Do You Know These Expressions?

| | | |
|---|---|---|
| _d_ | 1. My new co-worker is a real peach. | a. He's funny. |
| ____ | 2. She's the top banana in our company. | b. He's afraid. |
| ____ | 3. He's a real ham at office parties. | c. She's intelligent. |
| ____ | 4. He's a couch potato. | d. He's nice. |
| ____ | 5. She's a smart cookie. | e. He's lazy. |
| ____ | 6. He wants to ask for a raise, but he's chicken. | f. She's the boss. |

Dear Side by Side,

   We are students in Mr. Smith's class at the English Language Center, and we are very confused! We just don't understand the present perfect tense. We don't have this tense in our languages. We don't know when to use it, and we really don't like all these past participles, such as "given" and "driven." Why do we need this tense anyway? Why can't we just use the tenses we already know?

Sincerely,
"Perfectly Happy with the Present and the Past"

Dear "Perfectly Happy,"

   The present perfect tense has always been difficult for learners of English. We'll try to explain it to you with some examples.

We use the present perfect tense to talk about:

- things that happened (or didn't happen) sometime in the past, but the exact time isn't important. For example:

   I have (I've) already seen that movie.*
   He has (He's) never ridden a motorcycle.
   She hasn't gone to the bank yet.

\* If the exact time IS important, we use the past tense: "I saw a movie yesterday."

- things that happened many times in the past. For example:

   I have (I've) driven trucks for many years.
   We have (We've) eaten lunch there many times.

- things that happened in the past and are still happening in the present. For example:

   I have (I've) known them for two years.
   She has (She's) been sick since last Thursday.
   They have (They've) lived here for a year.

It's interesting how different languages express time in different ways, and we can understand why this tense is difficult for you. In your languages, you might say:

   ✗ I live here since last year.
   ✗ I am living here since last year.
   ✗ I lived here since last year.

In English, these are all wrong. Sorry! The correct way to say this is:

   ✓ I have (I've) lived here since last year.

This means "I lived here before, and I still live here now."

   So that's why we need the present perfect tense in English. Thanks for your question, and good luck!

Sincerely,
*Side by Side*

---

### Global Exchange

**Alex32:** I'm sorry I haven't written for a while. I've been very busy. I've taken four exams this week, and I have to take one more tomorrow. This weekend I'm going to relax. I'm going to see the new Julia Richards movie. (My sister saw it last week, and she says it's one of the best movies she's ever seen.) I'm also going to eat dinner with my family at a new Indian restaurant. I'm looking forward to it. We haven't been to a restaurant in a long time, and I've never eaten Indian food. And I'm going to visit our city's modern art museum. Believe it or not, I've lived here all my life, and I've never gone there! So, how have you been? Have you seen any movies recently? Have you eaten at any restaurants? Have you gone to any interesting places?

**Tell a keypal about some things you've done recently.**

### What Are They Saying?

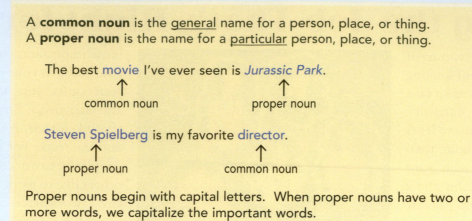

A **common noun** is the <u>general</u> name for a person, place, or thing.
A **proper noun** is the name for a <u>particular</u> person, place, or thing.

The best movie I've ever seen is *Jurassic Park*.
↑                              ↑
common noun              proper noun

Steven Spielberg is my favorite director.
↑                              ↑
proper noun              common noun

Proper nouns begin with capital letters. When proper nouns have two or more words, we capitalize the important words.

## Practice these conversations with a classmate.

| | |
|---|---|
| My favorite TV program is *Dancing with the Stars*. | Miami is the most interesting city I've ever visited. |

**A.** What's the sentence?

**B.** My favorite TV program is *Dancing with the Stars*.

**A.** What's the common noun in the sentence?

**B.** TV program.

**A.** What's the proper noun?

**B.** *Dancing with the Stars*.

**A.** What's the difference between the two nouns?

**B.** *Dancing with the Stars* is the name of a particular TV program.

**A.** What's the sentence?

**B.** Miami is the most interesting city I've ever visited.

**A.** What's the common noun in the sentence?

**B.** City.

**A.** What's the proper noun?

**B.** Miami.

**A.** What's the difference between the two nouns?

**B.** Miami is the name of a particular city.

**Underline each common noun once and each proper noun twice. Then practice new conversations about these sentences.**

1. My favorite <u>artist</u> is <u>Picasso</u>.

2. Ocean House has been our favorite restaurant for many years.

3. The supermarket where I buy groceries is called Big Value.

4. The best movie I've ever seen is *Titanic*.

5. *Don Quixote* is the best novel I've ever read.

6. Disney World is my children's favorite theme park.

7. The game our family has played every Sunday night for many years is Monopoly.

# Finding the Job That's Right for You

No matter how old you are, if you are thinking about looking for a new job, you need to take time to plan very carefully. This is important for students who are thinking about their future, for workers who want to change jobs, and for those who are unemployed. Before you begin to look for a new job, you need to evaluate your skills and your salary requirements. You should also think seriously about your future dreams. If you have a future job goal, you need to make a plan for how you can reach that goal.

A job that's right for you will depend on many things. For example, do you need a job with a special schedule or a location very close to your home? Do you need a part-time job while you are in school? Do you need a large salary, or are you more interested in what you will learn on the job? Often, a job is a steppingstone—a way to build experience to step up to a better job in the future. These are things to think about while you are looking for a job.

Make a list of your skills. What job skills do you already have? Are there skills you use in your hobbies? For example, you might know how to sew, draw, cook, or take photographs. These are skills you may be able to use in certain jobs. Also, make a list of your natural skills and talents—things you do well and are easy for you to do. For example, perhaps you know how to fix machines, sell things, or plan events. The best job for you uses your skills and talents. Make a different list of your interests. What activities and kinds of work have you enjoyed in the past? Keep these lists while you are thinking about your future job. If you have a good idea of your skills and interests, you will be able to find a good job match.

The right job for you will be a job that you enjoy. It will give you job satisfaction. There are three important ingredients for job satisfaction. First and most important, you need to use your skills in your job. If you use your skills, you will feel useful and satisfied. Second, your job should match your personality and interests. For example, some people like to work on a team, while others like to work alone. Finally, the workplace environment should be positive. When you have thoughtful co-workers and managers, you will feel more job satisfaction.

You should also think about your financial needs. What are your monthly expenses? How much income will you need every month? Look for a career that will give you a good salary. Although you may have to work your way up to a better job, you should have a plan and a goal in mind. When you find a job that interests you, find out about the starting salary. Then find out about the salary for an experienced worker. This is called the salary range—the range from the lowest to the highest salary. It's important to know the salary range of the job or career you are interested in.

For many people, a career test is very helpful. In a career test, you answer questions about your interests, your skills, your education, and your personality. There are many free tests available online and in schools, colleges, and libraries. If you have a career center or job center in your community or school, someone can help you find a good career test.

A career test will suggest jobs and careers that may be good for you. You might be surprised at the results. The test may suggest a job you haven't thought of before. Think about all possibilities. The test will give you information about the educational and skill requirements for different jobs. For example, a job may require vocational training or a special license or test. Read about different jobs and careers. You can find information online, at the library, or in a career center.

You may want to think about a vocational or technical program. Vocational programs teach you special skills for particular jobs. Vocational programs train medical assistants, hair stylists, automotive technicians, and truck drivers, for example. Technical programs are similar to vocational programs; however, they include more training in technology. They prepare students for jobs in areas such as information technology, nursing, criminal justice, and electronics. There are vocational and technical programs at community colleges, private schools, and even online. Find several programs and get information about each

one. Often community colleges have the best prices for vocational and technical training. Sometimes you can get financial assistance through a federal, state, or local government program.

Local job fairs are a good place to find out about jobs in your area. Many cities have several job fairs each year. They are free and open to the public. In a job fair, you can talk with representatives from many different companies. You can learn about job openings and ask questions. Sometimes you can even fill out an application for a job. Job fairs are a good place to talk with employers and learn about different types of jobs.

When you are looking for a position, don't just find a job. Find the *right* job! Before you start your job search, remember to think about your skills, your interests, and your future plans. Take some time to complete a career test and learn about other job possibilities. Find out about other training and education. When you do your job search carefully, you will hopefully find the job that's right for you.

1. According to the article, it's important to _____.
   Ⓐ find a job quickly
   Ⓑ make a plan to reach your job goal
   Ⓒ work on a team
   Ⓓ change jobs often so you can find the job that's right for you

2. According to the article, you have a good job match if _____.
   Ⓐ you have a hobby
   Ⓑ you earn a large salary
   Ⓒ your job makes use of your skills, talents, and interests
   Ⓓ your job has a special schedule and location

3. A salary range gives information about _____.
   Ⓐ how much money new and experienced workers make
   Ⓑ how much money everybody at a company earns
   Ⓒ a person's salary history over the years
   Ⓓ employees' work skills

4. Many people think it's important to take a career test because _____.
   Ⓐ it's available online
   Ⓑ it's free and easy to do
   Ⓒ it suggests a variety of jobs
   Ⓓ it gives information about your current job skills

5. Vocational and technical programs _____.
   Ⓐ train people for every kind of job
   Ⓑ are only at community colleges and online
   Ⓒ always offer students financial assistance
   Ⓓ are good places to learn special skills

6. This passage is about _____.
   Ⓐ new jobs in today's world
   Ⓑ how to plan before you begin a job search
   Ⓒ how to get good job training
   Ⓓ how to use your skills and talents

**Think & Share**

1. Make a list of your job skills and interests. In your opinion, what job is a good match for your skills and interests?
2. Do you agree that it's important to plan very carefully when you look for a job? Why or why not?
3. For you, what is the most useful information in this article? Why is it useful?

# THE WRITING PROCESS

## Purpose and Audience

Before you write, you need to think about your purpose and your audience.

**Purpose:** Why are you going to write? Do you want to give information? Do you want to express your feelings or ideas? Do you want to entertain?

**Audience:** Who are you writing for? Will your audience be your teacher? your classmates? your family members and friends? people in your community? anybody who reads your writing?

## Pre-writing

Pre-writing is the first step in the writing process. During this step, you **brainstorm**—you write down all your ideas about the topic. One way to brainstorm is to quickly make a **list** of your ideas, thoughts, and feelings about a topic. Don't write full sentences. Just write words and phrases. Don't take time to think about your ideas. Just write down everything.

Marcus is preparing to write a story with the title *My Bucket List*. He's going to write about the things he hasn't done in his life yet that he wants to do in the future. First, he brainstormed ideas for the story and made his list of ideas in a bucket.

**Things I Haven't Done Yet**

see the Grand Canyon
buy a house so we can stop paying rent
buy my first new car
go to Disney World with my children
become a U.S. citizen
send my children to college—first in my family to go
speak and write English perfectly
get a good job with a big salary
bring my parents and my wife's parents here to live with us

## Organizing Ideas

The second step in the writing process is to organize your ideas. You look at all the ideas you brainstormed and decide how you want to put them together. A **cluster map** is a good way to organize ideas by topics. You can write your title in the center, write your main topics in circles around the title, and then connect more circles to each topic.

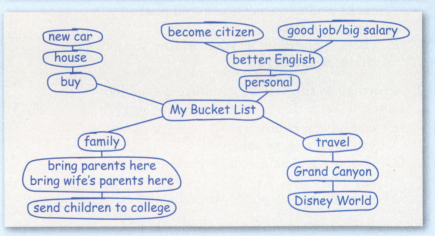

*Marcus made this cluster map to organize the ideas in his bucket.*

## Write your story.

**Purpose and Audience:** Your purpose is to share information about what you haven't done in your life yet that you want to do in the future. Your audience is your classmates, your teacher, and anyone else you want to share with.

**Pre-write:** Draw an empty bucket, brainstorm ideas, and list them in the bucket.

**Organize your ideas:** Make a cluster map to organize your bucket of ideas into topics.

**Write a first draft:** Write your story. Indent the first line of each paragraph. Use this title: *My Bucket List*.

**Share:** Share your story with your teacher and your classmates.

# Present Perfect Continuous Tense

- **Discussing Duration of Activity**
- **Reporting Household Repair Problems**
- **Describing Tasks Accomplished**
- **Reassuring Someone**
- **Describing Experiences**
- **Job Interviews**
- **Renting an Apartment**
- **Lease Information**
- **Apartment Rules**
- **Utility Bills**
- **Housing Maintenance and Repairs**
- **Yellow Pages**

## VOCABULARY PREVIEW

1. ask for a raise
2. complain
3. date
4. direct traffic
5. do sit-ups
6. leak
7. look for
8. mend
9. peel
10. pick apples
11. ring
12. stand in line

# How Long Have You Been Waiting?

| | | |
|---|---|---|
| (I have) | I've | |
| (We have) | We've | |
| (You have) | You've | |
| (They have) | They've | been working. |
| (He has) | He's | |
| (She has) | She's | |
| (It has) | It's | |

**A.** How long have you been waiting?

**B.** I've been waiting **for two hours**.

**A.** How long has your neighbor's dog been barking?

**B.** It's been barking **since this morning**.

**1.** How long has Yasmin been studying English?

*eight months*

**2.** How long have Mr. and Mrs. Green been living on School Street?

*1994*

**3.** How long has the phone been ringing?
*two minutes*

**4.** How long have you been feeling bad?
*yesterday morning*

**5.** How long have we been driving?
*five hours*

**6.** How long has it been snowing?
*late last night*

**7.** How long has Ted been having problems with his back?
*high school*

**8.** How long have you been practicing the piano?
*half an hour*

**9.** How long have Barry and Susan been dating?
*three and a half years*

**10.** How long has your baby son been crying?
*early this morning*

**11.** How long have I been running?
*twenty minutes*

**12.** How long have we been jogging?
*about an hour*

# They've Been Arguing All Day

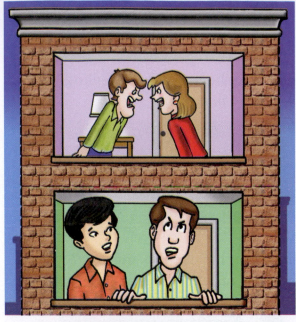

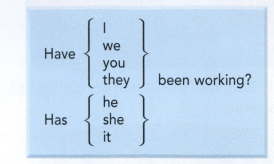

**A.** What are your neighbors doing?

**B.** They're arguing.

**A.** Have they been arguing for a long time?

**B.** Yes, they have.  They've been arguing all day.*

*Or:  all morning / all afternoon / all evening / all night

**1.** *you*
*studying*

**2.** *Gary*
*exercising*

**3.** *Brenda*
*waiting for the bus*

**4.** *your parents*
*watching the news*

**5.** *your car*
*making strange noises*

**6.** *Officer Lopez*
*directing traffic*

**7.** *Jim*
*looking for his keys*

**8.** *you and your friends*
*standing in line for*
*concert tickets*

**9.**

## APARTMENT PROBLEMS

Mr. and Mrs. Banks have been having a lot of problems in their apartment recently. For several weeks their bedroom ceiling has been leaking, their refrigerator hasn't been working, and the paint in their hallway has been peeling. In addition, they have been taking cold showers since last week because their water heater hasn't been working, and they haven't been sleeping at night because the heating system has been making strange noises.

Mr. and Mrs. Banks are furious. They have been calling the manager of their apartment building every day and complaining about their problems. He has been promising to help them, but they have been waiting for more than a week, and he still hasn't fixed anything at all.

## ✔ READING *CHECK-UP*

### Q & A

Mr. and Mrs. Banks are calling the manager of their apartment building for the first time about each of the problems in their apartment. Using this model, create dialogs based on the story.

A. Hello.
B. Hello. This is *Mrs.* Banks.
A. Yes, *Mrs.* Banks. What can I do for you?
B. We're having a problem with *our bedroom ceiling.*
A. Oh? What's the problem?
B. *It's leaking.*
A. I see. Tell me, how long *has it been leaking?*
B. *It's been leaking for about an hour.*
A. All right, *Mrs.* Banks. I'll take care of it as soon as I can.
B. Thank you.

**How About You?**

Have you been having problems in your apartment or house recently? Tell about some problems you've been having.

# No Wonder They're Tired!

A. You look tired. What have you been doing?

B. I've been writing letters since nine o'clock this morning.

A. Really? How many letters have you written?

B. Believe it or not, I've already written fifteen letters.

A. You're kidding! Fifteen letters?! NO WONDER you're tired!

A. Anthony looks tired. What has he been doing?

B. He's been making pizzas since ten o'clock this morning.

A. Really? How many pizzas has he made?

B. Believe it or not, he's already made seventy-five pizzas.

A. You're kidding! Seventy-five pizzas?! NO WONDER he's tired!

1. you
   plant flowers

2. Ms. Perkins
   give piano lessons

3. Dr. Chen
   see patients

4. your grandmother
   mend socks

5. you
   pick apples

6. Tom and Sally
   write thank-you notes

7. Chester
   take photographs

8. Thelma
   draw pictures

9. you
   go to job interviews

10. Jackie
    clean cages

11. Rick
    do sit-ups

12. Dr. Harris
    deliver babies

# How to Say It!

## Expressing Surprise

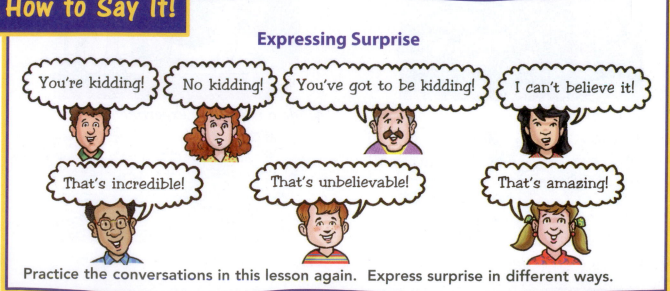

You're kidding!

No kidding!

You've got to be kidding!

I can't believe it!

That's incredible!

That's unbelievable!

That's amazing!

Practice the conversations in this lesson again. Express surprise in different ways.

# There's Nothing to Be Nervous About!

**A.** I'm nervous.

**B.** Why?

**A.** I'm going to **fly in an airplane** tomorrow, and I've never **flown in an airplane** before.

**B.** Don't worry! I've been **flying in airplanes** for years. And believe me, there's nothing to be nervous about!

**1.** *drive downtown*

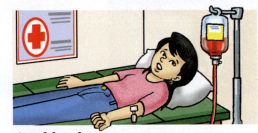

**2.** *give blood*

**3.** *buy a used car*

**4.** *do a chemistry experiment*

**5.** *run\* in a marathon*

**6.** *go to a job interview*

\*run – ran – run

**7.** *speak at a meeting*

**8.** *sing in front of an audience*

**9.** *take a karate lesson*

**10.** *ask for a raise*

**11.** *go out on a date*

**12.**

## INTERVIEW  *Have You Ever . . . ?*

Interview other students in your class about experiences they have had.  Ask these questions and make up your own questions.  Then tell the class about these experiences.

Have you ever met a famous person?
(Who did you meet?)

Have you ever spoken at a meeting?
(Where did you speak?  What did you say?)

Have you ever been in the hospital?
(Why were you there?)

Have you ever lost something important or
    valuable?
(What did you lose?)

Have you ever been very embarrassed?
(What happened?)

Have you ever been in an accident?
(What happened?)

Complete this conversation and act it out with another student.

**A.** Tell me, (Mr./Ms./Mrs./Miss _____), how long have you been living in _____?

**B.** I've been living in _____ (for/since) _____.

**A.** And where else have you lived?

**B.** I've also lived in _____.

**A.** Oh.  How long did you live there?

**B.** I lived there for _____.

**A.** Okay.  I see here on your resume that you're studying _____.

**B.** That's correct.

**A.** How long have you been studying _____?

**B.** (For/Since) _____.

**A.** Where?

**B.** At _____.

**A.** Tell me about your work experience.  Where do you work now?

**B.** I work at _____.

**A.** How long have you been working there?

**B.** I've been working there (for/since) _____.

**A.** And what do you do there?

**B.** I _____.

**A.** And where did you work before that?

**B.** I worked at _____.

**A.** How long did you work there?

**B.** For _____.

**A.** What did you do?

**B.** I _____.

**A.** Well, I don't have any more questions.

**B.** I appreciate the opportunity to meet with you.  Thank you very much.

**A.** It's been a pleasure.  We'll call you soon.

## READING

### IT'S BEEN A LONG DAY

Frank has been assembling cameras since 7 A.M., and he's very tired. He has assembled 19 cameras today, and he has NEVER assembled that many cameras in one day before! He has to assemble only one more camera, and then he can go home. He's really glad. It's been a long day.

Julie has been typing letters since 9 A.M., and she's very tired. She has typed 25 letters today, and she has NEVER typed that many letters in one day before! She has to type only one more letter, and then she can go home. She's really glad. It's been a very long day.

Officer Jackson has been writing parking tickets since 8 A.M., and he's exhausted! He has written 211 parking tickets today, and he has NEVER written that many parking tickets in one day before! He has to write only one more parking ticket, and then he can go home. He's really glad. It's been an extremely long day.

## ✔ READING CHECK-UP

### Q & A

Co-workers are talking with Frank, Julie, and Officer Jackson. Using this model, create dialogs based on the story.

**A.** *Frank*, you look tired.
**B.** I am. I've been *assembling cameras* since 7 A.M.
**A.** Really? How many *cameras* have you *assembled*?
**B.** Believe it or not, I've already *assembled 19 cameras* today.
**A.** That's a lot of *cameras*!
**B.** I know. I've never *assembled* that many *cameras* in one day before!

## LISTENING

### WHICH WORD DO YOU HEAR?

Listen and choose the correct answer.

1. a. gone          b. going
2. a. written       b. writing
3. a. seen          b. seeing
4. a. taken         b. taking
5. a. given         b. giving
6. a. driven        b. driving

### WHO IS SPEAKING?

Listen and decide who is speaking.

1. a. a landlord             b. a boss
2. a. a student              b. a teacher
3. a. a singer               b. a dentist
4. a. a window washer        b. a baby-sitter
5. a. a doctor               b. a bookkeeper
6. a. a movie theater        b. a police officer
      cashier

# PRONUNCIATION  Reduced *for*

**Listen.  Then say it.**

I've been working *for* two hours.

She's been waiting *for* the bus.

Have you been studying *for* a long time?

**Say it.  Then listen.**

He's been jogging *for* thirty minutes.

We've been looking *for* our keys.

Has she been exercising *for* a long time?

**SIDE by SIDE JOURNAL**

Write in your journal about places where you have lived, worked, and gone to school.

Where do you live now?  How long have you been living there?  Where else have you lived?  How long did you live there?

Where do you work or go to school now?  How long have you been working or going to school there?  Where else have you worked or gone to school?  How long did you work or study there?  What did you do?  What did you study?

# GRAMMAR FOCUS

### PRESENT PERFECT CONTINUOUS TENSE

| (I have) (We have) (You have) (They have) | I've We've You've They've | been working. |
|---|---|---|
| (He has) (She has) (It has) | He's She's It's | |

| Have | I we you they | been working? |
|---|---|---|
| Has | he she it | |

| Yes, | I we you they | have. |
|---|---|---|
| | he she it | has. |

**Complete the sentences with *since* or *for* and the correct forms of these verbs.**

| live   practice   stand   take   write |

**1.** A. How long _____ you and your husband _____ _____ in Los Angeles?

  B. _____ _____ _____ in Los Angeles ( since    for ) three years.

**2.** A. How long _____ your daughter _____ _____ the piano?

  B. _____ _____ _____ the piano ( since    for ) 9:00 A.M.

**3.** A. _____ your friends _____ _____ in line for a long time?

  B. Yes, _____ _____. _____ _____ _____ in line ( since    for ) about an hour.

**4.** Ms. Lee _____ _____ _____ photographs ( since    for ) early this morning.

  _____ already _____ more than fifty photographs!

**5.** I'm very busy. _____ _____ _____ letters ( for    since ) five hours.

  _____ already _____ twenty letters!

## 1 CONVERSATION  INQUIRING ABOUT LEASE INFORMATION

> A **lease** is a contract. It is a legal document that describes the rental agreement between a landlord and a tenant. A lease includes information about rent, the number of tenants who can live in an apartment, and the rules of the building. Make sure you understand a lease before you sign it! If you don't understand something, ask!

**Practice conversations with a classmate.**

**A.** I don't understand this line in the lease:

_____

What does it mean?

**B.** _____

**A.** Oh. I understand.

1.  ~~repair is not permitted on the property.~~ No refuse or trash will be permitted to be left at the building entrance. ~~It is strictly prohibited to place or hang~~ — You can't put garbage in front of the building.

2.  ~~be left at the building entrance.~~ Vehicle repair is not permitted on the property. ~~It is strictly prohibited to place or hang~~ — You're not allowed to fix your car in the parking lot.

3.  It is strictly prohibited to place or hang rugs, clothing, or laundry of any kind on the balcony. — You're not allowed to hang anything on the balcony.

4.  No dogs, cats, large birds, or any other animals shall be permitted, kept, or harbored in or about the leased premises. — You're not allowed to have pets.

5.  ~~or about the leased pr~~ Tenant shall carpet or rug a minimum of 80% of hardwood floor areas. ~~It is strictly prohibited to place~~ — You have to cover most of your floors with a rug.

**THINK & SHARE**  As a class, discuss rental agreements in different countries you know. Do all tenants have to sign a lease? What information and rules are in different leases? How long is a typical rental period?

## 2 TEAMWORK  APARTMENT RULES

Work with a classmate. Think about all the rules for tenants in an apartment building. Make a list of the rules. Then compare lists with your classmates.

Read the utility bills and answer the questions.

## California Power and Light
P.O. Box 3566
Los Angeles, CA 90016
Web address: www.cpl.com

**Account Number  235-12-55-78304**
Hector Nieves
15 Park Drive
Los Angeles, CA 90020

Customer assistance line
**1-800-555-7600**
To report a power outage
**1-800-555-3000**

Billing Date: 10/15/20
Payment Due: 11/10/20
Next Meter Read Date: 11/14/20

### Billing Summary
| | |
|---|---:|
| Amount of Previous Statement 9/15/20 | $ 94.32 |
| Payment Received— 10/08/20 Thank You | 94.32 |
| Balance Before Current Charges | 0.00 |
| Current Charges | 89.91 |
| Your Total Balance Due | $ 89.91 |

### Your current energy usage

| Meter Number | From | To | Usage |
|---|---|---|---|
| AB910731 | 9/14/20 | 10/14/20 | |
| | 50719 | 51291 | 572 kilowatt hours |

Reminder — a 9% late payment will be added to the total unpaid balance of your account if a full payment is not received by the due date on this bill.

---

## ≡SE  Southern Energy    P.O. Box 2569  Miami, FL 33101    Visit us at www.senergy.com

Samira Mohammed
23 McDonald Street
Miami FL 33121

**Statement Date**
8/23/20
**Past Due After**
9/12/20

**Account #456-382-09**

Meter Number
**H564364**

Service Address
23 McDonald Street
Miami, FL

Billing Period:
From 7/23/20 to 8/23/20

Days in Billing Period:  31

Total Gas Used:  35 Therms

Next Meter Reading:  9/23/20

**Account Activity**

| | |
|---|---:|
| BALANCE LAST STATEMENT | $ 45.19 |
| Credits and Adjustments | |
| GAS PAYMENT 9/04/20 | 45.19- |
| Current Charges | |
| PAST DUE LAST STATEMENT | 0.00 |
| GAS CHARGE | 38.63 |
| Balance Information | |
| TOTAL AMOUNT DUE | $ 38.63 |
| GAS BALANCE | $ 38.63 |
| SERVICE BALANCE | $  0.00 |

To avoid a late payment charge of 2%, please pay the total amount by 9/12/20.
Billing questions?  Call 1-800-327-3270
24-hour customer service  1-800-327-5000

## 🔔 Bell Telephone Statement

Account Number **5792104857**

**Lena James**
146 Grove Street
Long Beach, CA 90802

Customer Service 1-800-666-2901

**Summary of Charges**

| | |
|---|---:|
| Total charges from your last bill | $ 87.32 |
| Payments through 8/13 | 0.00 |
| Remaining balance | 87.32 |
| Current charges | |
| Local Services | 37.55 |
| Long Distance Services | 3.60 |
| Total Current Charges | 41.15 |
| Late Payment Charge | 2.75 |
| **Total Amount Due by 9/7/20** | **$ 131.22** |

If paid after 9/7/20, the amount due will be $141.22

Send payment to:
Bell Telephone
P.O Box 5683
Long Beach, CA 90745

**Long Distance Calls**

| Date | Number called | Where | Time | Rate | Mins. | Amount |
|------|---------------|-------|------|------|-------|--------|
| 7/29 | 212-873-9854 | NYC, NY | 8:20 p.m. | night | 40 | 2.50 |
| 8/06 | 307-760-4782 | Lar, WY | 5:00 p.m. | eve | 20 | 1.10 |

1. Hector has to pay his electric bill on or before _____.
   A. September 14
   B. October 15
   C. November 10
   D. November 14

2. Hector will pay _____ for the electricity he used from 9/14 to 10/14.
   A. $0.00
   B. $89.91
   C. $94.32
   D. $184.23

3. Samira has to pay the gas bill _____.
   A. on August 23
   B. on September 4
   C. after September 12
   D. before September 13

4. If Samira smells gas in her apartment, she should _____.
   A. call 1-800-327-5000
   B. call 1-800-327-3270
   C. write to Southern Energy
   D. visit www.senergy.com

5. The past balance on Lena's telephone bill is _____.
   A. $0.00
   B. $2.75
   C. $37.55
   D. $87.32

6. The total new charges for the current month on Lena's telephone bill are _____.
   A. $3.60
   B. $37.55
   C. $41.15
   D. $131.22

7. If Lena pays her bill after the due date, her late payment charge next month will be _____.
   A. $2.75
   B. $3.60
   C. $10.00
   D. $131.22

8. We can infer that utility company meters measure _____.
   A. due dates
   B. amounts of gas or electricity you use
   C. total amount due
   D. days in a billing period

**Consumer Tip**  If you want to rent an apartment or borrow money, you need a good *credit rating*. A credit rating is a grade that a credit agency gives you based on information from landlords, utility companies, and lenders about how you pay your bills and how you repay the money you borrow. To have a good credit rating, you must pay your bills on time.

## Hillside Apartments
### 3700 East 25th Avenue, Oakdale, CA 95361

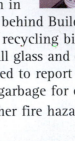

Dear Tenants:

The maintenance staff at Hillside Apartments works hard to keep things running smoothly. You can depend on us whenever you have a problem. Please do everything you can to help us keep Hillside Apartments clean and safe.

Keep the hallways and all common areas clear. Store your bicycles and other personal possessions in your storage area in the basement. Don't leave trash in the hallway. Throw it in the dumpster nearest to you. There are dumpsters behind Buildings A, C, and E, and there's a recycling collection site next to each dumpster. Use the green recycling bins that we provide to recycle newspaper, glass, cardboard, and metal cans. Be sure to rinse out all glass and cans before you recycle them. Recycling in Oakdale is mandatory. It's the law. We're pleased to report that we have reduced waste by 10% since the recycling program began. That's 10% less garbage for our landfill.

For everyone's safety, call us to report any broken smoke detectors or other fire hazards as soon as you discover them. We will respond immediately.

The pest control company comes the second Monday of each month. Call the rental office if you need this service. You will have to empty all your kitchen cabinets in preparation.

Please do not call us with routine maintenance requests. Fill out a maintenance request form instead. In our experience, this is a much more reliable system. We will try to get back to you as soon as possible. Call us at (310) 457-8923 only if we haven't contacted you within 24 hours.

Our tenants' most common maintenance problem is a jammed garbage disposal. To avoid this, always turn on the water when you operate your disposal. Don't throw bones or fruit with hard pits in the center down the disposal. Don't put large amounts of garbage down the disposal all at once.

If you have an emergency maintenance request, the emergency maintenance number is (310) 278-1489. You can call at any time. Please do not use the emergency number for routine requests.

Sincerely,

*Oscar Molina*
Building Manager

1. Tenants should _____.
   A. store bicycles in the hallway
   B. throw metal cans into the dumpster
   C. put their trash in the hallway
   D. call when a smoke detector is broken

2. Tenants should put old newspapers in the _____.
   A. dumpster
   B. landfill
   C. recycling bin
   D. garbage disposal

3. The pest control company _____.
   A. empties kitchen cabinets
   B. comes once a month
   C. comes twice a month
   D. comes every other Monday

4. Tenants should fill out a maintenance request form when _____.
   A. they have cockroaches in their apartment
   B. a smoke detector doesn't work
   C. their garbage disposal is broken
   D. there's no hot water in their apartment

5. Tenants should NOT _____.
   A. throw peaches down the disposal
   B. rinse out cans before they recycle them
   C. use storage areas for personal possessions
   D. turn on the water when they use the disposal

6. Tenants should call (310) 278-1489 when _____.
   A. the paint in their apartment is peeling
   B. they can't find a maintenance request form
   C. their kitchen faucet is leaking
   D. their toilet doesn't work

Look at the yellow pages listings and answer the questions.

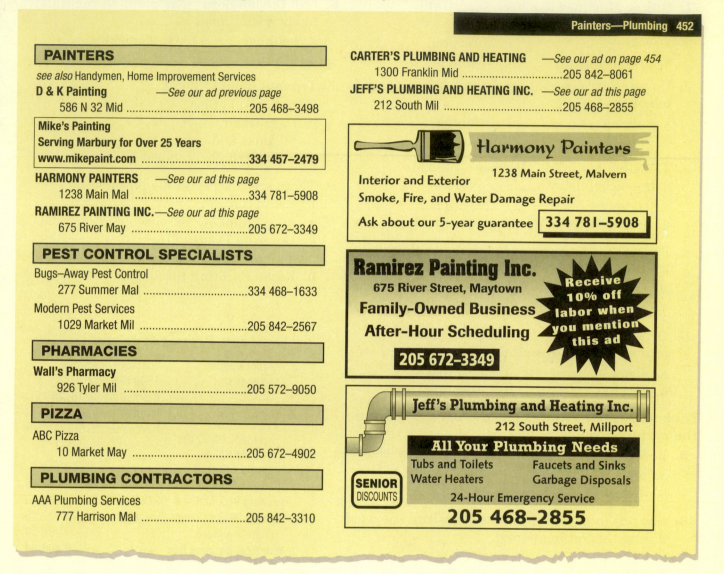

Painters—Plumbing 452

**PAINTERS**

*see also* Handymen, Home Improvement Services

**D & K Painting** *—See our ad previous page*
586 N 32 Mid ...................................205 468–3498

**Mike's Painting**
**Serving Marbury for Over 25 Years**
www.mikepaint.com ...........................**334 457–2479**

**HARMONY PAINTERS** *—See our ad this page*
1238 Main Mal ...................................334 781–5908

**RAMIREZ PAINTING INC.***—See our ad this page*
675 River May ...................................205 672–3349

**PEST CONTROL SPECIALISTS**

Bugs–Away Pest Control
277 Summer Mal ...............................334 468–1633

Modern Pest Services
1029 Market Mil ...............................205 842–2567

**PHARMACIES**

**Wall's Pharmacy**
926 Tyler Mil ...................................205 572–9050

**PIZZA**

ABC Pizza
10 Market May ...................................205 672–4902

**PLUMBING CONTRACTORS**

AAA Plumbing Services
777 Harrison Mal ...............................205 842–3310

CARTER'S PLUMBING AND HEATING *—See our ad on page 454*
1300 Franklin Mid ...............................205 842–8061

JEFF'S PLUMBING AND HEATING INC. *—See our ad this page*
212 South Mil ...................................205 468–2855

**Harmony Painters**
1238 Main Street, Malvern
Interior and Exterior
Smoke, Fire, and Water Damage Repair
Ask about our 5-year guarantee **334 781–5908**

**Ramirez Painting Inc.**
675 River Street, Maytown
**Family-Owned Business**
**After-Hour Scheduling**
**205 672–3349**
*Receive 10% off labor when you mention this ad*

**Jeff's Plumbing and Heating Inc.**
212 South Street, Millport
**All Your Plumbing Needs**
Tubs and Toilets      Faucets and Sinks
Water Heaters          Garbage Disposals
**SENIOR DISCOUNTS**
**24-Hour Emergency Service**
**205 468–2855**

1. You live in Maytown. The paint in your apartment is peeling. You should call _____.
   A. 334 781-5908      C. 334 457-2479
   B. 205 672-3349      D. 205 468-3498

2. You live in Midfield. Your water heater isn't working. You should call _____.
   A. 205 468-3498      C. 205 468-2855
   B. 205 842-3310      D. 205 842-8061

3. You need to paint the outside of your house. It's a big job, and you want a guarantee that the paint won't peel. You should call _____.
   A. 334 781-5908      C. 334 457-2479
   B. 205 672-3349      D. 205 468-3498

4. You live in Malvern. Your garbage disposal isn't working. You should call _____.
   A. 205 468-2855      C. 205 842-3310
   B. 205 842-8061      D. 334 468-1633

5. You live in Millport. There are roaches in your kitchen. You should call _____.
   A. 334 468-1633      C. 205 468-2855
   B. 205 842-2567      D. 205 572-9050

6. It's midnight. A pipe in your bathroom just broke, and water is leaking all over the floor. You should call _____.
   A. 205 842-3310      C. 334 781-5908
   B. 205 842-8061      D. 205 468-2855

## Choose the correct answer.

**1.** Officer Martinez has been _____ traffic all morning.
- A. taking
- B. disturbing
- C. directing
- D. standing

**2.** Do you hear something? I think the telephone is _____.
- A. talking
- B. ringing
- C. running
- D. barking

**3.** The students in Ms. Jackson's class are doing a chemistry _____.
- A. audience
- B. system
- C. experience
- D. experiment

**4.** I've worked here for a long time. I think it's time to ask my boss for a _____.
- A. raise
- B. job
- C. resume
- D. salary

**5.** Dr. Martinetti has _____ several babies at the Westside Hospital today.
- A. given
- B. decided
- C. delivered
- D. assembled

## Look at Beverly Wong's electric bill and choose the correct answer.

**9.** Beverly has to pay her electric bill on or before _____.
- A. May 15, 2020
- B. June 10, 2020
- C. June 14, 2020
- D. April 15, 2020

**10.** She has to pay _____ for the electricity she used during this billing period.
- A. $86.99
- B. $87.45
- C. $109.44
- D. $22.45

**6.** Call the landlord. The paint on the walls in our living room is _____.
- A. leaking
- B. peeling
- C. picking
- D. mending

**7.** Tenants should fill out _____.
- A. the rental office
- B. their trash
- C. all glass and cans
- D. a maintenance request form

**8.** There are roaches in my basement. I need to call _____.
- A. Ajax Plumbing Service
- B. Harrison Heating Inc.
- C. United Pest Control
- D. Rocha Painting Inc.

---

### Western Power & Light

| | |
|---|---|
| **Account Number** | **Customer Assistance:** |
| **444-229-8832** | **1-800-555-1212** |
| | Billing Date: **5/15/20** |
| Beverly Wong | Payment Due: **6/10/20** |
| 228 Ocean Ave | Next Meter Read: **6/14/20** |
| San Diego, CA 92101 | |

**Billing Summary**

| | |
|---|---|
| Amount of Previous Statement 4/15/20 | 87.45 |
| Payment Received — 4/09/20 Thank You | 65.00 |
| Balance Before Current Charges | 22.45 |
| Current Charges | 86.99 |
| **Your Total Balance Due** | **$ 109.44** |

---

## SKILLS CHECK ✓

**Words:**
- ☐ account number
- ☐ adjustments
- ☐ balance
- ☐ bill
- ☐ billing date
- ☐ billing period
- ☐ credit rating
- ☐ current charges
- ☐ due
- ☐ payment
- ☐ payment received
- ☐ late payment charge
- ☐ statement
- ☐ total amount
- ☐ common area
- ☐ dumpster
- ☐ fire hazard
- ☐ hallway
- ☐ lease
- ☐ maintenance
- ☐ mandatory
- ☐ recycling bin
- ☐ recycling collection site
- ☐ request form
- ☐ smoke detector
- ☐ storage area
- ☐ trash

**I can ask & answer:**
- ☐ How long have you been *waiting*?
- ☐ Have you been *waiting* for a long time?
- ☐ I've been *waiting* for *two hours*/since *10:00*.
- ☐ I've been *writing letters* since *9:00 A.M.*
- ☐ I've already *written twenty letters*.
- ☐ Have you ever *been in the hospital*?
- ☐ How long have you been living in *Easton*?
- ☐ Where else have you lived?
- ☐ How long have you been *studying English*?

**I can express surprise:**
- ☐ You're kidding!/No kidding!/You've got to be kidding!/ I can't believe it!/That's incredible!/ That's unbelievable!/That's amazing!

**I can write about:**
- ☐ places I have lived, worked, and gone to school

**I can:**
- ☐ inquire about lease information
- ☐ describe apartment building rules
- ☐ interpret utility bills
- ☐ interpret rules for housing maintenance and repairs
- ☐ interpret yellow pages listings

## 7

**Gerunds**

**Infinitives**

**Review: Present Perfect and Present Perfect Continuous Tenses**

- Discussing Recreation Preferences
- Discussing Things You Dislike Doing
- Habits
- Describing Talents and Skills
- Telling About Important Decisions
- Requests at Work
- Thanking Someone
- Borrow and Lending
- Workplace Notes and Messages
- "Small Talk" at Work

### VOCABULARY PREVIEW

1. enjoy / like
2. hate / can't stand
3. avoid
4. begin / start
5. continue / keep on
6. quit / stop
7. consider / think about
8. decide
9. learn
10. practice

# My Favorite Way to Relax

| to watch | watching |
|----------|----------|
| to dance | dancing |
| to swim | swimming |

**A.** Do you **like to watch TV**?

**B.** Yes. I **enjoy watching TV** very much. **Watching TV** is my favorite way to relax.

1. *you*
   *paint*

2. *Beverly*
   *knit*

3. *Kevin*
   *swim*

4. *your parents*
   *play golf*

5. *you and your friends*
   *dance*

6. *you*
   *listen to music*

7. *Hector*
   *go to the movies*

8. *Valerie*
   *browse the web*

9.

### ENJOYING LIFE

Howard enjoys reading. He likes to read in the park. He likes to read in the library. He even likes to read in the bathtub! As you can see, reading is a very important part of Howard's life.

Patty enjoys singing. She likes to sing in school. She likes to sing in church. She even likes to sing in the shower! As you can see, singing is a very important part of Patty's life.

Brenda enjoys watching TV. She likes to watch TV in the living room. She likes to watch TV in bed. She even likes to watch TV in department stores! As you can see, watching TV is a very important part of Brenda's life.

Tom enjoys talking about politics. He likes to talk about politics with his friends. He likes to talk about politics with his parents. He even likes to talk about politics with his barber! As you can see, talking about politics is a very important part of Tom's life.

## ✔️ READING *CHECK-UP*

### Q & A

The people in the story are introducing themselves to you at a party. Using this model, create dialogs based on the story.

**A.** Hello. My name is *Howard*.
**B.** Nice to meet you. My name is _____.
 Are you enjoying the party?
**A.** Not really. To tell you the truth, I'd rather be *reading*.
**B.** Oh? Do you like to *read*?
**A.** Oh, yes. I enjoy *reading* very much.
**B.** I like to *read*, too. In fact, *reading* is my favorite way to relax.
**A.** Mine, too. Tell me, what do you like to *read*?
**B.** I like to *read books about famous people*. How about you?
**A.** I enjoy *reading short stories*.
**B.** Well, please excuse me. I have to go now. It was nice meeting you.
**A.** Nice meeting you, too.

# She Hates to Drive Downtown

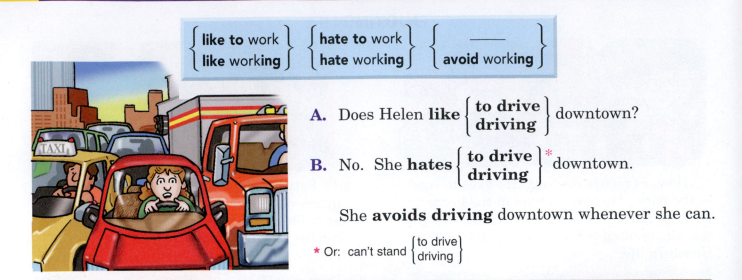

| like **to** work | | hate **to** work | | ——— |
| like work**ing** | | hate work**ing** | | avoid work**ing** |

**A.** Does Helen **like** { **to drive** / **driving** } downtown?

**B.** No. She **hates** { **to drive** / **driving** } * downtown.

She **avoids driving** downtown whenever she can.

\* Or: can't stand { to drive / driving }

**1.** *Albert*
*travel by plane*

**2.** *you*
*go to the mall*

**3.** *your parents*
*eat at fast-food restaurants*

**4.** *Carmen*
*sit in the sun*

**5.** *you and your friends*
*talk about politics*

**6.** *Kathy*
*use her cell phone*

**7.** *you*
*wear a suit and tie*

**8.** *the president*
*talk to reporters*

**9.**

**How About You?**

What do you enjoy doing?
What do you avoid doing whenever you can?

## BAD HABITS

Jill's co-workers always tell her to stop eating junk food. They think that eating junk food is unhealthy. Jill knows that, but she still keeps on eating junk food. She wants to stop, but she can't. Eating junk food is a habit she just can't break.

Vincent's friends always tell him to stop gossiping. They think that gossiping isn't nice. Vincent knows that, but he still keeps on gossiping. He wants to stop, but he can't. Gossiping is a habit he just can't break.

Jennifer's parents always tell her to stop interrupting people while they're talking. They think that interrupting people is very rude. Jennifer knows that, but she still keeps on interrupting people. She wants to stop, but she can't. Interrupting people is a habit she just can't break.

Walter's wife always tells him to stop talking about business all the time. She thinks that talking about business all the time is boring. Walter knows that, but he still keeps on talking about business. He wants to stop, but he can't. Talking about business is a habit he just can't break.

## ✔️ READING *CHECK-UP*

### Q & A

You're talking with the people in the story about their bad habits. Using this model, create dialogs based on the story.

**A.** *Jill?*
**B.** Yes?
**A.** You know . . . I don't mean to be critical, but I really think you should stop *eating junk food*.
**B.** Oh?
**A.** Yes. *Eating junk food is unhealthy*. Don't you think so?
**B.** You're right. The truth is . . . I want to stop, but I can't. *Eating junk food* is a habit I just can't break.

**How About You?**

Do you have any habits you "just can't break"? Tell about them.

# How Did You Learn to Swim So Well?

$$\left\{ \begin{array}{l} \textbf{start to } \text{swim} \\ \textbf{start } \text{swim\textbf{ing}} \end{array} \right\} \quad \left\{ \begin{array}{l} \textbf{learn to } \text{swim} \\ \underline{\qquad} \end{array} \right\} \quad \left\{ \begin{array}{l} \underline{\qquad} \\ \textbf{practice } \text{swim\textbf{ing}} \end{array} \right\}$$

**A.** How did you **learn to swim** so well?

**B.** Well, I **started** $\left\{ \begin{array}{l} \textbf{to swim} \\ \textbf{swimming} \end{array} \right\}$ when I was young,

and I've been **swimming** ever since.

**A.** I envy you. I've never **swum** before.

**B.** I'll be glad to teach you how.

**A.** Thank you. But isn't **swimming** very difficult?

**B.** Not at all. After you **practice swimming** a few times, you'll probably **swim** as well as I do.

**A.** How did you learn to _____ so well?

**B.** Well, I started { to _____ / _____ing } when I was young,

and I've been _____ing ever since.

**A.** I envy you. I've never _____ before.

**B.** I'll be glad to teach you how.

**A.** Thank you. But isn't _____ing very difficult?

**B.** Not at all. After you practice _____ing a few times,

you'll probably _____ as well as I do.

**1.** _draw_

**2.** _box_

**3.** _surf_

**4.** _figure skate_

**5.** _tap dance_

**6.**

## How to Say It!

### Expressing Appreciation

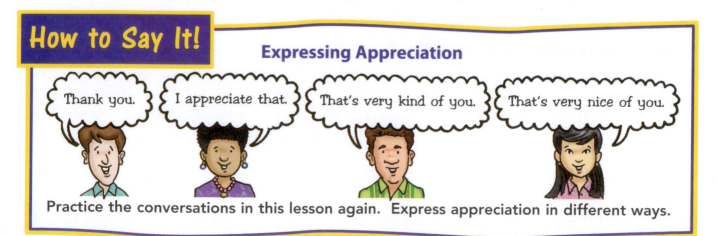

Thank you.

I appreciate that.

That's very kind of you.

That's very nice of you.

**Practice the conversations in this lesson again. Express appreciation in different ways.**

# Guess What I've Decided to Do!

decide to buy / _____    consider buying / _____    think about buying / _____

**A.** Guess what I've decided to do!

**B.** What?

**A.** I've **decided to get married**.

**B.** That's wonderful!  How long have you been **thinking about getting married**?

**A.** For a long time, actually.  I **considered getting married** a few years ago, but never did.

**B.** Well, I think you're making the right decision.  **Getting married** is a great idea.

**A.** Guess what I've decided to do!

**B.** What?

**A.** I've decided to _____.

**B.** That's wonderful! How long have you been thinking about _____ing?

**A.** For a long time, actually. I considered _____ing a few years ago, but never did.

**B.** Well, I think you're making the right decision. _____ing is a great idea.

**1.** *get a dog*

**2.** *buy a new car*

**3.** *move to New York*

**4.** *go on a diet*

**5.** *go back to college*

**6.** *start my own business*

**7.** *retire*

**8.** *become a vegetarian*

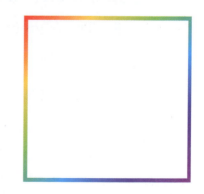

**9.**

# I've Made a Decision

$$\left\{ \begin{array}{l} \textbf{begin to } \text{eat} \\ \textbf{begin } \text{eating} \end{array} \right\} \quad \left\{ \begin{array}{l} \text{———} \\ \textbf{keep on } \text{eating} \end{array} \right\} \quad \left\{ \begin{array}{l} \textbf{quit } \text{eating} \end{array} \right\}$$

$$\left\{ \begin{array}{l} \textbf{start to } \text{eat} \\ \textbf{start } \text{eating} \end{array} \right\} \quad \left\{ \begin{array}{l} \textbf{continue to } \text{eat} \\ \textbf{continue } \text{eating} \end{array} \right\} \quad \left\{ \begin{array}{l} \text{———} \\ \textbf{stop } \text{eating} \end{array} \right\}$$

begin = start      keep on = continue      quit = stop

**A.** I've made a decision.

**B.** What is it?

**A.** I've decided to **quit eating** junk food.

**B.** That's great!  Have you ever tried to **stop eating** junk food before?

**A.** Yes.  Many times.  But every time I've **stopped eating** it,

I've **begun** $*$ $\left\{ \begin{array}{l} \textbf{to eat} \\ \textbf{eating} \end{array} \right\}$ it again after a few days.

**B.** Well, I hope you're successful this time.

**A.** I hope so, too.  After all, I can't **keep on eating** junk food for the rest of my life.

$*$ begin – began – begun

**A.** I've made a decision.

**B.** What is it?

**A.** I've decided to quit* _____ing.

**B.** That's great! Have you ever tried to stop* _____ing before?

**A.** Yes. Many times. But every time I've stopped* _____ing,

I've begun* { to _____ / _____ing } again after a few days.

**B.** Well, I hope you're successful this time.

**A.** I hope so, too. After all, I can't keep on* _____ing for the rest of my life.

\* quit = stop
  begin = start
  keep on = continue

**1.** *bite my nails*

**2.** *tease my little sister*

**3.** *worry about my health*

**4.** *argue with my neighbors*

**5.** *complain about my son-in-law*

**6.**

# IMPORTANT DECISIONS

Jim had to make an important decision recently. He made an appointment for an interview at the Tektron Internet Company, and he had to decide what to wear. First, he considered wearing a sweater to the interview. Then, he thought about wearing a sports jacket. Finally, he decided to wear a suit and tie. Jim thinks he made the right decision. He's glad he didn't wear a sweater or sports jacket. He feels that wearing a suit and tie was the best thing to do.

Emily had to make an important decision recently. Her landlord sold her apartment building, and she had to decide where to move. First, she considered moving to another apartment. Then, she thought about buying a small house. Finally, she decided to move home with her parents for a while. Emily thinks she made the right decision. She's glad she didn't move to another apartment or buy a small house. She thinks that moving home with her parents for a while was the right thing to do.

Nick had to make an important decision recently. He got out of the army, and he had to decide what to do next with his life. First, he considered working in his family's grocery store. Then, he thought about taking a job in a restaurant. Finally, he decided to enroll in college and study engineering. Nick thinks he made the right decision. He's glad he didn't work in his family's grocery store or take a job in a restaurant. He feels that enrolling in college and studying engineering was the smartest thing to do.

Maria had to make an important decision recently. She lost her job as a bookkeeper because her company went out of business, and she had to decide what to do. First, she considered looking for another job as a bookkeeper. Then, she thought about working as a secretary for a while. Finally, she decided to enroll in technical school and study network programming. Maria thinks she made the right decision. She's glad she didn't look for another job as a bookkeeper or work as a secretary for a while. She thinks that enrolling in technical school and studying network programming was the best thing to do.

## ✔ READING *CHECK-UP*

### TRUE, FALSE, OR MAYBE?

Answer True, False, or Maybe (if the answer isn't in the story).

1. Jim considered wearing a sweater to the interview.
2. He got the job at the Tektron Internet Company.
3. Emily decided not to move to another apartment.
4. Emily never considered buying a small house.
5. Emily's parents think that moving home was the right thing for her to do.
6. Nick's family is in the restaurant business.
7. Nick first became interested in engineering while he was in the army.
8. Maria wasn't a very good bookkeeper.
9. After Maria lost her job, she worked as a secretary for a while.
10. Maria feels she made the right decision.

## LISTENING

Listen and choose the correct answer.

1. a. She enjoys going to the mall.
   b. She hates going to the mall.

2. a. He sold his car.
   b. He's going to sell his car.

3. a. He bites his nails.
   b. He stopped biting his nails.

4. a. She likes traveling by plane.
   b. She can't stand traveling by plane.

5. a. They're going to move to Florida.
   b. They might move to Florida.

6. a. He's married.
   b. He isn't married.

7. a. She's going to keep on practicing.
   b. She isn't going to continue practicing.

8. a. He interrupts people.
   b. He doesn't interrupt people any more.

**Listen.  Then say it.**

I like **to** watch TV.

She hates **to** drive downtown.

How did you learn **to** draw?

I started **to** skate last year.

**Say it.  Then listen.**

We decided **to** move.

He can't stand **to** wear a tie.

They've already begun **to** eat.

I continue **to** worry about my health.

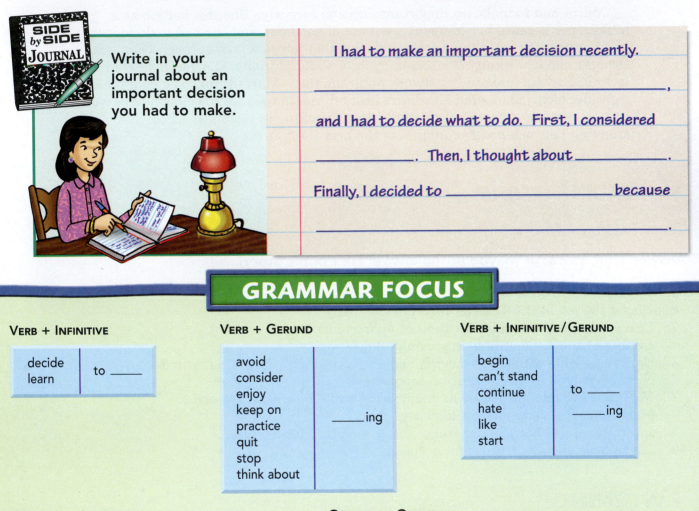

**SIDE by SIDE JOURNAL**

Write in your journal about an important decision you had to make.

I had to make an important decision recently.

_____ ,

and I had to decide what to do.  First, I considered

_____ . Then, I thought about _____ .

Finally, I decided to _____ because

_____ .

## GRAMMAR FOCUS

**VERB + INFINITIVE**

| decide<br>learn | to _____ |

**VERB + GERUND**

| avoid<br>consider<br>enjoy<br>keep on<br>practice<br>quit<br>stop<br>think about | _____ing |

**VERB + INFINITIVE/GERUND**

| begin<br>can't stand<br>continue<br>hate<br>like<br>start | to _____<br>_____ing |

**GERUND AS SUBJECT**

Watching TV is my favorite way to relax.

**GERUND AS OBJECT**

I'm thinking about **getting married**.

**Choose the correct word.**

1. I enjoy ( to listen    listening ) to music.

2. My daughter practices ( to skate    skating ) every weekend.

3. We've decided ( to move    moving ) to Florida.

4. I usually avoid ( to talk    talking ) about politics.

5. I really want to quit ( to bite    biting ) my nails.

6. You can't keep on ( to worry    worrying ) all the time.

7. Where did you learn ( to draw    drawing ) so well?

8. I know I have to stop ( to eat    eating ) junk food.

**1** **CONVERSATION**   **REQUESTS AT WORK**

Practice the conversations with a classmate.

**A.** Would you please lend me your pencil?

**B.** Sure.  I'll be happy to.

**A.** Thank you for lending me your pencil.

**B.** You're welcome.

Now work with other classmates.  Practice making requests and thanking co-workers.

| | |
|---|---|
| **A.** Would you please _____? | **A.** Thank you for _____ing. |
| **B.** Sure.  I'll be happy to. | **B.** You're welcome. |

**1.** clean table six

**2.** copy this report

**3.** set up the tables and chairs

**4.** hang the new coats on the racks

**5.** change the oil in the Ford

**6.** take the lunch trays to the fifth floor

**2** **TEAMWORK**   **ASKING TO BORROW SOMETHING**

Work with other classmates.
Practice both conversations.
Ask to borrow different items.

**A.** Would you please lend me _____?

**B.** Sure.  I'll be happy to.

**A.** Thank you.

**A.** Could I possibly borrow _____?

**B.** Sure.

**A.** Thanks.

**GWL**

Emily,

Would you be able to help me with the PowerPoint presentation I have to give next month? I've given a lot of presentations, but I haven't used PowerPoint before. I know exactly what I want to say and what pictures I want to show. I attended last month's computer training sessions, but I'm still having trouble making charts with PowerPoint, and I don't know how to add pictures to my presentation. I'd really appreciate your help. Would you have some time to meet with me this week?

Thanks,
Joe

**SHS SPRINGFIELD HIGH SCHOOL**

Roberto,

Thank you for staying late last week and helping to mail our school's annual fund-raising letter. You were an important part of the "assembly line" of employees who helped with this. We mailed 2,000 letters last week—500 more than last year!

We have already received more than $1,000 from students who read the letter. This is just the beginning! It looks like we'll finally be able to buy a new copy machine this year.

Thanks again for all your help.
Carol

From: George_Jensen@skillcorp.com
To: Linda_Chang@skillcorp.com
Subject: Request for day off

Ms. Chang,

Could I possibly take the day off next Wednesday, November 2? I'm asking because I have to take my daughter to a doctor's appointment in the morning and a dentist's appointment in the afternoon. I tried to schedule the appointments for an afternoon when I don't work, but these were the only times available. If the appointment at the dentist is quick, I might be able to come in for an hour of work at the end of the day. I've been making excellent progress on all my work, including the monthly report. I'm sure I'll be able to complete it by November 7. I'll come in and work on it this weekend if necessary.

Thanks,
George Jensen

1. Joe does NOT know _____.
   A. how to give presentations
   B. what pictures to use in his presentation
   C. how to make charts with PowerPoint
   D. what to say in his presentation

2. We can infer that _____.
   A. Joe doesn't use a computer at work
   B. everybody attended the training sessions
   C. Joe's presentation is about power
   D. PowerPoint is a computer program for presentations

3. Carol is thanking Roberto because he _____.
   A. assembled electronic equipment
   B. put letters into envelopes
   C. gave money for a new copy machine
   D. wrote a letter

4. We can infer from Carol's note that _____.
   A. a fund-raising letter asks for money
   B. Roberto works in a factory
   C. they mailed 2,500 letters last year
   D. more than 1,000 students have already read the letter

5. George wants to take time off _____.
   A. to make progress on all his work
   B. to work on the monthly report
   C. to work on the weekend
   D. to take his daughter to the doctor and dentist

6. George made appointments for November 2nd because _____.
   A. he doesn't usually work that afternoon
   B. his report is due on November 7th
   C. that's when the doctor and dentist can see his daughter
   D. the appointment at the dentist will be quick

**Read the article and answer the questions.**

## Small Talk

"How was your weekend?" "What are you going to do on your day off?" "Did you see the game on TV last night?" "Isn't the weather beautiful today?" These questions, and the answers to these questions, are examples of "small talk"—the short, friendly conversations that people have with friends and co-workers.

Some people avoid making small talk at work. They think they shouldn't chat about topics that aren't important on the job, or they believe their supervisors and co-workers will think they aren't serious about their work. Some people just don't enjoy making conversation about themselves.

But small talk is important! Knowing how to make small talk is a skill that can help you in your job. By making conversation, you show that you are friendly and interested in your co-workers. You become a better *team player*. If you don't make small talk, other workers might feel uncomfortable around you and think you're rude or unfriendly. Peter Harper, Director of Human Resources at the Apex Company, says, "We always look for friendly employees who know how to communicate with each other and with our customers."

Here are some tips for successful small talk. Talk about safe topics such as the weather, sports, hobbies, movies, TV programs, and celebrities (movie stars, singers, and other famous people). You can share some information about your family such as birthdays, anniversaries, and other family events, but don't share very personal information about family problems. You can talk about the news, but avoid conversations about politics. Other topics to avoid are money, religion, and illness. Don't ask personal questions such as "How old are you?" or "What's your salary?" And don't gossip. Co-workers won't want to talk with you if they think you will talk to other people about them.

Listening is an important part of small talk. Listen carefully to what the other person is saying and ask questions. Don't just talk about yourself. Show that you are interested in the other person. And remember to smile! Making conversation takes practice. The more you do it, the better you'll be at making small talk!

1. If you make small talk at work, _____.
   A. your supervisor will think you're serious
   B. your supervisor will be uncomfortable
   C. your co-workers will think you're friendly
   D. your co-workers will think you're rude

2. When you make small talk, don't _____.
   A. talk about sports
   B. talk about family problems
   C. talk about movies and TV shows
   D. smile

3. It's okay to ask, _____
   A. "What's your salary?"
   B. "How much do you weigh?"
   C. "Who's your favorite actor?"
   D. "How old are you going to be?"

4. _____ is a safe topic to talk about.
   A. The weather
   B. Religion
   C. Money
   D. Politics

5. In paragraph 2, *chat* means _____.
   A. to gossip
   B. to have serious conversations
   C. to have long conversations
   D. to make small talk

6. In paragraph 3, a *team player* refers to _____.
   A. a supervisor at work
   B. a person who works well with co-workers
   C. a celebrity player on a sports team
   D. a person who likes sports

**TEAMWORK** With a classmate, make a list of other topics for small talk. Then share with your classmates. As a class, vote for the best topics.

**Choose the correct answer.**

1. I enjoy _____ the web.
   A. traveling
   B. browsing
   C. watching
   D. following

2. It's impolite to _____ people while they're speaking.
   A. consider
   B. complain
   C. interrupt
   D. quit

3. I've been thinking about _____ my own business.
   A. starting
   B. going back
   C. keeping on
   D. liking

4. I'm considering _____ in a technical school.
   A. going
   B. deciding
   C. practicing
   D. enrolling

5. I just made an important _____. I'm going to retire this year.
   A. reason
   B. advice
   C. decision
   D. idea

6. Would you please _____ your pencil?
   A. lend you
   B. lend me
   C. borrow you
   D. borrow me

7. I attended a training _____ at my company last week.
   A. session
   B. section
   C. system
   D. line

8. I've been making good _____ on all my work.
   A. presentation
   B. appointments
   C. schedule
   D. progress

9. I enjoy _____ with my colleagues during breaks at work.
   A. arriving
   B. changing
   C. chatting
   D. listening

10. _____ is a safe topic for small talk at work.
   A. Politics
   B. The weather
   C. Your salary
   D. Gossip about co-workers

## SKILLS CHECK ✔

**Words:**
☐ begin/start
☐ can't stand/hate
☐ consider/think about
☐ continue/keep on
☐ enjoy/like
☐ quit/stop

☐ avoid
☐ borrow
☐ decide
☐ learn
☐ lend
☐ practice

**I can ask & answer:**
☐ Do you like to *swim*?
☐ Do you like *swimming*?
  I enjoy *swimming* very much.
  *Swimming* is my favorite way to relax.
  I avoid *swimming* whenever I can.

☐ How did you learn to *draw* so well?
  I started *drawing* when I was young.

☐ How long have you been thinking about *moving*?
  I considered *moving* a few years ago.

☐ Would you please lend me your *pencil*?
☐ Could I possibly borrow your *pencil*?

**I can express appreciation:**
☐ Thank you.
☐ I appreciate that.
☐ That's very kind of you.
☐ That's very nice of you.

**I can:**
☐ make and respond to requests at work
☐ ask to borrow something
☐ interpret workplace notes and messages
☐ make small talk at work and understand its importance

**I can write about:**
☐ an important decision I had to make

## Past Perfect Tense
## Past Perfect Continuous Tense

- **Discussing Things People Had Done**
- **Discussing Preparations for Events**
- **Describing Consequences of Being Late**
- **Discussing Feelings**
- **Describing Accomplishments**

- **Scheduling Medical Appointments**
- **Medical Appointment Cards**
- **Medical History Forms**
- **Preventive Care Recommendations**
- **Public Health Information**
- **Nutrition: The Food Pyramid**
- **Reading a Health Textbook Lesson**

### VOCABULARY PREVIEW

1. discuss
2. fly a kite
3. go canoeing
4. go window-shopping
5. pack

6. purchase
7. realize
8. shine
9. water
10. wrestle

11. forget
12. remember
13. memorize
14. rehearse
15. perform

# They Didn't Want to

| I |  |
|---|---|
| He | |
| She | |
| It | had eaten. |
| We | |
| You | |
| They | |

the weekend before

**A.** Why didn't Mr. and Mrs. Henderson **see** a movie last weekend?

**B.** They didn't want to. They **had seen** a movie the weekend before.

the evening before

**1.** Why didn't your parents eat out yesterday evening?

the Saturday before

**2.** Why didn't Barry go canoeing last Saturday?

the morning before

**3.** Why didn't Martha make eggs for breakfast yesterday morning?

the night before

**4.** Why didn't you have pizza for dinner last night?

the Sunday before

5. Why didn't you and your friends drive to the beach last Sunday?

the day before

6. Why didn't Paul wear his polka dot shirt to work yesterday?

the semester before

7. Why didn't Susan take a psychology course last semester?

the month before

8. Why didn't your neighbors give a party last month?

the week before

9. Why didn't Mozart write an opera last week?

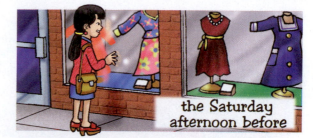

the Saturday afternoon before

10. Why didn't you go window-shopping last Saturday afternoon?

the day before

11. Why didn't Monica fly her kite yesterday?

the evening before

12. Why didn't you and your family discuss politics at the dinner table yesterday evening?

the weekend before

13. Why didn't George do card tricks for his friends last weekend?

14.

## THE MOST IMPORTANT THING

Roger thought he was all prepared for his dinner party last night. He had sent invitations to his boss and all the people at the office. He had looked through several cookbooks and had found some very interesting recipes. He had even gone all the way downtown to buy imported fruit, vegetables, and cheese, which he needed for his dinner. However, as soon as Roger's doorbell rang and his guests arrived, he realized that he had forgotten to turn on the oven. Roger felt very foolish. He couldn't believe what he had done. He thought he was all prepared for his dinner party, but he had forgotten to do the most important thing.

Mr. and Mrs. Jenkins thought they were all prepared for their vacation. They had packed their suitcases several days ahead of time. They had gone to the bank and purchased traveler's checks. They had even asked their next-door neighbor to water their plants, feed their dog, and shovel their driveway if it snowed. However, as soon as Mr. and Mrs. Jenkins arrived at the airport, they realized that they had forgotten to bring their plane tickets with them, and there wasn't enough time to go back home and get them. Mr. and Mrs. Jenkins were heartbroken. They couldn't believe what they had done. They thought they were all prepared for their vacation, but they had forgotten to do the most important thing.

Harold thought he was all prepared for his job interview yesterday. He had gone to his barber and gotten a very short haircut. He had bought a new shirt, put on his best tie, and shined his shoes. He had even borrowed his brother's new suit. However, as soon as Harold began the job interview, he realized that he had forgotten to bring along his resume. Harold was furious with himself. He thought he was all prepared for his job interview, but he had forgotten to do the most important thing.

Janet thought she was all prepared for the school play. She had memorized the script several weeks in advance. She had practiced her songs and dances until she knew them perfectly. She had even stayed up all night the night before and rehearsed the play by herself from beginning to end. However, as soon as the curtain went up and the play began, Janet realized that she had forgotten to put on her costume. Janet was really embarrassed. She couldn't believe what she had done. She thought she was all prepared for the play, but she had forgotten to do the most important thing.

✔️ **READING** *CHECK-UP*

### True, False, or Maybe?

**Answer True, False, or Maybe (if the answer isn't in the story).**

1. Roger had remembered to buy the ingredients he needed.
2. Roger hadn't remembered to cook the food.
3. Roger's guests couldn't believe what he had done.
4. Mr. and Mrs. Jenkins had forgotten to buy their plane tickets.
5. When Mr. and Mrs. Jenkins realized what had happened, they felt very sad and upset.
6. Harold thinks it's important to bring a resume to a job interview.
7. Harold doesn't have a suit.
8. Janet hadn't seen the script until the night before the play.
9. Before the play began, Janet hadn't realized that she had forgotten to put on her costume.

### Which Is Correct?

1. Before Barbara went on her vacation, she went to the bank and bought ( tickets   traveler's checks ).
2. Peter wanted his boss to come over for dinner, but he forgot to send him ( a resume   an invitation ).
3. Sheila ( borrowed   bought ) her roommate's laptop for a few days.
4. Our grandchildren were ( heartbroken   foolish ) when our dog ran away.
5. At the supermarket next to the United Nations, ( imported   important ) people buy ( imported   important ) food.

## How About You?

Have you ever thought you were all prepared for something, but you realized you had forgotten to do something important?
What were you preparing for?
What had you done?
What had you forgotten to do?

# They Didn't Get There on Time

**A.** Did you get to the **concert** on time?

**B.** No, I didn't. By the time I got to the **concert**, it had already **begun**.

**1.** *post office*
   *closed*

**2.** *plane*
   *take off*

**3.** *movie*
   *start*

**4.** *train*
   *leave*

**5.** *lecture*
   *end*

**6.** *meeting*
   *finish*

**7.** *library*
   *close*

**8.** *boat*
   *sail away*

**9.** *parade*
   *go by*

# He Hadn't Gone Fishing in a Long Time

I
He
She
It
We
You
They
} hadn't eaten.
(had not)

**A.** Did Grandpa enjoy **going fishing** last weekend?

**B.** Yes, he did. He hadn't **gone fishing** in a long time.

**1.** Did Natalie enjoy swimming in the ocean last weekend?

**2.** Did you enjoy seeing a movie yesterday evening?

**3.** Did Mr. and Mrs. Ramirez enjoy taking a walk along the beach yesterday?

**4.** Did you and your friends enjoy eating at Burger Queen yesterday?

**5.** Did Henry enjoy singing with the choir last Sunday?

**6.** Did you enjoy having strawberry shortcake for dessert last night?

**7.** Did Jim and Tess enjoy riding on a roller coaster this afternoon?

**8.** Did Kevin enjoy playing "hide and seek" with his children last night?

**9.** Did Mrs. Kramer enjoy reading her old love letters last weekend?

## DAYS GONE BY

Michael took a very special trip last month. He went back to Fullerton, his home town. Michael's visit to Fullerton was very special to him. He was born there, he grew up there, but he hadn't been back there since he finished high school.

He went to places he hadn't gone to in years. He walked through the park in the center of town and remembered the days he had walked through the same park with his first girlfriend. He passed by the empty field where he and his friends had played baseball every day after school. And he stood for a while in front of the movie theater and thought about all the Saturday afternoons he had spent there sitting in the balcony, watching his favorite movie heroes and eating popcorn.

He did things he hadn't done in a long time. He had some homemade ice cream at the ice cream shop, he rode on the merry-go-round in the park, and he went fishing at the lake on the outskirts of town. For a while, he felt like a kid again. He hadn't had homemade ice cream, ridden on a merry-go-round, or gone fishing since he was a young boy.

He also saw people he hadn't seen in years. He visited several of his old neighbors who had never moved out of the neighborhood. He said hello to the owners of the candy store near his house. And he even bumped into Mrs. Riley, his tenth-grade science teacher.

During his visit to his home town, Michael remembered places he hadn't gone to, things he hadn't done, and people he hadn't seen since his childhood. Michael's trip back to Fullerton was a very nostalgic experience for him. Going back to Fullerton brought back many memories of days gone by.

# READING CHECK-UP

## TRUE, FALSE, OR MAYBE?

Answer True, False, or Maybe (if the answer isn't in the story).

1. Michael moved back to Fullerton last month.
2. He hadn't seen Fullerton in years.
3. When Michael passed by the field last month, children were playing baseball.
4. Michael enjoyed going to the movies when he was young.
5. The ice cream shop was near Michael's home in Fullerton.
6. Michael rode on the merry-go-round when he was a young boy.
7. Some of Michael's old neighbors still live in the same neighborhood.
8. Mrs. Riley still teaches science.

## WHICH IS CORRECT?

1. I always enjoy eating Aunt Betty's ( home town    homemade ) food.
2. The new shopping mall is located in the ( outskirts    outside ) of our city.
3. She recently visited the town where she had ( spent    grown up ) her childhood.
4. I bumped ( through    into ) an old friend on the street the other day.
5. They hadn't been ( back    by ) to their old neighborhood in several years.
6. Seeing my old college friends was a ( nauseous    nostalgic ) experience for me.

# LISTENING

Listen and choose the correct answer.

1. a. Yes.  They've never eaten there.
   b. Yes.  They had never eaten there.

2. a. I had already seen it.
   b. I've already seen it.

3. a. No.  It had already started.
   b. No.  It has already started.

4. a. But I had already done it.
   b. But I've already done it.

5. a. She had memorized all the important names and dates.
   b. She's going to study very hard.

6. a. Have you ever stayed there before?
   b. Had you ever stayed there before?

# THINK ABOUT IT!   *Feelings and Experiences*

Think about times you have had these feelings.  Share your experiences with other students.

I was heartbroken when . . .

I was furious when . . .

I felt foolish when . . .

I always feel nostalgic when . . .

# Have You Heard About Harry?

**A.** Have you heard about Harry?

**B.** No, I haven't. What happened?

**A.** He broke his leg last week.

**B.** That's terrible! How did he do THAT?

**A.** He was roller-skating . . . and he had never roller-skated before.

**B.** Poor Harry! I hope he feels better soon.

---

**A.** Have you heard about _____?

**B.** No, I haven't. What happened?

**A.** (He/She) _____ last week.

**B.** That's terrible! How did (he/she) do THAT?

**A.** (He/She) was _____ing . . . and (he/she) had never _____ before.

**B.** Poor _____! I hope (he/she) feels better soon.

**1.** _twist his ankle_
   _fly a kite_

**2.** _injure her knee_
   _ski_

**3.** _burn himself_
   _bake brownies_

**Louise**

**4.** sprain her wrist
play squash

**Howard**

**5.** get a black eye
box

**Abby**

**6.** hurt her arm
wrestle

**Victor**

**7.** lose his voice
sing opera

**Shirley**

**8.** dislocate her shoulder
do gymnastics

**Ann**

**9.** get hurt in an accident
ride a motorcycle

**Bruce**

**10.** sprain his back
do the tango

**Rex**

**11.** break his front teeth
chew on a steak bone

**12.**

---

## How to Say It!

### Sharing News About Someone

A. { Have you heard about
Have you heard the news about
Have you heard what happened to } *Harry?*

B. No, I haven't. What happened?

**Practice the conversations in this lesson again. Begin your conversations in different ways.**

# It's Really a Shame

I
He
She
It
We
You
They
} had been eating.

**A.** I heard that Arnold failed his driver's test last week.  Is it true?

**B.** Yes, it is . . . and it's really a shame.  He had been practicing for a long time.

---

**A.** I heard that _____ last week.  Is it true?

**B.** Yes, it is . . . and it's really a shame.  (He/She/They) had been _____ing for a long time.

I heard that . . .

**1.** Fred lost his job at the factory
*work there*

**2.** Larry and Jane broke up
*go together*

**3.** Mona had to cancel her trip to France
*plan it*

**4.** Pam and Bob canceled their wedding
*plan to get married*

**5.** Mr. and Mrs. Williams moved
*live in this neighborhood*

**6.** Walter had another heart attack
*feel better*

**7.** Alex did poorly on his science exam
*study for it*

**8.** Penny twisted her ankle and couldn't run in the marathon
*train for it*

**9.** Your daughter got sick and couldn't perform in her piano recital
*rehearse for it*

**10.** Herbert caught a cold and couldn't go camping
*look forward to it*

## READING

### THEIR PLANS "FELL THROUGH"

Patty had planned to have a party last weekend. She had been getting ready for the party for a long time. She had invited all of her friends and several co-workers, she had cooked lots of food, and she had cleaned her apartment from top to bottom. But at the last minute, she got sick and had to cancel the party. Poor Patty! She was really disappointed.

John and Julia had planned to get married last month. They had been planning their wedding for more than a year, and all of their friends and relatives had been looking forward to the ceremony. Julia had bought a beautiful wedding gown, John had rented a fancy tuxedo, and they had sent invitations to 150 people. But at the last minute, John "got cold feet"* and they had to cancel the wedding.

\* got scared

Michael had planned to ask his boss for a raise last week. He had been preparing to ask his boss for a raise for a long time. He had come to work early for several weeks, he had worked late at the office every night, and he had even bought a new suit to wear to the appointment with his boss. Unfortunately, before Michael could even ask for a raise, his boss fired him.

## IN YOUR OWN WORDS

### FOR WRITING AND DISCUSSION

**Tell about plans YOU had that "fell through."**

What had you planned to do?
How long had you been planning to do it?
What had you done beforehand?
What went wrong? What happened?
Were you upset? disappointed?

When Stella Karp won the marathon last week, nobody was surprised. She had been getting up early and jogging every morning. She had been eating health foods and taking vitamins for several months. And she had been swimming fifty laps every day after work. Stella Karp really deserved to win the marathon. After all, she had been preparing for it for a long time.

When my friend Stuart finally passed his driver's test the other day, nobody was surprised. He had been taking lessons at the driving school for several months. He had been practicing driving with his father for the past several weeks. And he had been studying the "rules of the road" since he was a little boy. My friend Stuart really deserved to pass his driver's test. After all, he had been preparing for it for a long time.

When Sally Compton got a promotion last week, nobody was surprised. She had been working overtime every day for several months. She had been studying computer programming in the evening. And she had even been taking extra work home on the weekends. Sally Compton really deserved to get a promotion. After all, she had been working hard to earn it for a long time.

We all feel proud when we accomplish something that we have prepared for. Tell other students about an accomplishment you're proud of.

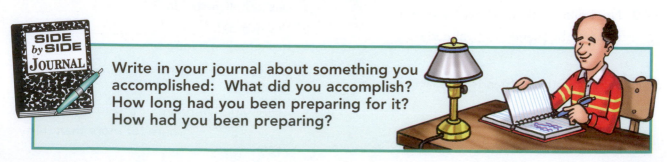

Write in your journal about something you accomplished: What did you accomplish? How long had you been preparing for it? How had you been preparing?

**Listen.  Then say it.**

She **had** seen a movie the day before.

We **had** never roller-skated before.

It **had** already begun.

Patty **had** planned to have a party.

**Say it.  Then listen.**

He **had** gone fishing the week before.

We **had** been studying for several hours.

I **had** forgotten to do it.

Tom **had** been practicing for a long time.

## GRAMMAR FOCUS

PAST PERFECT TENSE

| I<br>He<br>She<br>It<br>We<br>You<br>They | had eaten. |
|---|---|

| I<br>He<br>She<br>It<br>We<br>You<br>They | hadn't eaten. |
|---|---|

PAST PERFECT CONTINUOUS TENSE

| I<br>He<br>She<br>It<br>We<br>You<br>They | had been eating. |
|---|---|

**Complete the conversations.  Use the correct forms of these verbs in your answers.**

| forget | go | have | live | plan | play | ride | see | take off | work |
|---|---|---|---|---|---|---|---|---|---|

1. A. Why didn't you see a movie last weekend?
   B. I didn't want to. _____ _____ _____ a movie the weekend before.

2. A. Why was your brother upset during his job interview yesterday?
   B. _____ _____ _____ to bring along his resume.

3. A. Did your daughter enjoy having chocolate cake for dessert last night?
   B. Yes, she did. _____ _____ _____ chocolate cake for dessert in a long time.

4. A. Did you get to the airport on time?
   B. No, I didn't.  By the time I got to the airport, the plane _____ already _____.

5. A. Why didn't your friends go sailing with us last Sunday?
   B. They didn't want to. _____ _____ _____ sailing the weekend before.

6. A. How did Roberta hurt herself?
   B. She was _____ a motorcycle, and _____ _____ never _____ a motorcycle before.

7. A. Did you hear that Gregory and Isabelle canceled their wedding?
   B. No, I didn't.  What a shame! _____ _____ _____ _____ it for a long time.

8. A. Is it true that Bruno lost his job at the factory?
   B. Yes, it is . . . and it's really a shame. _____ _____ _____ _____ there for many years.

9. A. Did you and your friends enjoy playing basketball yesterday?
   B. Yes, we did. _____ _____ _____ basketball in a long time.

10. A. Did you hear that Mrs. Ramirez moved last weekend?
    B. Yes, I did.  I'm really surprised. _____ _____ _____ _____ here for more than thirty years.

## 1 CONVERSATION  MAKING, CONFIRMING, RESCHEDULING, & CANCELING APPOINTMENTS

Practice conversations with your classmates. For each conversation, use the information on any of these medical appointment cards or your own information.

### MAKING AN APPOINTMENT

**A.** Hello. This is ___(first & last name)___. I'd like to make an appointment.

**B.** All right. Can you come in on ___(day)___ ___(date)___ at ___(time)___?

**A.** ___(day)___ ___(date)___ at ___(time)___? Yes. That would be fine. Thank you.

### CONFIRMING AN APPOINTMENT

**A.** Hello. This is ___(first & last name)___. I'm calling to confirm my appointment on ___(day)___ ___(date)___ at ___(time)___.

**B.** Let me check. Yes, you have an appointment on ___(day)___ ___(date)___ at ___(time)___. We'll see you then.

**A.** Thank you.

### RESCHEDULING AN APPOINTMENT

**A.** Hello. This is ___(first & last name)___. I need to reschedule an appointment.

**B.** When are you scheduled to come in?

**A.** On ___(day)___ ___(date)___ at ___(time)___.

**B.** Okay. We have an opening on ___(day)___ ___(date)___ at ___(time)___. Is that a convenient time?

**A.** Yes. Thank you.

### CANCELING AN APPOINTMENT

**A.** Hello. This is ___(first & last name)___. I need to cancel an appointment.

**B.** What's the date and time of the appointment?

**A.** ___(day)___ ___(date)___ at ___(time)___.

**B.** Would you like to reschedule that appointment?

**A.** Not at this time. Thanks very much.

---

**COMMUNITY MEDICAL CLINIC**
4600 N. Federal Highway, Miami, FL 33137

*Ana Ramirez*

**HAS AN APPOINTMENT ON**

Tue.    Nov.    12th  at  3  A.M. / P.M.
DAY    MONTH    DATE

IF UNABLE TO KEEP THIS APPOINTMENT, PLEASE GIVE ONE DAY ADVANCE NOTICE.
TELEPHONE: (305) 576-7000

---

**APPOINTMENT**

FOR ___Abdul Asmal___

ON ___Mon.___  ___Feb.___  ___4___  AT ___11:30___ A.M. / P.M.
    DAY    MONTH    DATE

**GLENDALE HEALTH CENTER**
501 North Glendale Avenue
Glendale, CA 91206
(818) 500-8762

IF UNABLE TO KEEP THIS APPOINTMENT, KINDLY GIVE 24 HOURS NOTICE.

---

M ___Clara Wong___

**HAS AN APPOINTMENT ON**

☐ MON  ☐ TUE  ☐ WED  ☐ THU  ☑ FRI  ☐ SAT

OCT    24    AT  1:15  A.M. / P.M.
MONTH    DATE

**SUNNYSIDE HEALTH CENTER**
9314 Cullen Blvd.    TEL (713) 732-5000
Houston, TX 77051

PATIENTS WILL BE CHARGED FOR APPOINTMENTS
NOT CANCELED AT LEAST 24 HOURS IN ADVANCE.

---

KOMED HOLMAN HEALTH CENTER
4259 S. Berkelely Street
Chicago, Illinois 60653
TEL 773.268.7600

HAS AN APPOINTMENT ON

_____ AT _____ A.M.
DAY  MONTH  DATE             P.M.

IF APPOINTMENT CANNOT BE KEPT, NOTIFICATION
SHOULD BE MADE ONE DAY IN ADVANCE.

---

## 2 COMMUNITY CONNECTIONS  MEDICAL CARE

Where can people go for free or inexpensive medical care in your community? Are there public health clinics or other medical offices? Is it difficult to get medical services? Discuss as a class.

## MEDICAL HISTORY

**Name** _Lena Kosta_      **Date of Birth** _5/15/68_

**List the medications you are now taking. Include non-prescription drugs and vitamins.**
_insulin, aspirin, multivitamins, calcium_

**List any allergies you have to drugs, food, or other items.**
_strawberries, cats, dogs, dust, bee stings_

**List any operations you have had, including the year.** _broken leg (2011),_
_gall bladder (2015)_

**Please check if you have had any of the following health problems.**

| | | |
|---|---|---|
| ✓ chicken pox | ✓ diabetes | ___ depression |
| ✓ measles | ___ tuberculosis | ___ frequent earaches |
| ✓ mumps | ___ cancer | ✓ severe headaches |
| ___ asthma | ___ AIDS | ___ back problems |
| ___ heart disease | ___ kidney disease | ___ frequent colds |
| ✓ high blood pressure | ___ liver disease (hepatitis) | ___ stomach problems |
| ___ pneumonia | ___ influenza | ___ loss of appetite |

### FAMILY HISTORY

**Please check if anyone in your family (parents, siblings, grandparents, children) has had any of the following illnesses.**

| | | |
|---|---|---|
| ___ asthma | ✓ diabetes | ___ AIDS |
| ✓ heart disease | ___ tuberculosis | ___ kidney disease |
| ✓ high blood pressure | ___ cancer | ___ liver disease |

### RECORD OF IMMUNIZATIONS

**Please check if you had any of the following vaccinations or tests, and fill in the year of the most recent ones.**

| | Year |
|---|---|
| ___ measles | |
| ___ mumps | |
| ___ chicken pox | |
| ✓ tetanus | 2016 |

| | Year |
|---|---|
| ✓ tuberculosis test | 2009 |
| ___ hepatitis B | |
| ✓ influenza | 2016 |
| ___ pneumonia | |

# LEGACY HEALTH PLAN

## Preventive Care Guidelines for Staying Healthy

Legacy Health Plan recommends the following examinations and screening tests to keep our adult members healthy. Talk with your doctor about these recommendations.

| What to do: | How often: | | |
| --- | --- | --- | --- |
| | Ages 18–39 | Ages 40–49 | Ages 50 & older |
| Have a physical examination | Every 1–3 years | Every year | Every year |
| Check your blood pressure | Every 1–2 years | Every year | Every year |
| Have an eye examination | Every 1–2 years | Every year | Every year |
| Have a hearing test | Every 10 years | Every 10 years | Every 10 years |
| See a dentist | 1–2 times a year | 1–2 times a year | 1–2 times a year |
| Get a tetanus shot | Every 10 years | Every 10 years | Every 10 years |
| Have a skin examination | Every 3 years | Every year | Every year |
| Have a cholesterol blood test | Every 5 years | Every 5 years | Every 5 years |
| Have a flu shot | If doctor advises | If doctor advises | Every year |
| Have a pneumonia vaccination | If doctor advises | If doctor advises | Once after age 65 |
| Have a colonoscopy to check for colon cancer | If doctor advises | If doctor advises | Every 10 years |

**Answer these questions about the medical history form and the preventive care guidelines.**

1. What allergies does Lena have?
2. What prescription and non-prescription drugs does she take?
3. Has she had any operations? When, and what for?
4. What childhood diseases has she had?
5. What other medical problems does she have?
6. What illnesses have people in her family had?
7. When did Lena have her most recent flu shot?
8. When did she have her most recent tetanus shot?
9. According to the clinic guidelines, when should she get her next tetanus shot?
10. How often should adults between the ages of 18 and 39 have an eye examination?
11. How often should adults have a cholesterol blood test?
12. At what age should adults start having a yearly flu shot?
13. How often should adults have a dental examination?
14. How often should adults have a hearing test?
15. How often should a senior citizen have a colonoscopy?
16. When should an adult below the age of fifty get a pneumonia vaccination?

**COMMUNITY CONNECTIONS**  You can sometimes get free medical screening tests at street festivals, community fairs, and other events. Drug stores and supermarkets sometimes offer these tests. It's a cheap and easy way to check your blood pressure, your cholesterol, your risk of heart disease, and other aspects of your health. Where can you get free tests in your area? Discuss as a class.

## NORTHDALE PUBLIC HEALTH DEPARTMENT
### Guide to Services

The Northdale health clinics and Northdale City Hospital provide outstanding health care to all city residents at a cost everyone can afford. Fees are on a sliding scale. The amount you pay is based on how much you earn. Northdale City Hospital is  a full-service hospital with 350 beds, a family clinic, and 24-hour emergency care. The emergency room is for serious problems that put your life in danger. Do NOT call 911 or go to the emergency room with routine health problems such as an earache or a bad cough. If you do not speak English well, ask for an interpreter. Translation in 25 languages is available by phone or in person 24 hours a day.

At the Northdale Hospital Family Clinic, adults and children receive a full range of medical services including eye care. The Carter Clinic  at 179 Pine Street provides medical care for children up to the age of seventeen. This is a drop-in clinic. No appointment is necessary. The multilingual staff speaks Spanish, Mandarin, and Vietnamese.

At the High School Health Center, students get free medical services that include physical exams and immunizations.

Immunizations protect your child from serious diseases such as measles and hepatitis B. All children entering kindergarten are required to already have the following vaccinations:

- Hepatitis B—3 doses
- Polio—4 doses
- Measles, mumps, rubella—2 doses
- Chicken pox—one dose
- Diphtheria, tetanus, pertussis*—5 doses
  *pertussis is also called whooping cough

Make sure your child's vaccinations are up-to-date. The following chart shows the immunization schedule that doctors recommend.

| Immunization | At What Ages? |
|---|---|
| hepatitis B | birth, 1–4 months, and 6–18 months |
| DTaP (diphtheria, tetanus, pertussis) | 2 months, 4 months, 6 months, 15–18 months, and 4–6 years |
| polio | 2 months, 4 months, 6–18 months, and 4–6 years |
| MMR (measles, mumps, rubella) | 12–15 months and 4–6 years |
| chicken pox (varicella) | 12–18 months and 4–6 years |
| influenza | from 6 months to 5 years, every fall |

1. *Fees are on a sliding scale* means _____.
   A. the more you earn, the less you pay
   B. everyone pays the same amount
   C. the more you earn, the more you pay
   D. the more you weigh, the more you pay

2. When you have a bad cough, _____.
   A. call 911
   B. call the Northdale Hospital Family Clinic
   C. get a diphtheria, tetanus, pertussis shot
   D. go to the emergency room

3. When you can't meet with an interpreter at Northdale City Hospital, _____.
   A. your family members will have to translate
   B. a nurse will translate
   C. you have to go to the Carter Clinic
   D. you can talk to an interpreter on the phone

4. A *drop-in clinic* is a clinic that _____.
   A. sees patients without appointments
   B. is for children only
   C. is multilingual
   D. is open 24 hours a day

5. Medical services are free at the _____.
   A. Northdale City Hospital
   B. Northdale Hospital Family Clinic
   C. High School Health Center
   D. Carter Clinic

6. Four-month old children should get a _____.
   A. flu shot
   B. chicken pox vaccination
   C. measles, mumps, rubella vaccination
   D. diphtheria, tetanus, pertussis vaccination

## HEALTHY EATING AND A BALANCED DIET

The MyPlate symbol can help us understand how to choose the foods we need to stay healthy. The four sections of the plate represent four different food groups—fruits, vegetables, grains, and protein. A separate plate represents dairy foods. The symbol shows us that we should eat foods from all of these groups every day.

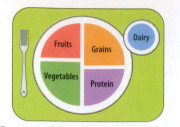

U.S. Department of Agriculture  www.choosemyplate.gov

Fruits and vegetables are on half the plate, and grains and proteins are on the other half of the plate. The vegetables section is larger than the fruits section because we should eat more vegetables than fruit. The grains section is larger than the protein section because we should eat more grains than protein.

The fruits group (the red section of the plate) includes fruit and 100% fruit juice. However, most 100% fruit juice does not have fiber. Therefore, it's healthier to eat fruit than to drink fruit juice. The average adult should eat 2 cups of fruit a day.

The vegetables group (the green section of the plate) includes dark green vegetables, orange vegetables, and starchy vegetables such as corn and potatoes. It's important to eat vegetables from all three of these groups each week, but we should eat dark green and orange vegetables more often than starchy vegetables because they contain more nutrients and fewer calories. The average adult should eat 2 ½ cups of vegetables a day.

The grains group (the orange section of the plate) consists of foods made from wheat, like bread and spaghetti, or from rice or corn. Some of these foods, such as whole wheat bread and brown rice, are whole grains. They have important vitamins, minerals, and fiber. Fiber helps keep blood cholesterol low and prevent heart disease. Most of the grains we eat should be whole grains.

The protein group (the purple section of the plate) consists of meat, chicken, fish, beans, eggs, and nuts. Protein is important for the body, but this plate section isn't as large as the green and orange sections because the average adult needs less protein than vegetables or grains.

The dairy group (the separate blue plate) consists of dairy foods that are high in calcium, a mineral that builds strong bones. Milk products such as yogurt and cheese are part of this group. Other dairy products such as cream, butter, and cream cheese are not as good because they have little or no calcium. Adults need three cups of dairy products each day. To keep blood cholesterol low and protect against heart disease, it's important to choose low-fat or fat-free dairy products.

### DID YOU UNDERSTAND?

1. What four food groups do the sections of the plate represent?
2. What does the blue plate represent?
3. Why are the green and orange sections larger than the red and purple sections?
4. Why is calcium an important mineral?

### APPLYING YOUR KNOWLEDGE

1. What vegetables do you eat?
2. How much fruit do you eat in a day?
3. What grains do you eat?
4. What protein foods do you eat?
5. What foods should you eat more of?
6. What foods should you eat less of?

**Choose the correct answer.**

1. We need to ____ traveler's checks before our trip.
   A. rehearse
   B. purchase
   C. perform
   D. send

2. I enjoy ____ politics with my friends.
   A. discussing
   B. realizing
   C. believing
   D. memorizing

3. By the time I got to the airport, my plane had ____.
   A. sailed away
   B. gone by
   C. taken off
   D. started

4. I ____ my wrist while I was playing tennis.
   A. packed
   B. sprained
   C. passed by
   D. bumped into

5. Sally and Sam broke up and ____ their wedding.
   A. called
   B. closed
   C. dislocated
   D. canceled

6. I'm calling to ____ my appointment with Dr. Tanaka on Tuesday at 10:30.
   A. have
   B. need
   C. confirm
   D. check

7. The nurse gave me ____ for tetanus.
   A. an immunization
   B. insulin
   C. an allergy
   D. influenza

8. Do you have a family history of ____?
   A. vaccinations
   B. bee stings
   C. high blood pressure
   D. skin examinations

9. Fees at this clinic are on a ____ scale.
   A. drop in
   B. sliding
   C. full-service
   D. multilingual

10. Eating a lot of whole grains and following a low-fat diet will protect you against ____.
    A. a healthy plate
    B. food groups
    C. nutrients and calories
    D. heart disease

## SKILLS CHECK ✓

**Words:**
- allergy
- disease
- drop-in clinic
- fee
- illness
- immunization
- interpreter
- medical care
- medical services
- multilingual staff
- non-prescription drug
- routine health problem
- sliding scale
- vaccination
- blood cholesterol
- bones
- calcium
- calories
- fat-free
- fiber
- food group
- healthy plate
- low-fat
- minerals
- nutrients
- oils
- protein
- vitamins
- whole grains

**I can say:**
- I had *skied* the *day* before.
- By the time I got there, *it* had already *begun*.
- I hadn't *gone fishing* in a long time.
- I was *skiing* . . . and I had never *skied* before.
- I had been *working there* for a long time.

**I can share news:**
- Have you heard about/Have you heard the news about/Have you heard what happened to *Harry*?

**I can:**
- make, confirm, reschedule, and cancel medical appointments
- interpret medical appointment cards
- identify medical care facilities in my community
- complete a medical history form
- interpret preventive care guidelines
- interpret community health care information
- interpret nutrition guidelines

**I can write about:**
- something I accomplished

| Feature Article
Fact File
Around the World
Interview
We've Got Mail! | **SIDE** *by* **SIDE Gazette** | Global Exchange
Listening
Fun with Idioms
What Are They
Saying? |

Volume 3                                                                                           Number 3

# The Jamaican Bobsled Team

### Amazing athletes from a Caribbean island

An unusual group of athletes arrived in Calgary, Canada for the 1988 Winter Olympic Games—the Jamaican Bobsled Team. Many people were surprised. How could the Caribbean island of Jamaica have a bobsled team? Jamaica doesn't have any snow!

The Jamaican athletes had never competed in the Winter Olympics before. In fact, most of them hadn't ever been on a bobsled or seen snow before they began to prepare for the Olympics. But by the time the team members arrived in Calgary, they had trained hard for their first Olympic event. They had been running and weight training in Jamaica. Then they had gone to a training center in Lake Placid, New York. Unfortunately, they had poor equipment, and their bobsled crashed a lot during training.

They didn't do well in the Olympics. Most people were sure they had seen the Jamaican

Bobsled Team for the first and last time! But the team didn't give up. They had lost, but they had been in the Olympics, and they wanted to go back and compete again.

The team went to a special training center in Germany. They trained there four to eight hours a day. By the time these athletes arrived at the 1994 Olympic Winter Games in Lillehammer, France, they had become a much stronger bobsled team. They had practiced for years. They were also very famous because a movie about the team, *Cool Runnings*, had been in theaters around the world the year before.

At the 1994 games, the team came in 14th in the four-person bobsled event, and they placed 10th in the two-person event. The team had done the impossible! They had competed well in the Olympics, and they had won the hearts of fans around the world.

The movie *Cool Runnings* tells the story of a Jamaican bobsled team at the Olympics. The movie is part fact and part fiction. The popular movie soundtrack has reggae music by famous Jamaican musicians.

The first modern Olympics were in Athens, Greece in 1896. Now there are Summer Olympics and Winter Olympics every four years. Athletes represent their countries in different events. Summer Olympic events include track, gymnastics, and swimming. Winter Olympic events include skiing, skating, and the bobsled competition.

## Children and Sports Training

**I**n different countries around the world, children begin training at an early age to compete in different popular sports.

hockey in Canada

baseball in Japan

soccer in Brazil

gymnastics in Russia

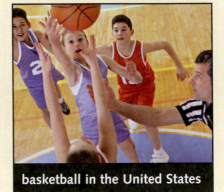
basketball in the United States

distance running in Kenya

What sports are popular in your country? At what age do children start training to compete in these sports?

# Interview

A Side by Side Gazette reporter interviewed Olga Petrova last week. Olga had just won the Women's Regional Figure Skating Competition.

**Q:** Olga, I'm sure you're very happy about today's competition.

**A:** Oh, yes. I'm very happy. You know, I had been preparing for this day for a long time.

**Q:** How had you been preparing?

**A:** In the months before the competition, I had been training with my coach ten hours a day. I had been getting up early, and I had been practicing my routines over and over again.

**Q:** When did you first know you wanted to compete as a skater?

**A:** I began to skate back in Russia when I was four years old. By the time I was seven, I had already skated in many competitions, and I had won several medals. We moved here when I was ten, and I began to take lessons at a skating program in our city. By the time I was eleven, I had finished all the levels of this program. My parents found a professional coach, Mr. Gary Abrams, and I've been training with him ever since.

**Q:** Now that you have won this regional competition, what's next?

**A:** The National Competition. It's in three months. I have to work very hard to prepare for that. My dream is to be in the Olympics next winter. I must do very well in the Nationals.

**Q:** Good luck, Olga! We'll see you in the Olympics!

**A:** Oh, I hope so.

## Countries in the Olympics

Only 14 countries competed in the first modern Olympics in 1896. Over the years, the number of participating countries has grown. Does your country compete in the summer or winter games? In which events does your country do well?

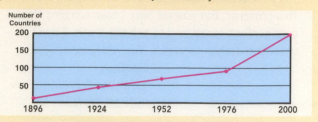

Number of Countries

| | 1896 | 1924 | 1952 | 1976 | 2000 |
|---|---|---|---|---|---|

200
150
100
50

## LISTENING

## Olympic Game Highlights

| | | | |
|---|---|---|---|
| _b_ | **1** | **a.** | figure skating |
| ___ | **2** | **b.** | basketball |
| ___ | **3** | **c.** | running |
| ___ | **4** | **d.** | gymnastics |
| ___ | **5** | **e.** | swimming |

# FUN with IDIOMS

## Do You Know These Expressions?

| | | | | |
|---|---|---|---|---|
| _c_ | **1.** | Break a leg! | **a.** | Don't be sad! |
| ___ | **2.** | Hold your tongue! | **b.** | Try hard! |
| ___ | **3.** | Keep your chin up! | **c.** | Good luck! |
| ___ | **4.** | Keep your eye on the ball! | **d.** | Pay attention! |
| ___ | **5.** | Put your best foot forward! | **e.** | Don't bother me! |
| ___ | **6.** | Get off my back! | **f.** | Be quiet! |

## We've Got Mail!

Dear Side by Side,

I have a question about gerunds and infinitives after verbs. I'm very confused. I know that after some verbs, I must use a gerund, such as "practice swimming" and "consider buying." After other verbs, I must use an infinitive, such as "learn to swim" and "decide to buy." And finally, I know that after some verbs, I can use either a gerund or an infinitive, such as "like to swim" and "like swimming." Are there any rules that will tell me what to do with different verbs?

Sincerely,

"Worrying About the Rules"

Dear "Worrying About the Rules,"

You seem to understand how to use gerunds and infinitives. Unfortunately, we're sorry to tell you that there aren't any rules about what to do with different verbs. You just have to learn about each verb. Keep on practicing gerunds and infinitives, and stop worrying about the rules! Using these verbs is a lot better than thinking about them too much! Good luck!

Sincerely,

*Side by Side*

Dear Side by Side,

We've been studying the present perfect and present perfect continuous tenses in our class for the past several weeks. I think I finally understand this grammar, but now we have begun learning the past perfect tense, and to tell the truth, I don't understand when to use it. Can you help?

Sincerely,

"Life Was Perfect Before the Past Perfect"

Dear "Life Was Perfect,"

We understand your problem because we use both the present perfect and past perfect tenses to talk about things that happened in the past. Here's the difference. We use the present perfect tense to talk about things that happened before now. For example:

I don't want to see that movie today.
I have already seen it.

We use the past perfect tense to talk about things that happened before another time in the past. For example:

I didn't want to see that movie yesterday.
I had already seen it.

We're glad you have learned the present perfect tense, and we're sure you'll do well with the past perfect!

Best wishes,

*Side by Side*

### Global Exchange

**Stamp4:** Have I told you about my hobby? I've been collecting stamps since I was a little kid. I began to collect stamps when I was eight years old. At that time, my mother worked at an international bank. Every Friday, she brought home stamps from all the letters she had received during that week. I also had many penpals in different countries, and we wrote letters to each other very often. By the time I was twelve, I had collected more than 1000 stamps from 50 different countries! I've continued collecting stamps, but now it's more difficult. My mother retired from her job, and my penpals send me e-mail messages instead of letters. (The Internet has been very bad for my stamp collection!) Tell me, do you have a hobby? What do you enjoy doing in your free time? How long have you been doing that? Write and tell me about it.

Send a message to a keypal. Tell about your favorite hobby.

### What Are They Saying?

**Gerunds** and **infinitives** are **verbals**. They are nouns formed from verbs.
A **gerund** ends in *-ing*. A **gerund phrase** is a gerund and its related words.
An **infinitive** consists of the word *to* and the base form of the verb.
An **infinitive phrase** is an infinitive and its related words.

I began working at this store a year ago.          I began to work at this store a year ago.

↑                                                                    ↑

gerund                                                        infinitive

Gerund phrases and infinitive phrases can be used in different ways in sentences.

**Subject:**                     *Eating junk food* is unhealthy.
                                      *To go on a diet* is difficult.

**Direct object:**            I started *swimming in the ocean* when I was young.
                                      I began *to play the piano* when I was five years old.

**Subject complement:**   My favorite weekend activity is *dancing*.
                                      My father's favorite weekend activity is *to play golf*.

A gerund phrase can also be used in the following way:

**Object of a preposition:**   We've been thinking about *getting married* for a long time.

**Practice these conversations with a classmate.**

| Painting is my favorite way to relax. | I learned to dance when I was young. |
|---|---|

**A.** What kind of verbal does the sentence have?

**B.** A gerund.

**A.** What is it?

**B.** Painting.

**A.** How is it used in the sentence?

**B.** It's the subject.

**A.** What kind of verbal does the sentence have?

**B.** An infinitive.

**A.** What is it?

**B.** To dance.

**A.** How is it used in the sentence?

**B.** It's the direct object.

**Underline the verbal in each sentence and decide how it is used. Then practice new conversations about these sentences.**

1. <u>Singing</u> is an important part of my life.

2. I hate to drive downtown.

3. He's been thinking about getting a new job for a long time.

4. Our family's decision is to get a dog.

5. I enjoy listening to classical music.

6. Enrolling in college was a good idea.

# Immunizations and Vaccines

Regular immunizations are an important part of health throughout the world. An immunization is an injection of a vaccine, a special medicine that protects a person against an infectious disease. Infectious diseases are dangerous and they can be deadly. They pass quickly from person to person, but regular immunizations prevent this. Immunizations are one of the greatest improvements in modern medicine.

Before today's immunizations, many people around the world died from common diseases. For example, during the 1920s in the United States, over 10,000 children died each year just from diphtheria. Now children in the United States rarely die from childhood diseases. Today's parents are less worried about these terrible illnesses. This is because of the many important scientific discoveries that have resulted in better immunizations and better health.

## History of Vaccines and Immunizations

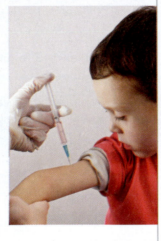

There are early records of vaccines in China over 1000 years ago. They developed a medicine to protect people against smallpox. Chinese doctors made vaccines from material that came from sick cows. Early scientists in Turkey and Africa made a similar medicine. Later, scientists in Europe and America developed medicines for smallpox. However, these early vaccines were not always good and they were not easy to make. In 1796, British scientist Edward Jenner finally developed the first true smallpox vaccination.

Since then, scientists have made more improvements to the smallpox vaccination. As doctors around the world gave smallpox vaccinations, there were fewer and fewer cases. In fact, there have been no cases of smallpox in the United States since 1949, and according to health experts, in 1980, there was no more smallpox in

*diphtheria*—a serious infectious throat disease that makes it difficult to breathe

*pertussis*—an infectious disease, mostly in children, that makes them cough; also called whooping cough

*polio*—a serious infectious disease of the spine that makes a person unable to move certain muscles

*smallpox*—a serious disease that causes permanent spots on the skin

*tetanus*—a serious disease that comes from an infection in a cut

the world. Now only two science laboratories have samples of smallpox for scientific research.

The next important vaccine invention was in 1885, when Louis Pasteur developed the rabies vaccine. A rabid dog bit a small boy, but after Pasteur's vaccination, the boy did not get sick. Now most dogs and cats in the U.S. receive a rabies vaccination, so people do not need the rabies vaccine after a dog or cat bites them if they know the animal had the vaccination. However, if they do not know the vaccination history of the dog or cat, or if a raccoon or other animal bites them, the rabies vaccination is absolutely necessary. In some areas of the world, many dogs and cats still get rabies. When people travel to these countries, they may need to get the human rabies vaccine, which can protect them from this deadly disease.

Another important vaccine was for polio. This terrible disease resulted in death or a lifetime in a wheelchair. Before 1952, there were 13,000 to 20,000 cases of polio in the United States every year. Most of the cases were children. In 1952, Doctor Jonas Salk and Albert Sabin developed life-saving polio vaccines. Since the 1950s, these polio vaccines have protected children's lives in the United States and throughout the world. There has been no polio in the United States since 1979.

## Immunizations around the World

Since the 20th century, there have been many improvements in vaccines. As a result of modern immunizations, many serious diseases have now become rare. In countries with good immunization programs, children and adults are healthy. However, in some areas of the world, good health care is not available. There are not enough doctors, nurses, clinics, or vaccinations. People are poor and do not have good medical care. In addition, in some areas there is not enough clean water or good nutrition. In some countries, thousands of children and adults still get sick and die from diseases. The World Health Organization (WHO) is working hard to give immunizations to people in all countries. It is also working to improve health with better housing, water, nutrition, and education.

## Immunizations in the United States

In the United States, there are guidelines for childhood and adult immunizations. The CDC (Centers for Disease Control and Prevention) recommends that all babies get immunizations. Regular immunizations start at 3 months of age. They protect babies from diseases such as measles, mumps, and rubella. Children must have immunization records when they register for school. Adults should also receive immunizations. For example, adults should receive immunizations for tetanus, diphtheria, pertussis, chickenpox, and Hepatitis A and B. Senior citizens should receive yearly vaccinations for the flu and for pneumonia.

Although some people worry that vaccinations can cause other health problems, doctors and experts recommend regular immunizations. People who do not get vaccinations can get a disease and pass it on to other people. According to the CDC and the WHO, everyone should get immunizations to protect against these serious diseases. For this reason, there has been a federal vaccination program for children in the United States since 1962. Doctors and clinics follow federal guidelines for immunizations. In addition, students, teachers, health care workers, and food service workers must receive immunizations.

## DID YOU UNDERSTAND?

1. What is an immunization?
2. What is a vaccine?
3. Why are infectious diseases dangerous?
4. Where were some of the earliest vaccines?
5. Who developed the first true smallpox vaccine?
6. Why are there no cases of smallpox in the world today?
7. Why are cases of human rabies rare in the United States?
8. What important work did Doctors Salk and Sabin do?
9. In some places around the world, people still suffer from many serious diseases. What are the reasons for this?
10. When did the U.S. federal vaccination program start?
11. Why is the federal vaccination program important for everyone's health?

## WHAT'S YOUR EXPERIENCE?

1. Do children and adults in your family get immunizations? Why or why not?
2. What immunizations have you had?
3. Will you get more immunizations in the future? Which ones? Why?

## WHAT'S YOUR OPINION?

1. Some parents refuse vaccinations for their children. Do you think these parents have good reasons to refuse the vaccinations?
2. If a child does not receive immunizations, he or she may pass a disease to other unvaccinated children. Should children attend school if they have not received vaccinations? Why or why not?
3. Do you think the number of serious diseases in the United States will grow if some children do not receive immunizations?

**Revising** is an important step in the writing process. After you write a first draft, you need to revise your writing. When you revise, you reread and rethink your writing, and you make changes to improve it.

First, read your writing to yourself silently, or read it aloud. Think about your purpose and your audience. Does your writing do what you want it to do? Will your readers like it? Will they understand it? What should you add or delete? What should you move to a different place? Do you have a strong beginning? Do you have a good ending? What changes should you make?

Next, have a **peer conference**. Read your writing aloud to a classmate, or have your classmate read it silently. Then ask for *feedback*—suggestions. Does your classmate understand your writing? What does your classmate like about it? How can you improve it?

---

### Peer Conference Questions

Is the purpose of my writing clear?
Did I accomplish my purpose?
What do you like about it?
Will my audience understand it?
Are any parts of the writing unclear?
What should I add?
What should I delete?
What should I move?
Do I have a strong beginning?
Do I have a good ending?
What other changes should I make?

### Peer Conference Suggestions*

I suggest *shortening this very long sentence.*
I recommend *breaking this large paragraph into two separate paragraphs.*
Consider *adding more information in this paragraph.*
Think about *starting with a stronger beginning sentence.*
Try *moving this sentence from your last paragraph to the middle paragraph.*

\* "You should" is very direct advice. It's like an instruction. Instead, use these expressions with "softer" verbs followed by gerund forms.

---

### Revising your writing.

**Write:** Did you write in your journal about the topic on page 109? If you did, revise and expand your writing. If you didn't, write it now. Give your story this title: *Something I Accomplished.* Write about what you accomplished. How long had you been preparing for it? How had you been preparing? Was it difficult to accomplish? How did you feel after you accomplished it?

**Revise:** Reread and rethink your first draft. Make some changes to improve it, or wait until after the peer conference.

**Peer conference:** Discuss your writing with a classmate. Use the Peer Conference Questions above to ask about your writing. Your classmate can use the Peer Conference Suggestions as examples of how to give feedback. After the peer conference, make more changes to improve your writing.

## Two-Word Verbs: Separable
## Inseparable

- **Discussing Future Events**
- **Remembering and Forgetting**
- **Discussing Obligations**
- **Asking for and Giving Advice**
- **School Assignments**
- **Making Plans by Telephone**

- **Shopping for Clothing**
- **Identifying Bargains**
- **Returning and Exchanging Defective Items**
- **Advertisements**
- **Store Coupons**

## VOCABULARY PREVIEW

1. cross out
2. fill out
3. hand in
4. hang up
5. hook up

6. pick out
7. put away
8. put on
9. take down
10. take off

11. throw away
12. try on
13. turn on
14. turn off
15. wake up

# Sometime Next Week

| | |
|---|---|
| **bring back** the TV | **bring** it **back** |
| **call up** Sally | **call** her **up** |
| **throw out** the newspapers | **throw** them **out** |

**A.** When is the repairman going to **bring back** our TV?

**B.** He's going to **bring** it **back** sometime next week.

---

**1.** When are you going to **call up** your uncle in Ohio?

**2.** When is Ted going to **throw out** his old newspapers?

**3.** When is your daughter going to **fill out** her college application forms?

**4.** When is Jeff going to **pick up** his clothes at the cleaner's?

**5.** When is Vicky going to **take back** her library books?

**6.** When are you going to **hook up** your new computer?

**7.** When is Howard going to **hang up** his new portrait?

**8.** When is Gloria going to **take down** her Christmas decorations?

**9.** When is Mr. Grumpkin going to **turn on** the heat in the building?

# Oh, No! I Forgot!

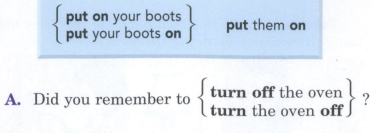

{ **put on** your boots
**put** your boots **on** }   **put** them **on**

**A.** Did you remember to { **turn off** the oven
**turn** the oven **off** } ?

**B.** Oh, no! I forgot! I'll **turn** it **off** right away.

---

**1.** *take back*
*videos*

**2.** *fill out*
*the accident report*

**3.** *turn on*
*the alarm*

**4.** *put away*
*your toys*

**5.** *hand in*
*your English homework*

**6.** *wake up*
*the kids*

**7.** *put on*
*your raincoat*

**8.** *take off*
*your boots*

**9.** *take out*
*the garbage*

---

## How to Say It!

### Remembering & Forgetting

**A.** Did you remember to *turn off the oven?*

**B.** Oh, no! { I forgot!
I forgot all about it!
I completely forgot!
It slipped my mind!
It completely slipped my mind! }

Practice the conversations in this lesson again. Tell that you forgot in different ways.

## A BUSY SATURDAY

Everybody in the Peterson family is very busy today. It's Saturday, and they all have to do the things they didn't do during the week.

Mr. Peterson has to fill out his income tax form. He didn't have time to fill it out during the week.

Mrs. Peterson has to pick up her clothes at the cleaner's. She was too busy to pick them up during the week.

Their son Steve has to take his library books back. He forgot to take them back during the week.

Their other son, Michael, has to throw out all the old newspapers in the garage. He didn't have time to throw them out during the week.

Their daughter Stacey has to hook up the new modem for her computer. She was too busy to hook it up during the week.

And their other daughter, Abigail, has to put her toys away. She didn't feel like putting them away during the week.

As you can see, everybody in the Peterson family is going to be very busy today.

## ✔️ READING CHECK-UP

### Q & A

You're inviting somebody in the Peterson family to do something with you. Using this model, create dialogs based on the story.

**A.** Would you like to *play tennis* with me this morning?
**B.** I'd like to, but I can't. I have to *fill out my income tax form.*
**A.** That's too bad.
**B.** I know, but I've really got to do it. I *didn't have time to fill it out during the week.*
**A.** Well, maybe some other time.

**How About You?**

What do YOU have to do on your next day off from work or school?

# I Don't Think So

**A.** Do you think I should keep these old love letters?

**B.** No, I don't think so. I think you should **throw** them **away**.

**1.** *hand in my homework*
   *do over*

**2.** *use up this old milk*
   *throw out*

**3.** *erase all my mistakes*
   *cross out*

**4.** *leave the air conditioner on*
   *turn off*

**5.** *try to remember Amy's telephone number*
   *write down*

**6.** *ask the teacher the definition of this word*
   *look up*

**7.** *make my decision right away*
   *think over*

**8.** *keep my ex-boyfriend's ring*
   *give back*

**9.** *accept this invitation to my ex-girlfriend's wedding*
   *turn down*

119

# READING

## LUCY'S ENGLISH COMPOSITION

Lucy is very discouraged. She handed in her English composition this morning, but her English teacher gave it back to her and told her to do it over. Apparently, her English teacher didn't like the way Lucy had done it. She hadn't erased her mistakes. She had simply crossed them out. Also, she had used several words incorrectly. She hadn't looked them up in a dictionary. And finally, she hadn't written her homework on the correct paper because she had accidentally thrown her notebook away. Poor Lucy! She didn't feel like writing her English composition in the first place, and now she has to do it over!

## ✔ READING *CHECK-UP*

### TRUE, FALSE, OR MAYBE?

**Answer True, False, or Maybe (if the answer isn't in the story).**

1. Lucy gave her composition to her English teacher this morning.
2. Lucy's English teacher was satisfied with Lucy's composition.
3. The teacher gave back other students' compositions.
4. Lucy had made some mistakes in her composition.
5. Lucy knew the definitions of all the words she used in her composition.
6. Lucy is going to hand in her composition again tomorrow.

### WHAT'S THE WORD?

**Choose the correct words to complete the sentences.**

| cross ___ out | do ___ over | give ___ back | hand ___ in | look ___ up | throw ___ away |
| --- | --- | --- | --- | --- | --- |

1. I need the dictionary you borrowed from me. Please _____.
2. I want to check your homework. Please _____.
3. Ms. Smith, there are too many mistakes in this letter. Please _____.
4. I haven't read today's newspaper yet. Please don't _____.
5. I don't remember his phone number. I've got to _____.
6. You should erase your mistakes. Don't just _____.

# COMPLETE THE LETTERS

Complete these letters with the correct form of the verbs.

| call ___ up | give ___ back | think ___ over | throw ___ away | turn ___ down |

Dear Alice,

   I'm very discouraged. I'm having a lot of trouble with my girlfriend, and I don't know what to do. The problem is very simple. I'm in love with her, but she isn't in love with me. A few weeks ago, I gave her a ring, but she _____ [1] to me. During the past few months, I have written several love letters to her, but she has _____ [2]. Recently I asked her to marry me. She _____ [3] for a while, and then she _____ [4]. Now when I try to _____ [5], she doesn't even want to talk to me. Please help me! I don't know what to do.

                              "Discouraged Donald"
                              Denver, Colorado

| hang ___ up | put ___ away | take ___ down | take ___ out | turn ___ off | turn ___ on |

Dear Alice,

   I'm extremely frustrated. My husband is a very difficult person. Every time I do something, he does the opposite. For example, every time I turn on the stereo system to listen to music, he _____ [1]. Every time I turn off the air conditioner in our apartment, he _____ [2]. Last week I bought a beautiful new painting for our bedroom. The day after I _____ [3], he _____ [4]. We had a lot of old photographs on a table in our living room. I decided to _____ [5] in a closet, but two hours later he _____ [6]. Please help me! I don't know what to do.

                              "Frustrated Fran"
                              Phoenix, Arizona

What should "Discouraged Donald" and "Frustrated Fran" do? Write answers to their letters.

# Would You Like to Get Together Today?

> **take back** my library books = **take** my library books **back**

> ☑ **take** my library books **back**
> ☑ **pick up** my car at the repair shop
> ☑ **drop** my sister **off** at the airport

**A.** Would you like to get together today?

**B.** I'm afraid I can't. I have to **take** my library books **back**.

**A.** Are you free after you **take** them **back**?

**B.** I'm afraid not. I also have to **pick up** my car at the repair shop.

**A.** Would you like to get together after you **pick** it **up**?

**B.** I'd really like to, but I can't. I ALSO have to **drop** my sister **off** at the airport.

**A.** You're really busy today! What do you have to do after you **drop** her **off**?

**B.** Nothing. But by then I'll probably be exhausted. Let's get together tomorrow instead.

**A.** Fine. I'll call you in the morning.

---

**A.** Would you like to get together today?

**B.** I'm afraid I can't. I have to _____.

**A.** Are you free after you _____?

**B.** I'm afraid not. I also have to _____.

**A.** Would you like to get together after you _____?

**B.** I'd really like to, but I can't. I ALSO have to _____.

**A.** You're really busy today! What do you have to do after you _____?

**B.** Nothing. But by then I'll probably be exhausted. Let's get together tomorrow instead.

**A.** Fine. I'll call you in the morning.

**1.**
- ☑ **clean up** my living room
- ☑ **throw out** all my old newspapers
- ☑ **pick** my brother **up** at the train station

**2.**
- ☑ **figure out** my hospital bill
- ☑ **fill out** my insurance form
- ☑ **call** the doctor **up**

**3.**
- ☑ **take down** my Christmas decorations
- ☑ **hang up** my New Year's decorations
- ☑ **drop** my suit **off** at the cleaner's

**4.**
- ☑ **pick out** my wedding dress
- ☑ **write down** the names of all the wedding guests
- ☑ **pick** the wedding invitations **up**

**5.**
- ☑ **clean up** my room
- ☑ **put** my toys **away**
- ☑ **do** my math homework **over**

**6.**
- ☑ _____
- ☑ _____
- ☑ _____

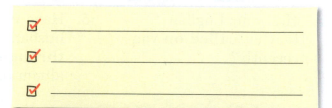

# I Heard from Her Just Last Week

| | |
|---|---|
| hear from Aunt Betty | hear from her |
| ~~hear Aunt Betty from~~ | ~~hear her from~~ |

**A.** Have you **heard from** Aunt Betty recently?

**B.** Yes, I have. I **heard from** her just last week.

1. Have you **run into** Mr. Clark recently?

2. Have you **run out of** paper recently?

3. Has Martha **gotten over** the flu yet?

4. Has your English teacher **called on** you recently?

5. Have you and your husband **looked through** your photo album recently?

6. Has Ricky been **picking on** his little sister recently?

## How About You?

Tell about some of the people in your life.
  Do you have a good friend in another city? Who is he/she?
  How often do you hear from him/her? How long have you known each other?
  Who do you get along with very well? Why?
  Who do you take after? How?
  Who do you look up to? Why?

## A CHILD-REARING PROBLEM

Timothy and his little sister, Patty, don't get along with each other very well. In fact, they fight constantly. He picks on her when it's time for her to go to bed. She picks on him when his friends come over to play.

Timmy and Patty's parents are very concerned. They don't know what to do about their children. They have looked through several books on child rearing, but so far they can't seem to find an answer to the problem. They're hoping that eventually their children will learn to get along with each other better.

## ✓ READING CHECK-UP

### TRUE, FALSE, OR MAYBE?

Answer True, False, or Maybe (if the answer isn't in the story).

1. Patty picks on Timmy when it's time for her go to bed.
2. Timmy is Patty's older brother.
3. Timmy and Patty's parents have a child-rearing problem.
4. They can't seem to find any books about child rearing.
5. Timmy and Patty will eventually learn to get along with each other better.

### CHOOSE

1. Please don't _____ your little sister.
   a. pick on
   b. get along with

2. We've been _____ these old family pictures.
   a. looking through
   b. taking after

3. My history teacher _____ me three times today.
   a. looked up to
   b. called on

4. I haven't _____ my aunt and uncle recently.
   a. gotten over
   b. heard from

5. Everybody thinks I _____ my mother.
   a. take after
   b. look through

6. I really _____ my older sister because she's so smart.
   a. run into
   b. look up to

7. I _____ my cousin Jane on Main Street yesterday.
   a. ran into
   b. heard from

8. Don't kiss me! I haven't _____ my cold yet.
   a. gotten along with
   b. gotten over

You're looking for clothing in a department store. Complete this conversation and act it out with another student.

**A.** May I help you?

**B.** Yes, please. I'm **looking for** (a/an) _____ .

**A.** What size do you wear?

**B.** { Size 32/34/36/ . . .
     { Small/Medium/Large/Extra Large.

**A.** Here. How do you like (this one/these)?

**B.** Hmm. I think (it's/they're) a little too _____ .* Do you have any _____ s that are a little _____ er?*

**A.** Yes. We have a wide selection. Why don't you **look through** all of our _____ s and **pick out** the (one/ones) you like?

**B.** Can I **try** (it/them) **on**?

**A.** Of course. You can **try** (it/them) **on** in the dressing room over there.

\* fancy – plain
   dark – light

*[5 minutes later]*

**A.** Well, how (does it/do they) fit?

**B.** I'm afraid (it's/they're) a little too _____.* Do you have any _____s that are a little _____er*?

**A.** Yes, we do. I think you'll like (THIS/THESE) _____. (It's/They're) a little _____er* than the one(s) you just **tried on**.

**B.** Will you **take** (it/them) **back** if I decide to return (it/them)?

**A.** Of course. No problem at all. Just **bring** (it/them) **back** within _____ days, and we'll **give** you your money **back**.

**B.** Fine. I think I'll take (it/them). How much (does it/do they) cost?

**A.** The usual price is _____ dollars. But you're in luck! We're having a sale this week, and all of our _____s are _____ percent off the regular price.

**B.** That's a real bargain! I'm glad I decided to buy (a/an) _____ this week. Thanks for your help.

**\*** large – small
long – short
wide – narrow
tight – loose (baggy)

**1.** *suit*          **2.** *jeans*          **3.** *sweater*          **4.**

## How About You?

Where do you shop for clothing?
What kind of clothing do you like to wear?

Think about clothing you own:
  What's your favorite clothing item?
  How long have you had it?
  Where did you get it?
  Why is it your favorite?

## ON SALE

Gary went to a men's clothing store yesterday. He was looking for a new sports jacket. He looked through the entire selection of jackets and picked out a few that he really liked. First, he picked out a nice blue jacket. But when he tried it on, it was too small. Next, he picked out an attractive red jacket. But when he tried it on, it was too large. Finally, he picked out a very fancy brown jacket with gold buttons. And when he tried it on, it seemed to fit perfectly.

Then he decided to buy a pair of trousers to go with the jacket. He looked through the entire selection of trousers and picked out several pairs that he really liked. First, he picked out a light brown pair. But when he tried them on, they were too tight. Next, he tried on a dark brown pair. But when he tried them on, they were too loose. Finally, he picked out a pair of brown-and-white plaid pants. And when he tried them on, they seemed to fit perfectly.

Gary paid for his new clothing and walked home feeling very happy about the jacket and pants he had just bought. He was especially happy because the clothing was on sale, and he had paid fifty percent off the regular price. However, Gary's happiness didn't last very long. When he got home, he noticed that one arm of the jacket was longer than the other. He also realized very quickly that the zipper on the pants was broken.

The next day Gary took the clothing back to the store and tried to get a refund. However, the people at the store refused to give him his money back because the clothing was on sale and there was a sign that said "All Sales Are Final!" Gary was furious, but he knew he couldn't do anything about it. The next time he buys something on sale, he'll be more careful. And he'll be sure to read the signs!

## ✔️ READING CHECK-UP

### WHAT'S THE SEQUENCE?

Put these events in the correct order, based on the story.

____ Gary picked out a few jackets he really liked.
____ Gary went back and asked for a refund.
_1_ Gary went shopping for clothes yesterday.
____ He walked home feeling very happy.
____ He walked home feeling very upset and angry.
____ The brown jacket seemed to fit perfectly.
____ The store refused to give him back his money.
____ A pair of plaid pants fit very well.
____ He paid only half of the regular price.
____ He picked out several pairs of trousers.
____ But then, Gary noticed a few problems with the jacket and the pants.

**How About You?**

Have you ever bought something you had to return?
What did you buy?
Where?
What was wrong with it?
What did you do?
Were you successful?

## LISTENING

Listen and choose what the people are talking about.

1. a. shorts
   b. a blouse

2. a. shoes
   b. a library book

3. a. an application form
   b. a math problem

4. a. homework
   b. children

5. a. pictures
   b. pants

6. a. the flu
   b. a decision

7. a. a coat
   b. the heat

8. a. milk
   b. the garbage

9. a. a telephone number
   b. an invitation

**Listen.  Then say it.**

Turn it on!

Turn it off!

Clean it up!

Throw it away!

**Say it.  Then listen.**

Fill it out!

Do it over!

Drop it off!

Hand it in!

**SIDE by SIDE JOURNAL**

Write in your journal about someone you look up to—a member of your family, a person in your community, or a famous person in your country or in history.  Who do you look up to?  Why do you admire this person?

## GRAMMAR FOCUS

### TWO-WORD VERBS: SEPARABLE

| I'm going to | **put on** my boots.<br>**put** my boots **on**.<br>**put** them **on**. |
|---|---|

### TWO-WORD VERBS: INSEPARABLE

| I | **hear from** Aunt Betty<br>**hear from** her<br>~~hear Aunt Betty from~~<br>~~hear her from~~ | very often. |
|---|---|---|

**Complete the sentences.**

1. A. When are you going to throw out those old magazines?
   B. I'll _____ _____ _____ this weekend.

2. A. Have you heard from your cousins in Detroit recently?
   B. Yes, I have.  I _____ _____ _____ a few weeks ago.

3. A. Did you hook up your new computer?
   B. Not yet.  I'm going to _____ _____ _____ tonight.

4. A. Did you fill out the insurance form?
   B. Oh, no!  I forgot.  I'll _____ _____ _____ right away.

5. A. Does your English teacher call on you a lot in class?
   B. Yes.  She _____ _____ _____ all the time.

6. A. I hope you get over the flu soon.
   B. I'm sure I'll _____ _____ _____ in a few days.

7. A. Please take out the garbage!
   B. I _____ _____ _____ a few minutes ago.

8. A. Lilly, did you put away your toys?
   B. Yes, I did.  I _____ _____ _____ a little while ago.

9. A. Have you run into your old friend Bob recently?
   B. Yes, I have.  I _____ _____ _____ just the other day.

10. A. How do you get along with your neighbors?
    B. I _____ _____ _____ _____ very well.

11. A. Don't forget to take back the videos.
    B. Don't worry.  I'll _____ _____ _____ today.

## 1 CONVERSATION Identifying Sale Prices & Bargains

Look at the sale signs. Practice conversations with your classmates.

**A.** Excuse me. I think that price is wrong.

**B.** It is?

**A.** Yes. The sign on the rack says "_____________."

**B.** Okay. Let me check.

Special Sale!
20% OFF

1.

REDUCED!
TAKE
15% OFF

2.

BUY 1, GET 1
FREE!

3.

Bargain!
Half-Price

4.

CLEARANCE
50% OFF

5.

**THINK & SHARE** Do you buy things when they're on sale? Which stores in your community have sales? How much can you save when you buy something on sale?

## 2 CONVERSATION Returning & Exchanging Defective Products

Practice conversations. Return these defective items to a store.

**A.** I'd like to return this/these _________.

**B.** What's the matter with it/them?

**A.** _____________________________

**B.** Would you like to exchange it/them?

**A.** No, thank you. I'd like a refund, please. Here's my receipt.

1. coat
Two buttons are missing.

2. pants
The zipper is broken.

3. blouse
The sleeve is stained.

**TEAMWORK** Work with a classmate. Make a list of items you buy in a store and the reasons you might return them. Practice conversations about these items.

Look at the store advertisements and answer the questions.

**Perry's DISCOUNT STORE**

Save up to **80%** on Select Merchandise

**TWO DAYS ONLY** FRIDAY AND SATURDAY, SEPTEMBER 22 & 23

**CLEARANCE**
**75%** Savings on all Vera West skirts
**Now $8-$18**
Were $32-$72

**$9.99**
**50%-80% OFF**
Designer dress shirts
Orig. $20-$50

NOW **$30** - All Pairs

**Save 25%-60%**
Running Shoes
Rockwell & Adressa
Reg. $40-$75

**40%** off
Lexis Men's Jeans
orig. $40.00
**now $24.00**

All Ellen Clare tee shirts
Reg. $20
**Sale 2/$20 or $10.99 ea.**

**Watson's 25th Anniversary Sale**
Super Discounts All Week!
MONDAY, SEPTEMBER 18–SATURDAY, SEPTEMBER 23

**1/3 OFF**

**ENTIRE STOCK Men's Jeans**
On Sale $24-$46
Buy one pair, get second pair 50% off sale price

**1/3 Off Men's dress shirts**
Were $39  Sale $25.99

**All Karen James skirts**
**HALF PRICE**
Reg $22-$80
**Sale $11-$40**

**HALF PRICE**

**40% OFF**

**40% Off Rockwell Running Shoes**
Orig $75
**Sale $45**

**Women's tee shirts**
Orig $15
**Reduced to $8**

1. The sale price for a $72 Vera West skirt is ____.
   - A. $8
   - B. $18
   - C. $32
   - D. $36

2. You get a ____ discount on $60 running shoes at Perry's.
   - A. 25%
   - B. 40%
   - C. 50%
   - D. 60%

3. When you buy 2 pairs of $46 jeans on sale at Watson's, the second pair costs ____.
   - A. $23
   - B. $24
   - C. $50
   - D. $92

4. You pay ____ when you buy four tee shirts on sale at Perry's.
   - A. $20.00
   - B. $30.00
   - C. $40.00
   - D. $43.96

5. During the sale at Perry's, Lexis Men's Jeans are ____ off the regular price.
   - A. $16
   - B. $24
   - C. $40
   - D. 24%

6. On September 22, a dress shirt at Watson's costs ____ than a dress shirt at Perry's.
   - A. $5.99 less
   - B. $25.99 more
   - C. $16 less
   - D. $16 more

**TEAMWORK** Cut out some newspaper ads for department store sales. Bring the ads to class and work with a classmate. Compare the products on sale at these stores. Which sale is better? Why? Share your ads and opinions with the class.

Look at the coupons and answer the questions.

1. You save $1.00 when you buy _____ with a coupon.
   A. a quart of yogurt
   B. 2 pints of ice cream
   C. a can of coffee
   D. 3 cans of tomatoes

2. A can of Farini Tomatoes costs $1.50. With a coupon you pay _____ for 3 cans.
   A. 75¢
   B. $3.00
   C. $3.50
   D. $3.75

3. A can of Crandall Soup costs $1.65. If you buy ten cans with a coupon, you pay _____.
   A. $5.50
   B. $8.90
   C. $15.40
   D. $15.50

4. You bought a jar of Pollyanna Jam with a coupon and paid $1.85. The original price was _____.
   A. $1.50
   B. $2.20
   C. $2.35
   D. $2.60

5. You can use a coupon for _____ on November 12, 2020.
   A. Crandall Soup
   B. Maxima Coffee
   C. Alan's Bread
   D. Eggtown Eggs

6. You bought two pints of Bob and Joe's Chocolate Ice Cream with a coupon and paid $5.00. The regular price for a pint is _____.
   A. $2.50
   B. $2.75
   C. $3.00
   D. $4.00

7. A 6 oz. container of Farmtown Yogurt costs 90¢. With a coupon you pay _____ for each container when you buy ten.
   A. 80¢
   B. 85¢
   C. 90¢
   D. $1.00

8. Happy Heart Cereal costs $2.79. With a coupon you can get _____ for $5.58.
   A. one box
   B. two boxes
   C. three boxes
   D. four boxes

**TEAMWORK** Bring food product coupons to class and work with a classmate. Compare coupons for similar products. Which coupons offer the best bargains? Share your information with the class. Then use some coupons to save money at the supermarket!

## Choose the correct answer.

1. Could you possibly help me _____ my new computer?
   A. hear from          C. hook up
   B. hang up           D. hand in

2. Do you have a dictionary? I need to _____ a word I don't know.
   A. look through      C. look up to
   B. look up           D. call on

3. I'm going to _____ my clothes at the cleaner's this morning.
   A. pick up           C. pick out
   B. pick on           D. put away

4. Please _____ the garbage before you leave.
   A. take after        C. take out
   B. take back         D. take off

5. I _____ an old friend while I was walking down the street today.
   A. got over          C. ran out of
   B. got along with    D. ran into

6. It's very hot today. Let's _____ the air conditioner all afternoon.
   A. drop off          C. do over
   B. use up            D. leave on

7. I don't want to exchange it. I'd like _____, please.
   A. a sign            C. a refund
   B. a receipt         D. a clearance

8. Shirts are usually $48. They're on _____ today for $28.
   A. sale price        C. bargain
   B. sale              D. discount

## Look at the food coupons. Choose the correct answer.

9. A container of Fieldstone Yogurt costs $1.00. With a coupon, you pay _____ for each container when you buy ten.
   A. 80¢
   B. 90¢
   C. 95¢
   D. $1.00

10. Healthy Start Cereal costs $2.99. With a coupon, you can get _____ for $5.98.
    A. one box
    B. two boxes
    C. three boxes
    D. four boxes

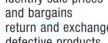

**$2.00 OFF**
10 Fieldstone
SINGLE YOGURT CUPS (6 oz.)
OR 2 QUARTS (32 oz.)

**Buy Two, Get One FREE**
Purchase TWO boxes of
**HEALTHY START**
Cereal and get one free

## Connectors: And . . . Too
## And . . . Either
## So, But, Neither

- Coincidences
- Asking for and Giving Reasons
- Describing People's Backgrounds, Interests, and Personalities
- Looking for a Job
- Referring People to Someone Else
- Discussing Opinions

- Requesting Help at Work
- Giving and Following a Sequence of Instructions
- Operating Equipment
- Career Advancement
- Continuing Education
- Developing a Personal Education Plan

## VOCABULARY PREVIEW

| | | |
|---|---|---|
| 1. allergic | 6. alarm clock | 11. enroll |
| 2. athletic | 7. army | 12. hide |
| 3. frightened | 8. lightning | 13. kiss |
| 4. strict | 9. parking space | 14. walk *my* dog |
| 5. lenient | 10. want ad | 15. work out |

# What a Coincidence!

| | |
|---|---|
| I'm hungry. | { I am, too. / So am I. } |
| I can swim. | { I can, too. / So can I. } |
| I've seen that movie. | { I have, too. / So have I. } |

| | |
|---|---|
| I have a car. | { I do, too. / So do I. } |
| I worked yesterday. | { I did, too. / So did I. } |

**A.** I'm allergic to cats.

**B.** What a coincidence!
{ I am, too. / So am I. }

**1.** I'm a vegetarian.

**2.** I like peppermint ice cream.

**3.** I can speak four languages fluently.

**4.** I just got a raise.

**5.** I'll be on a business trip next week.

**6.** I've been feeling tired lately.

**7.** I have to work late at the office tonight.

**8.** I forgot my umbrella this morning.

**9.**

# What a Coincidence!

| | |
|---|---|
| I'm not hungry. | { I'm not either. / Neither am I. } |
| I can't swim. | { I can't either. / Neither can I. } |
| I haven't seen that movie. | { I haven't either. / Neither have I. } |

| | |
|---|---|
| I don't have a car. | { I don't either. / Neither do I. } |
| I didn't work yesterday. | { I didn't either. / Neither did I. } |

**A.** I'm not a very good dancer.

**B.** What a coincidence!
{ I'm not either. / Neither am I. }

**1.** I don't like macaroni and cheese.

**2.** I didn't see the stop sign.

**3.** I can't skate very well.

**4.** I haven't seen a movie in a long time.

**5.** I wasn't very athletic when I was younger.

**6.** I won't be able to go bowling next Saturday.

**7.** I don't have a date for the prom.

**8.** I've never kissed anyone before.

**9.**

# And They Do, Too

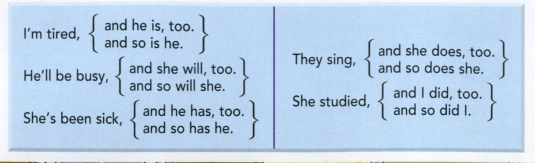

I'm tired, { and he is, too. / and so is he. }

He'll be busy, { and she will, too. / and so will she. }

She's been sick, { and he has, too. / and so has he. }

They sing, { and she does, too. / and so does she. }

She studied, { and I did, too. / and so did I. }

**A.** Why can't you or the children help me with the dishes?

**B.** I have to study, { **and they do, too.** / **and so do they.** }

**1.** Why weren't you and Bob at the meeting this morning?

*I missed the bus, _____.*

**2.** Why are you and Vanessa so nervous today?

*I have two final exams tomorrow, _____.*

**3.** What are you and your brother going to do when you grow up?

*I'm going to start an Internet company, _____.*

**4.** Where were you and your wife when the accident happened?

*I was standing on the corner, _____.*

**5.** How do you know Mr. and Mrs. Crandall?

*They walk their dog in the park, ____.*

**7.** Why haven't you and your brother been in school for the past few days?

*I've been sick, ____.*

**9.** How did you meet your wife?

*I was working out at the health club, ___.*

**11.** Why don't you or your neighbors complain about this leak?

*I've already spoken to the landlord, ____.*

**13.** Why are you and your cats hiding under the bed?

*I'm afraid of thunder and lightning, ____.*

**6.** Why can't you or your roommates come to my party?

*I'll be out of town, ____.*

**8.** Could you or your friend help me take these packages upstairs?

*I'll be glad to help you, ____.*

**10.** What are you two arguing about?

*He wants this parking space, ____.*

**12.** How did you and your husband like the play?

*I fell asleep during the first act, ____.*

**14.**

## "MADE FOR EACH OTHER"

Louise and Brian are very compatible people. They have a lot in common. For example, they have similar backgrounds. He grew up in a small town in the South, and so did she. She's the oldest of four children, and he is, too. His parents own their own business, and so do hers.

They also have similar academic interests. She's majoring in chemistry, and he is, too. He has taken every course in mathematics offered by their college, and so has she. She enjoys working with computers, and he does, too.

In addition, Louise and Brian like the same sports. He goes swimming several times a week, and so does she. She can play tennis very well, and so can he. His favorite winter sport is ice skating, and hers is, too.

Louise and Brian also have the same cultural interests. She has been to most of the art museums in New York City, and so has he. He's a member of the college theater group, and she is, too. She has a complete collection of Beethoven's symphonies, and so does he.

In addition, they have similar personalities. She has always been very shy, and he has, too. He tends to be very quiet, and so does she. She's often nervous when she's in large groups of people, and he is, too.

Finally, they have very similar outlooks on life. She has been a vegetarian for years, and so has he. He supports equal rights for women and minorities, and so does she. She's opposed to the use of nuclear energy, and he is, too.

As you can see, Louise and Brian are very compatible people. In fact, everybody says they were "made for each other."

 **READING** *CHECK-UP*

### TRUE, FALSE, OR MAYBE?

**Answer True, False, or Maybe (if the answer isn't in the story).**

1. Louise spent her childhood in the South.
2. Brian has older brothers and sisters.
3. Louise and Brian are both students in college.
4. They both ski very well.
5. They haven't been to all the art museums in New York City.
6. They both like to be in large groups of people.
7. They both feel that people shouldn't eat vegetables.

## LISTENING

**Listen and choose what the people are talking about.**

1. a. personality
   b. background

2. a. sports
   b. cultural interests

3. a. academic interests
   b. outlook on life

4. a. personality
   b. background

5. a. sports
   b. academic interests

6. a. cultural interests
   b. outlook on life

# And She Hasn't Either

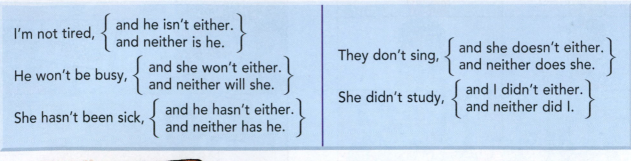

I'm not tired, { and he isn't either. / and neither is he. }

He won't be busy, { and she won't either. / and neither will she. }

She hasn't been sick, { and he hasn't either. / and neither has he. }

They don't sing, { and she doesn't either. / and neither does she. }

She didn't study, { and I didn't either. / and neither did I. }

**A.** Why do you and your sister look so frightened?

**B.** I've never been on a roller coaster before, { **and she hasn't either.** / **and neither has she.** }

---

**1.** Why haven't you and your roommate hooked up your new DVD player?

*I don't understand the instructions, _____.*

**2.** Why didn't you or your parents answer the telephone all weekend?

*I wasn't home, _____.*

**3.** Why did you and your wife move to the center of the city?

*She didn't like living in the suburbs, _____.*

**4.** What do you and Greg want to talk to me about?

*I won't be able to work overtime this weekend, _____.*

**5.** Why do you and your husband want to enroll in my dance class?

*I don't know how to dance, ____.*

**6.** Why does the school nurse want to see us?

*I haven't had an eye examination, ____.*

**7.** Why didn't you or Mom wake us up on time this morning?

*I didn't hear the alarm clock, ____.*

**8.** Why did you and your husband leave the concert so early?

*I couldn't stand the loud music, ____.*

**9.** What are you and your sister arguing about?

*She doesn't want to take the garbage out, ____.*

**10.** Why don't you and your friends want to come to the game?

*They aren't very interested in football, ____.*

**11.** Why were you and your wife so nervous during the flight?

*I had never flown before today, ____.*

**12.** Why have you and your friends stopped shopping at my store?

*I can't afford your prices, ____.*

**13.** Why don't you and your sister want me to read "Little Red Riding Hood"?

*I don't like fairy tales very much, ____.*

**14.**

## LAID OFF

Jack and Betty Williams are going through some difficult times. They were both laid off from their jobs last month. As the days go by, they're becoming more and more concerned about their futures, since he hasn't been able to find another job yet, and neither has she.

The layoffs weren't a surprise to Jack and Betty. After all, Jack's company hadn't been doing very well for a long time, and neither had Betty's. However, Jack had never expected both of them to be laid off at the same time, and Betty hadn't either. Ever since they have been laid off, Jack and Betty have been trying to find new jobs. Unfortunately, she hasn't been very successful, and he hasn't either.

The main reason they're having trouble finding work is that there simply aren't many jobs available right now. He can't find anything in the want ads, and neither can she. She hasn't heard about any job openings, and he hasn't either. His friends haven't been able to help at all, and neither have hers.

Another reason they're having trouble finding work is that they don't seem to have the right kind of skills and training. He doesn't know anything about computers, and she doesn't either. She can't type very well, and neither can he. He hasn't had any special vocational training, and she hasn't either.

A third reason they're having trouble finding work is that there are certain jobs they prefer not to take. He doesn't like working at night, and neither does she. She isn't willing to work on the weekends, and neither is he. He doesn't want to commute very far to work, and she doesn't either.

Despite all their problems, Jack and Betty aren't completely discouraged. She doesn't have a very pessimistic outlook on life, and neither does he. They're both hopeful that things will get better soon.

✅ **READING** *CHECK-UP*

### TRUE, FALSE, OR MAYBE?

Answer True, False, or Maybe (if the answer isn't in the story).

1. Betty quit her job last month.
2. Jack and Betty had been working for the same company.
3. Some of their friends have been laid off, too.
4. Typing skills are important in certain jobs.
5. Jack and Betty will find jobs soon.

**A Job Interview**

You're at a job interview. Role-play with another student, using the interviewer's questions below.

Tell me about your skills.
Tell me about your educational background.
Have you had any special vocational training?
Are you willing to work at night or on the weekend?
When can you start?

# You Should Ask Them

I don't sing, **but** my sister does.
She didn't know the answer, **but** I did.

He can play chess, **but** I can't.
We're ready, **but** they aren't.

**A.** Can you baby-sit for us tomorrow night?

**B.** No, I can't, but my SISTER can.  You should ask HER.

**1.** Have you heard the weather forecast?
*my father*

**2.** Do you have a hammer?
*my upstairs neighbors*

**3.** Are you interested in seeing a movie tonight?
*Maria*

**4.** Did you write down the homework assignment?
*Jack*

**5.** Have you by any chance found a brown-and-white dog?
*the woman across the street*

**6.** Were you paying attention when the salesman explained how to assemble this?
*the children*

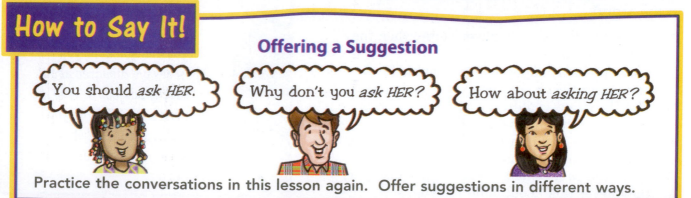

## How to Say It!

### Offering a Suggestion

You should *ask HER.*

Why don't you *ask HER?*

How about *asking HER?*

Practice the conversations in this lesson again.  Offer suggestions in different ways.

## "TOUCHY SUBJECTS"

Larry and his parents always disagree when they talk about politics. Larry is very liberal, but his parents aren't. They're very conservative. Larry thinks the president is doing a very poor job, but his parents don't. They think the president is doing a fine job. Also, Larry doesn't think the government should spend a lot of money on defense, but his parents do. They think the country needs a strong army. You can see why Larry and his parents always disagree when they talk about politics. Politics is a very "touchy subject" with them.

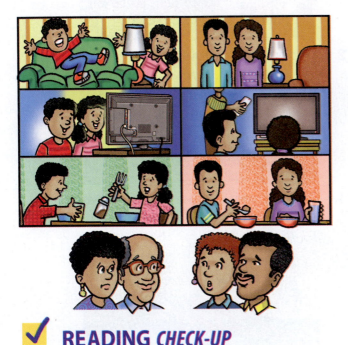

The Greens and their next-door neighbors, the Harrisons, always disagree when they talk about child rearing. The Greens are very lenient with their children, but the Harrisons aren't. They're very strict. The Greens let their children watch television whenever they want, but the Harrisons don't. They let their children watch television for only an hour a day. Also, the Harrisons have always taught their children to sit quietly and behave well at the dinner table, but the Greens haven't. They have always allowed their children to do whatever they want at the dinner table. You can see why the Greens and the Harrisons always disagree when they talk about child rearing. Child rearing is a very "touchy subject" with them.

✔️ **READING** *CHECK-UP*

### TRUE, FALSE, OR MAYBE?

Answer True, False, or Maybe (if the answer isn't in the story).

1. Larry and his parents never agree when they talk about politics.
2. Larry probably supports equal rights for women and minorities.
3. The Harrisons' children watch television more often than the Greens' children.
4. The Greens' children probably go to bed later than the Harrisons' children.
5. Since the Greens and the Harrisons disagree, they never talk about child rearing.

**How About You?**

Do you and someone you know always disagree about a "touchy subject"? Who is this person? What do you disagree about? In what ways do you disagree?

In many ways, my sister and I are exactly the same.
    I'm tall and thin, and she is, too.
    I have brown eyes and curly black hair, and so does she.
    I work in an office downtown, and she does, too.
    I'm not married yet, and neither is she.
    I went to college in Boston, and so did she.
    I wasn't a very good student, and she wasn't either.

And in many ways, my sister and I are very different.
    I like classical music, but she doesn't.
    She enjoys sports, but I don't.
    I've never traveled overseas, but she has.
    She's never been to New York, but I have many times.
    She's very outgoing and popular, but I'm not.
    I'm very quiet and philosophical, but she isn't.

Yes, in many ways, my sister and I are exactly the same, and in many ways, we're very different. But most important of all, we like and respect each other. And we're friends.

**Tell other students about somebody you are close to—a friend, a classmate, or someone in your family. Tell how you and this person are the same, and tell how you are different.**

**Write in your journal about somebody you are close to—a friend, a classmate, or someone in your family. Tell how you and this person are the same, and tell how you are different.**

In many ways, _____ and I are exactly the same.

_____

_____

_____

And in many ways, _____ and I are very different.

_____

_____

_____

**Listen.  Then say it.**

No, I can't, but my SISTER can.

No, I don't, but my NEIGHBORS do.

You should ask HER.

Why don't you ask THEM?

**Say it.  Then listen.**

No, I haven't, but my FATHER has.

No, I wasn't, but my CHILDREN were.

You should ask HIM.

How about asking THEM?

## GRAMMAR FOCUS

**CONNECTORS:**
**Too/So**

| I'm hungry. | { I am, too. / So am I. } |
| I can swim. | { I can, too. / So can I. } |
| I've seen that movie. | { I have, too. / So have I. } |
| I have a car. | { I do, too. / So do I. } |
| I worked yesterday. | { I did, too. / So did I. } |

**EITHER/NEITHER**

| I'm not hungry. | { I'm not either. / Neither am I. } |
| I can't swim. | { I can't either. / Neither can I. } |
| I've haven't seen that movie. | { I haven't either. / Neither have I. } |
| I don't have a car. | { I don't either. / Neither do I. } |
| I didn't work. | { I didn't either. / Neither did I. } |

**BUT**

I don't sing, **but** my sister does.

She didn't know the answer, **but** I did.

He can play chess, **but** I can't.

We're ready, **but** they aren't.

| I'm tired, | { and he is, too. / and so is he. } |
| He'll be busy, | { and she will, too. / and so will she. } |
| She's been sick, | { and he has, too. / and so has he. } |
| They sing, | { and she does, too. / and so does she. } |
| She studied, | { and I did, too. / and so did I. } |

| I'm not tired, | { and he isn't either. / and neither is he. } |
| He won't be busy, | { and she won't either. / and neither will she. } |
| She hasn't been sick, | { and he hasn't either. / and neither has he. } |
| They don't sing, | { and she doesn't either. / and neither does she. } |
| She didn't study, | { and I didn't either. / and neither did I. } |

**Complete the sentences.**

1. She just got a raise, and _____ _____ I.
2. He hasn't arrived yet, and _____ _____ they.
3. They can't lift it, and we _____ _____.
4. I have to work late, and you _____, _____.
5. She's leaving soon, and _____ _____ we.
6. He doesn't like to swim, and I _____ _____.
7. A. Are you interested in sports?
   B. No, _____ _____, but my sister _____.

8. I'm going to a meeting, and they _____, _____.
9. He hadn't been there before, and she _____ _____.
10. I won't be able to go, and _____ _____ you.
11. She types very well, and he _____, _____.
12. We've been very busy, and _____ _____ she.
13. You aren't allergic to anything, and _____ _____ I.
14. A. Do you have a ladder?
    B. No, I _____, but my neighbor _____.

## 1 CONVERSATION   REQUESTING HELP; SEQUENCES OF INSTRUCTIONS

**Practice the conversation with a classmate.**

**How to make coffee:**

- ☐ take out the old filter
- ☐ put in a new filter
- ☐ add the coffee
- ☐ press the ON button

**A.** Excuse me. Can you help me?

**B.** Sure. How can I help?

**A.** Can you show me how to make coffee?

**B.** Sure. I'll be happy to.
First, take out the old filter.
Then, put in a new filter.
After that, add the coffee.
And finally, press the ON button.

**A.** I see.
First, I take out the old filter.
Then, I put in a new filter.
After that, I add the coffee.
And finally, I press the ON button.
Is that right?

**B.** Yes. That's correct.

**A.** Thanks very much.

**Look at the instructions. Practice conversations with your classmates.**

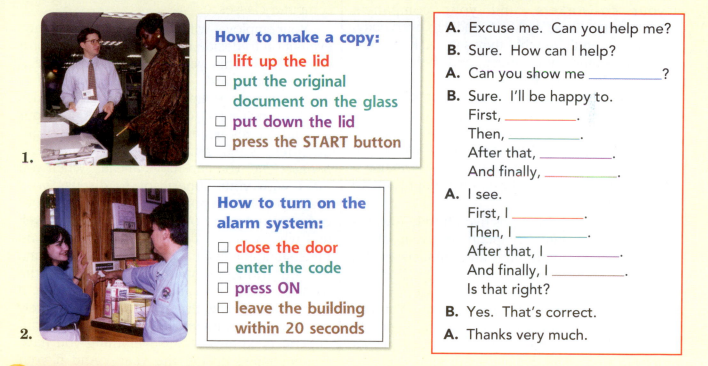

**1.**

**How to make a copy:**

- ☐ lift up the lid
- ☐ put the original document on the glass
- ☐ put down the lid
- ☐ press the START button

**2.**

**How to turn on the alarm system:**

- ☐ close the door
- ☐ enter the code
- ☐ press ON
- ☐ leave the building within 20 seconds

**A.** Excuse me. Can you help me?

**B.** Sure. How can I help?

**A.** Can you show me _____?

**B.** Sure. I'll be happy to.
First, _____.
Then, _____.
After that, _____.
And finally, _____.

**A.** I see.
First, I _____.
Then, I _____.
After that, I _____.
And finally, I _____.
Is that right?

**B.** Yes. That's correct.

**A.** Thanks very much.

## 2 TEAMWORK   INSTRUCTIONS FOR OPERATING EQUIPMENT

Work with a classmate. Think of a procedure for operating equipment at work, at school, or at home. Write down the instructions. Then practice a conversation and present it to the class.

144a

Read the article and answer the questions.

# Getting a Promotion

You've worked in the same job at the same company for many years. Many of your co-workers have gotten promotions to better jobs with higher pay. When will it be *your* turn? What can you do to get the promotion you've been waiting for?

First, check your appearance. Do you look professional? Are the clothes you wear appropriate for work? Dress for success! Look at what the successful people in your company wear and copy them. Good grooming is also an important part of your appearance. Take care of your hair, skin, and fingernails, and make sure that your clothes are clean and ironed. You can't look professional if you aren't well groomed.

If you want to move ahead in your company, you have to get along well with your supervisor, your co-workers, and your company's customers. Smile and be friendly to everybody. Listen carefully to what they say. Ask for their opinions, and try to understand their point of view. We all see things differently. Learn to communicate clearly. When you think your co-workers have done something well, tell them. Everybody likes to receive a compliment. Offer to help others, and be sure to say thank you when someone helps you. If you make a mistake, say you're sorry. It's important to apologize.

Above all, have a positive attitude towards your work. Don't complain or gossip about other people. Work hard and enthusiastically. This will show your supervisor that you like your job and care about the company. Get to work early before your co-workers arrive. You can accomplish a lot when nobody is there to interrupt you. If you start to lose interest in your job because you've had the same responsibilities for a long time, you need to bring new energy to your work. Ask for more responsibilities. Volunteer to work on difficult projects that can teach you new skills. Be creative. Try to find new and more efficient ways to work that will save you time. *Think outside the box.* Look for new ways to solve problems. Employees who can solve problems creatively are valuable. Speak up at meetings. Your supervisor will begin to notice and appreciate you.

Think ahead and prepare for the next job you want. Find out what skills you'll need and do what you can to develop them. For example, if the job you want requires report writing, register for an evening class in business English and volunteer to work on projects that give you the opportunity to write. In addition, check to see what training programs your company offers. It's important to continue your education both on the job and on your own time outside of work. Most jobs these days require strong computer skills, so it's a good idea to take computer classes.

Your employer will use your job performance evaluation to decide if you deserve a raise or a promotion. This yearly evaluation is like a school report card. It compares you to other workers in your group. Workers with low grades can lose their jobs. On the other hand, if your evaluation shows that you have the right qualities, such as being *dependable* and *hardworking*, you can move ahead. When you meet with your supervisor to discuss your evaluation, have a positive attitude. This is your opportunity to find out what you've done well and what you can do better. Make sure you understand the evaluation. Listen carefully and ask questions so you can learn from the feedback you receive about your performance. If you don't agree with your supervisor, politely explain your point of view. Make sure your supervisor knows about everything you have accomplished during the year. And if your evaluation is good, this is an excellent time to talk about your future at the company and a promotion.

# TEST YOURSELF! Do You Deserve a Promotion?

Give yourself one point for every Yes answer.
If you have a score of 14 or higher, you
probably deserve a promotion!

| | Yes | No |
|---|---|---|
| 1. Do you dress appropriately? | | |
| 2. Are you well groomed? | | |
| 3. Do you get along with your co-workers? | | |
| 4. Do you get along with customers? | | |
| 5. Are you friendly? | | |
| 6. Do you communicate clearly? | | |
| 7. Are you helpful? | | |
| 8. Do you have a positive attitude? | | |
| 9. Do you work hard? | | |
| 10. Do you get to work early? | | |
| 11. Do you ask for more responsibilities? | | |
| 12. Do you find new ways to solve problems? | | |
| 13. Do you speak up at meetings? | | |
| 14. Do you take classes to learn new skills? | | |
| 15. Are you dependable and hardworking? | | |
| 16. Do you learn from the feedback you receive? | | |

1. To be *well groomed* means ____.
   A. to dress for success
   B. to wear the right clothes
   C. to be clean and neat
   D. to be successful

2. When you *apologize* to someone, ____.
   A. you give the person a compliment
   B. you say you're sorry
   C. you say thank you
   D. you smile

3. When you work *enthusiastically*, people will see that ____.
   A. you like your job
   B. you look professional
   C. you are creative
   D. you communicate clearly

4. When you *think outside the box*, ____.
   A. you work outside
   B. you find new ways to solve problems
   C. you have the same responsibilities for a long time
   D. you copy successful people

5. When someone is *efficient*, he or she ____.
   A. works slowly
   B. works extra hours
   C. uses time well at work
   D. makes a lot of mistakes

6. If you want a promotion, you should NOT ____.
   A. volunteer for difficult projects
   B. get to work before your co-workers
   C. discuss your evaluation with your boss
   D. complain about your job

7. The main idea of paragraph 5 is ____.
   A. it's important to learn new skills
   B. it's important to volunteer
   C. companies offer training programs
   D. it's important to take classes after work

8. If your job performance evaluation is poor, ____.
   A. don't show it to your supervisor
   B. complain to your co-workers
   C. ask for a promotion
   D. learn from the feedback

## WESTVILLE VALLEY ADULT EDUCATION COURSES—FALL TERM

### BUSINESS

**BUS 101  Business Procedures**—M, W, F
Become familiar with the procedures in a business office.  Topics include filing, telephone skills, receiving and sending mail, organizing meetings and conferences, scheduling appointments, making travel reservations, and time management.

**BUS 103  Customer Service**—Tu, Th
In this course students will discuss and analyze common customer complaints and develop ways to deliver better customer service.

**BUS 105 Business Writing**—M, W
In the business world, time is money.  Learn to write clear and concise business letters, memos, and reports.

**BUS 106 Public Speaking**—W, F
This course helps students develop the ability to speak confidently in a variety of public speaking situations.  Participants will prepare and present a speech each week.

**BUS 201 Bookkeeping**—M, Tu, W, Th, F
This course prepares students for the national Certified Bookkeeper examination.  Topics include payroll (paying wages, reporting taxes) and inventory.

**BUS 205 Entrepreneurship**—W, F
Learn how to start and operate your own business. Each student will develop a business plan.

### COMPUTERS

**COM 101 Microsoft Word I**—Tu, Th
Students will learn to create documents with today's most popular word processing software.

**COM 102 Microsoft Outlook**—F
Learn to use Microsoft Outlook to send, receive, and organize electronic mail.

**COM 103 Introduction to the Internet**—M, F
Learn how to search the World Wide Web to find information online.  Students will get hands-on experience when they research a topic that interests them.

**COM 106 Excel Spreadsheets**—Tu, Th
You don't have to be good with numbers to balance a checkbook or calculate how you spend your money each month.  Learn how to enter the information and let Excel software do the math for you.  This course covers the basics of spreadsheets.  Students will learn how to create worksheets and charts.

**COM 201 Microsoft Word II**—W, Th, F
Use the advanced features of Word to create documents with charts.  Students will also learn to create newsletters and flyers.

**COM 203 PowerPoint Presentations**—M, F
Learn to create professional-looking presentations that include graphs, charts, and pictures using PowerPoint.  Prerequisite: Students must have keyboarding skills to take this course.

### CULINARY ARTS

**CA 100 Food Preparation**—M, Tu, W, Th, F
This course introduces students to the culinary arts profession and prepares them for an entry-level position as a Food and Beverage Specialist in a hotel, hospital, or restaurant kitchen. Participants will learn kitchen procedures and how to follow basic recipes.

**CA 104 Food Sanitation**—W, F
Learn how to prepare food safely.  This course teaches health regulations and procedures and the reasons for them.

### HEALTH SCIENCE

**HS 101 CPR (Cardiopulmonary Resuscitation)**—M
This course covers emergency procedures to follow when someone has stopped breathing or the heart has stopped beating.  Red Cross certification.

**HS 102 Basic Emergency Care**—Tu, W
Learn how to prevent accidents and give first aid. Students learn to recognize and respond to emergencies including shock, breathing emergencies, poison, cuts, and burns.

**Look at the adult education course catalog and answer the questions.**

1. The _____ course helps students learn how to start a business.
   A. Business Procedures
   B. Bookkeeping
   C. Entrepreneurship
   D. Business Writing

2. Business Procedures prepares students for a job as a _____.
   A. manager
   B. bookkeeper
   C. programmer
   D. secretary

3. Students learn research skills in course number _____.
   A. COM 102
   B. COM 103
   C. COM 106
   D. COM 203

4. In Business Writing, students do NOT learn to write _____.
   A. reports
   B. letters
   C. resumes
   D. memos

5. We can infer that a concise business letter _____.
   A. is short
   B. has many long words
   C. is hard to understand
   D. is long

6. Students have to be able to type on a computer before they can take _____.
   A. Microsoft Word I
   B. Microsoft Outlook
   C. Introduction to the Internet
   D. PowerPoint Presentations

7. After students complete _____, they will be ready to take a national exam.
   A. HS 102
   B. BUS 201
   C. CA 100
   D. CA 104

8. Microsoft Outlook is software for _____.
   A. word-processing
   B. spreadsheets
   C. e-mail
   D. presentations

9. Culinary Arts 100 does NOT prepare students for a job in _____.
   A. a hospital
   B. an office
   C. a restaurant
   D. a hotel

10. Students learn how to take care of bad burns when they take _____.
    A. CA 104
    B. CA 100
    C. HS 101
    D. HS 102

## YOUR EDUCATION PLAN

What classes do you plan to take in the future? When and where will you take these classes? Fill in the chart.

| MY EDUCATION PLAN | | |
|---|---|---|
| WHAT I PLAN TO STUDY | WHEN | WHERE |
| | | |
| | | |
| | | |

**CLASS DISCUSSION** Where in your community can you learn about different careers? Where can you go for help with career planning? Where can you take courses to learn new skills? Discuss as a class.

144e

**Choose the correct answer.**

1. This table is very expensive. I don't think we can _____ it.
   A. allow
   B. afford
   C. spend
   D. support

2. Marco plays soccer very well. He's very _____.
   A. athletic
   B. available
   C. compatible
   D. lenient

3. I'm very _____ about the environment.
   A. opposed
   B. allergic
   C. concerned
   D. similar

4. My sister likes science, and so do I. We have the same academic _____.
   A. instructions
   B. decisions
   C. collections
   D. interests

5. It's important to _____ when the teacher is talking.
   A. explain
   B. respect
   C. pay attention
   D. express

6. You and I have very similar _____ on life.
   A. outlooks
   B. personalities
   C. backgrounds
   D. reasons

7. I always try to have a positive _____ towards my work.
   A. appearance
   B. attitude
   C. quality
   D. grooming

8. Be creative. Try to look for new ways to _____ problems.
   A. accomplish
   B. volunteer
   C. develop
   D. solve

9. In this course, you will become familiar with common _____ in a business office.
   A. inventory
   B. procedures
   C. information
   D. service

10. I'm learning to use PowerPoint to _____ professional-looking graphs and charts.
    A. prevent
    B. search
    C. create
    D. balance

## SKILLS CHECK ✓

**Words:**

- [ ] appropriate
- [ ] creative
- [ ] dependable
- [ ] efficient
- [ ] hardworking
- [ ] professional
- [ ] valuable
- [ ] well groomed

- [ ] appearance
- [ ] attitude
- [ ] co-worker
- [ ] energy
- [ ] feedback
- [ ] grooming

- [ ] job performance evaluation
- [ ] opportunity
- [ ] performance
- [ ] point of view
- [ ] positive attitude
- [ ] project
- [ ] promotion
- [ ] qualities
- [ ] responsibility
- [ ] training program

- [ ] accomplish
- [ ] apologize
- [ ] appreciate

- [ ] care about
- [ ] communicate
- [ ] compare
- [ ] develop
- [ ] *dress for success*
- [ ] find out
- [ ] move ahead
- [ ] register
- [ ] solve problems
- [ ] speak up
- [ ] think ahead
- [ ] *think outside the box*
- [ ] volunteer

**I can say:**

- [ ] I'm a *vegetarian*. I am, too./So am I.
- [ ] I'm not *a good dancer*. I'm not either./ Neither am I.
- [ ] I don't *have a dog*, but *my neighbor* does.
- [ ] Can you show me *how to make coffee*? First, _____. Then, _____. After that, _____. And finally, _____.

**I can offer a suggestion:**

- [ ] You should *ask* HER.
- [ ] Why don't you *ask* HER?
- [ ] How about *asking* HER?

**I can:**

- [ ] request help at work
- [ ] give & follow a sequence of instructions
- [ ] identify important factors for career advancement
- [ ] interpret an adult education course catalog
- [ ] complete an education plan

**I can write about:**

- [ ] somebody I am close to

Feature Article
Fact File
Around the World
Interview
We've Got Mail!

Global Exchange
Listening
Fun with Idioms
What Are They
Saying?

**SIDE** *by* **SIDE Gazette**

Volume 3

Number 4

# From Matchmakers to Dating Services

## Traditions, customs, modern life, and the ways people meet

Marriage traditions and customs are very different around the world. In many cultures, young people meet at school, at work, or in other places; they decide to go out together; they fall in love; and they get married. In other cultures, parents or other family members arrange a match between two young people.

In India, for example, a father traditionally finds his daughter a husband. The father might ask friends or relatives to recommend a possible husband, and he might put an ad in the newspaper. The father looks for someone with a good education, occupation, and salary. When he finds a possible match, he sends his daughter's horoscope to the boy's family. An astrologer reads the horoscope and decides if there is a good astrological match between the young man and woman. If the astrologer approves, the families then discuss the marriage arrangements.

In many cultures around the world, families use a matchmaker to bring young people together and arrange marriages. This is especially common in rural areas of many countries. Families pay the matchmaker to find a partner for their child. Sometimes, the matchmaker also helps families with the "business" part of a marriage agreement. For example, a family may give or receive animals, products, or other valuable things as part of the marriage arrangement. In some cultures, parents even arrange marriages between children before they are born.

*An astrologer approved the marriage of these newlyweds from India. The astrologer examined their horoscopes to decide if the date and time of their births were a good match.*

These traditions and customs are changing in many places, especially in the modern cities of the world. Young people want the freedom to choose their own partners. Many, however, actually use modern-day versions of the traditional matchmaking services! For example, some people put personal ads in newspapers or magazines. In these ads, people describe themselves and tell what kind of person they're looking for. Others use dating services—companies that bring people together. Most dating services ask people to submit a photograph and fill out a long questionnaire about their background and interests. Some dating services even make videos of their customers. People who use a dating service can usually browse through the company's information to find a possible partner.

## FACT FILE

### When People Get Married

People around the world get married at different ages. At what age do men and women usually get married in different countries you know?

Age of Bride

Countries

| Swaziland | India | Mexico | Brazil | Saudi Arabia | Russia | Korea | Greece | Australia | Japan | Sweden |
|---|---|---|---|---|---|---|---|---|---|---|
| 16 | 20 | 21 | 21 | 22 | 23 | 25 | 25 | 26 | 27 | 28 |

## Wedding Customs and Traditions

a wedding ceremony in the United States

a Hindu ceremony

a wedding in the Slovak Republic

a ceremony in a Korean village

**W**edding customs and traditions are very different around the world. In many cultures, weddings happen in churches or other places of worship. In other cultures, people get married outdoors, in their homes, in special reception halls for family celebrations, or in other places. The bride and the groom usually wear clothing that is traditional for weddings in their culture. The type of clothing and the colors are very different around the world. Brides often wear a veil or a crown on their heads. Some weddings are private—just for family members and friends. Other weddings are public. Everybody in the neighborhood or the entire town might attend the celebration. Some weddings are short, and other weddings can last for hours, days, or even a week!

a traditional Romanian dance

musicians leading a wedding procession

**M**usic and dancing are an important part of wedding celebrations in different cultures. There are often special dances for the bride and groom, their parents, and other family members. Musicians might play special wedding music during the ceremony, at the celebration after the ceremony, or even in the street!

confetti

flower petals

rice

**I**n some cultures, people like to throw things at weddings! Before or after the ceremony, it is often traditional for guests to shower the bride and groom with something to wish them good luck.

Guests have pinned money on this bride and groom in Cyprus.

a wedding couple in Colombia lighting candles during the ceremony

cutting the cake at a U.S. wedding celebration

a Japanese bride arriving at her wedding by boat

a bride in the U.S. throwing a bouquet of flowers (According to tradition, the person who catches it will get married next.)

**M**any cultures around the world have special wedding customs. These traditions often involve candles, flowers, special foods, money, and the ways that couples get to their wedding ceremonies.

**What wedding customs and traditions in different cultures do you know?**

# Interview

A **Side by Side Gazette** reporter spoke with several young couples.

**Q:** "How did you meet?"

**A:** We met in college.

**A:** We met at work.

**A:** We met at a bookstore.

**A:** We were high school "sweethearts."

**A:** We met on a "blind date" that our friends arranged.

**A:** We met through a dating service.

**A:** Our parents arranged our marriage through a matchmaker.

## FUN with IDIOMS

He's nuts about me.

She gave me the cold shoulder.

I fell for him the moment I met him.

We had planned to go on a date, but she stood me up.

### Do You Know These Expressions?

_____ 1. He's nuts about me.

_____ 2. She gave me the cold shoulder.

_____ 3. I fell for him the moment I met him.

_____ 4. We had planned to go on a date, but she stood me up.

a. I liked him right away.

b. He likes me a lot.

c. She didn't meet me.

d. She didn't pay attention to me.

## We've Got Mail!

Dear Side by Side,

I'm trying to figure out two-word verbs. Is there a rule that will tell me which two-word verbs are separable and which are inseparable? I hope to <u>hear you from</u> soon.

Sincerely,

"Looking for an Answer"

Dear "Looking for an Answer,"

We're sorry to tell you that there isn't a rule for this. You need to learn about each verb separately. Here's a suggestion. On a piece of paper, make two lists. Write down separable two-word verbs in one list and inseparable two-word verbs in the other. Then look up the words on your lists when you can't remember them.

By the way, we've circled some words in the last sentence of your letter because "hear from" is an inseparable two-word verb. The correct way to say this is "I hope to hear from you soon." Thanks for writing, and good luck with two-word verbs!

Sincerely,

*Side by Side*

Dear Side by Side,

I think two-word verbs are very difficult. The verb in a two-word verb has one meaning, but the whole two-word verb often has a different meaning. For example, "I <u>turned on</u> the light," but "I <u>turned down</u> the invitation"; "I <u>take out</u> the garbage," but "I <u>take after</u> my father." In my language, we have different words for all these expressions. Why does English use the same words over and over again?

Sincerely,

"Turned Off by Two-Word Verbs"

Dear "Turned Off,"

We're sorry to hear you're unhappy. Two-word verbs are very common in everyday English. We actually have special words for many of these meanings, but these words are more formal. For example, you can say, "I <u>declined</u> the invitation" and "I <u>resemble</u> my father." Most English speakers, however, prefer to use informal language, so they use lots of two-word verbs. With time, we're sure you'll get over this problem with two-word verbs. Thanks for your question.

Sincerely,

*Side by Side*

---

### Global Exchange

**PedroJ:** Let me tell you about my best friend. His name is Marco. People think we're brothers because we look alike. He's short and thin, and so am I. I have curly brown hair, and he does, too. We also have similar backgrounds. He's originally from Peru, and I am, too. He moved to this country when he was a little boy, and so did I. His parents work in factories, and so do mine. Marco and I have very different interests. He enjoys playing sports, but I don't. I play a musical instrument, but he doesn't. I've been in several plays in school, but he hasn't. How about you? Tell me about your best friend.

**Tell a keypal about your best friend.**

---

### LISTENING

## "Telephone Tag" True or False?

_____ ❶ Mary likes jazz, and Jim does, too.

_____ ❷ Mary likes to play tennis, and so does Jim.

_____ ❸ Jim wants to go to the ballet, but Mary doesn't.

_____ ❹ Jim hasn't seen the movie, and neither has Mary.

_____ ❺ Jim doesn't like Italian food, but Mary does.

## What Are They Saying?

HILL

A **run-on sentence** is an error.  It happens when two or more complete sentences are not separated by correct punctuation or connecting words.

Here are two ways to correct a run-on sentence:    I'm a good singer I'm not a very good dancer.

Separate the sentences with a period.    I'm a good singer.  I'm not a very good dancer.

Separate the sentences with a comma and add a conjunction that is appropriate:  *and, or, but*.    I'm a good singer, but I'm not a very good dancer.

## Practice these conversations with a classmate.

I've had special vocational training I know how to repair car engines.

**A.** What's wrong with this sentence?

**B.** It's a run-on sentence.

**A.** What's one way to correct it?

**B.** We can separate the sentences with a period.

**A.** So, what's the correction?

**B.** *I've had special vocational training.* Period.  *I know how to repair car engines.*

I've been to Los Angeles several times Hollywood is one of my favorite places to visit.

**A.** What's wrong with this sentence?

**B.** It's a run-on sentence.

**A.** What's one way to correct it?

**B.** We can separate the sentences with a comma and add the conjunction *and*.

**A.** So, what's the correction?

**B.** *I've been to Los Angeles several times,* comma, *and Hollywood is one of my favorite places to visit.*

### Correct these run-on sentences.*  Then practice new conversations about them.

1. I get along with my co-workers I get along with my customers.

2. Be friendly with your co-workers don't complain or gossip about other people.

3. My sister lets her children use their cell phones while they eat dinner my husband and I don't allow our children to do that.

4. My son might stay in his current job he might look for a new job.

5. Marriage customs are different around the world these traditions are changing in many cultures.

6. Wedding ceremonies can be very short wedding ceremonies can last for hours or days.

* There are different ways to correct each sentence.

# The Daily Voice

*Journalism student Samantha Hoang interviewed Career Counselor Becky Aranda about services that the Career Center provides for students. Mrs. Aranda has worked at the Career Center for over 10 years.*

**SH:** Mrs. Aranda, when should students visit the Career Center? Should we wait until we have decided on a major?

**BA:** Oh, no! Don't wait that long! You should come to the Career Center during your first semester at the college. It's important to think about your career before you choose your major. We start by helping you identify your skills and interests. This is because we want your studies to lead you to the best possible job in the future. You can come into the Career Center and complete some online questionnaires. Then you make an appointment to meet with a career counselor to discuss the results. You can sign up for an appointment online or call us.

**SH:** What do you usually discuss in your first meeting with a student?

**BA:** During our first meeting, I want to get to know a student. We talk about previous education and employment and goals for the future. We discuss short-term goals, such as successfully completing first-year courses. We also talk about long-term goals—perhaps completing a training program or a graduate degree after college. Of course, we talk about employment goals, too.

Next, we look at the results of the interests and skills questionnaire. With this information, I can give suggestions about types of jobs to think about. And, I can provide information about different certificates and programs we have here at the college.

**SH:** Can you offer academic advice as well as career advice?

**BA:** Yes, absolutely. I can give information about courses required for different majors or certificates. I also know what courses will be good preparation for certain types of jobs. However, the Academic Counseling Office can provide much more detailed information about specific courses.

**SH:** What about certificate programs?

**BA:** Our college has a wide variety of certificate programs. For example, we have certificates in Accounting, Private Security, Automotive Technology, Early Childhood Education, TV Production, Medical Technology, and Real Estate. After completing 6 to 12 courses to prepare you for a specific type of job, you receive a certificate. These programs are good preparation for immediate employment or as a way of improving your job skills.

**SH:** In general, what are the most important skills to have these days?

**BA:** Of course, computer skills are important in all types of jobs these days. We make sure all students have strong computer skills. However, employers are also looking for workplace skills, such as strong communication skills, dependability, teamwork skills, and the ability to supervise others. So, in our certificate courses and in the Career Center, we help students with both computer skills and workplace skills.

**SH:** Can you help students get an internship?

**BA:** Yes. We have a very strong internship program. An internship allows you to experience working in a business or service. It's a short-term position, but you can learn a lot on the job. It's also an excellent way to see how to improve your workplace skills. It's not a job, so you don't get paid. However, you can get valuable training and hopefully a good recommendation. Sometimes an internship can eventually become a permanent position. We work together with local businesses and companies to help students find internships. Right now we have about 30 internships available starting in January.

**SH:** What about finding a job?

**BA:** We know that finding the right job is more than

just going to an interview. The job search should be a learning experience. First, you have to be prepared. You need to understand your skills, your interests, and what types of jobs are best for you. At the Career Center, we help you through the entire job search. First, we help you get the training and education you need. Then, we help you fill out applications, write a resume, and contact employers. We also teach you how to do well in an interview.

We offer workshops on preparing for interviews, writing resumes and cover letters, and completing applications—all the things that are important in helping you find a job. There are several workshops every week. Dates and times for the workshops are on our website. Twice a year we have a big job fair in the Student Activity Center. At a job fair, students can talk with company representatives about job openings. There are usually about 30 companies at the job fair. We have strong relationships with employers in the community, and so our students often find jobs in this area. Companies know that our students are well prepared and well trained.

We post new job openings on our website every day. There is a special Web page for our students, and you can see all of the latest job postings there. So, we teach you how to look for work from start to finish.

**SH:** Thank you so much for your time, Mrs. Aranda. I've never used the services at the Career Center, but I plan to come in next week.

**BA:** You're very welcome. I look forward to seeing you here. Even if you have already chosen your major, we can help you get the skills and experience you need to find a great job!

(The Career Center is on the first floor of Mead Hall. Hours: Monday–Thursday 8:00 A.M. to 6:00 P.M. and Friday 8:00 A.M. to 4:00 P.M. Phone: 999-777-6666)

*Samantha Hoang, a junior, is a reporter for The Daily Voice. She's majoring in journalism and wants to work as a TV news writer after graduation.*

## DID YOU UNDERSTAND?

1. How long has Mrs. Aranda been a counselor at the Career Center?
2. Why does she say that students should come to the center during their first semester?
3. What should students do before they make an appointment to speak with a career counselor?
4. What does a career counselor usually ask about during the first meeting?
5. Where can students get information about courses?
6. What is a certificate program?
7. What two skills does Mrs. Aranda believe are the most important?
8. Why is an internship a good idea for some students?
9. How does the Career Center help students find a job?
10. How can a job fair be helpful to people who are looking for work?
11. Has the interviewer ever used the Career Center services?

## DISCUSS AND REFLECT

1. Is there a career center in your school or community? What do you know about it?
2. What services in the Career Center in the article are the most interesting to you? Why?
3. Do you agree that students should think about their job futures as soon as they begin college? Why or why not?
4. Imagine that you have the opportunity to do an internship at a local business or service for two months. What business will you choose? Why?
5. Who can give you good advice about your job future? Think of three people, and tell why you think they can help you.

**Proofreading** is an important step in the writing process. After you write and revise a first draft, you need to **proofread** your writing. When you proofread, you look for errors in capitalization, punctuation, spelling, and paragraph formation, and you fix the errors that you find.

When you proofread, read your work two or three times. You can check your work for all the types of errors each time you read, or you can focus on one type of error at a time. For example, first look for spelling mistakes. Then look for errors in capitalization, punctuation, and paragraph formation. Some people use a ruler to read one line at a time easily when they proofread. Other people like to read sentence by sentence from the ending to the beginning. This helps to focus on the errors instead of the meaning.

## Proofreading Marks

You can use **proofreading marks** to mark the mistakes that you find. This student has written a composition about an experience she had, and her teacher has marked the errors in spelling, capitalization, punctuation, and paragraph formation. Rewrite the composition and fix the errors.

> When I was sixteen year old I had an experience that that change my life. One morning my aunt Rosa called. My uncle was sick, and aunt Rosa had to take him to Hospital. She needed a baby sitter for my two little cusins. I sayed I could come, but I had never take care of little children never. I arrived at there house in five minutes my aunt and uncle left immediately. The kids hadnt eaten yet, so I made them brekfast. I played with them, I read books to them, I took to them the Park, and I made them lunch and diner. Late that night my aunt called. She sayed my uncle was going to by fine. She thanked mi for baby sitting. She had worryed about my uncle, but she hadnt worryed about her kids. She trusted me compleatly. That night I sleept like I had never sleept before!

| Proofreading Marks | |
|---|---|
| ≡ | capital letter |
| / | small letter |
| ⌃ | add comma |
| ⊙ | add period |
| ⌄ | add apostrophe |
| ⏌ | indent paragraph |
| ¶ | new paragraph |
| ◯ or sp. | check spelling |
| ⩗⩗ | wrong word |
| ⌒ | close up space |
| ⌇ | transpose/reverse |
| ⟋ | delete |
| ⋀ | insert |

## Cooperative Proofreading

**Write:** Did you write in your journal about the topic on page 130 or on page 143? If you didn't, write about one of these topics now. (Page 130 asks you to write about someone you look up to. Page 143 asks you to write about how you and another person are the same and different.)

**Revise:** Reread your first draft. Make some changes to improve it.

**Proofread:** Exchange compositions with a classmate. Read and proofread each other's work. Use proofreading marks to mark errors. Then meet with the classmate and discuss the errors you have found in each other's writing.

**Rewrite:** Finally, rewrite your composition and fix the errors.

# Listening Scripts

## Unit 1 – Page 6

*Listen and choose the correct answer.*

1. What are you doing?
2. Do you watch the news very often?
3. Are you a good swimmer?
4. What's Cathy reading?
5. Who cooks in your family?
6. Do they like to skate?
7. Does your sister want to be a ballet dancer?
8. Do you and your friends play basketball very often?
9. Are your parents good dancers?
10. What does Peter want to be when he grows up?

## Unit 2 – Page 17

*Listen and choose the correct answer.*

1. Did you do well at your job interview yesterday?
2. Were your children tired last night?
3. What was he doing when he broke his leg?
4. Did you finish your dinner last night?
5. How did your husband lose his wallet?
6. What was your supervisor doing?
7. Did you do well on the exam?
8. What happened while you were preparing lunch?

## Unit 3 – Page 24

*Listen to the conversation and choose the answer that is true.*

1. A. Are you going to wear your brown suit today?
   B. No, I don't think so. I wore my brown suit yesterday. I'm going to wear my gray suit.
2. A. Let's make beef stew for dinner!
   B. But we had that last week. Let's make spaghetti and meatballs instead.
   A. Okay.
3. A. Do you want to watch the game show on Channel 5 or the news program on Channel 9?
   B. Let's watch the news program.
4. A. What's the matter with it?
   B. The brakes don't work, and it doesn't start very well in the morning.
5. A. What are you going to do tomorrow?
   B. I'm going to plant carrots, tomatoes, and lettuce.
6. A. This computer is very powerful, but it's too expensive.
   B. You're right.

## Side by Side Gazette – Page 35

*Listen to the messages on Dave's machine. Match the messages.*

You have five messages.

Message Number One: "Hi, Dave. It's Sarah. Thanks for the invitation, but I can't come to your party tomorrow. I'll be taking my uncle to the hospital. Maybe next time." [beep]

Message Number Two: "Hello, Dave. It's Bob. I'm sorry that my wife and I won't be able to come to your party tomorrow. We'll be attending a wedding out of town. I hope it's a great party. Have fun!" [beep]

Message Number Three: "Dave? It's Paula. How's it going? I got your message about the party tomorrow. Unfortunately, I won't be able to go. I'll be studying all weekend. Talk to you soon." [beep]

Message Number Four: "Hi, Dave. It's Joe. Thanks for the invitation to your party. I'll be visiting my parents in New York City, so I'm afraid I won't be around. I'll call you when I get back." [beep]

Message Number Five: "Hello, Dave? It's Carla. Thanks for the invitation to your party. I don't have anything to do tomorrow night, so I'll definitely be there. I'm really looking forward to it. See you tomorrow." [beep]

## Unit 4 – Page 49

1. *Linda is on vacation in San Francisco. This is her list of things to do. Check the things on the list Linda has already done.*

   Linda has already seen the Golden Gate Bridge. She hasn't visited Golden Gate Park yet. She took a tour of Alcatraz Prison yesterday. She's going to go to Chinatown tomorrow. She hasn't ridden a cable car yet. She's eaten at Fisherman's Wharf, but she hasn't had time to buy souvenirs.

2. *Alan is a secretary in a very busy office. This is his list of things to do before 5 P.M. on Friday. Check the things on the list Alan has already done.*

   Alan has already called Mrs. Porter. He has to type the letter to the Mervis Company. He hasn't taken the mail to the post office yet. He's gone to the bank. He hasn't sent an e-mail to the company's office in Denver, and he's going to speak to the boss about his salary next week.

3. *It's Saturday, and Judy and Paul Johnson are doing lots of things around the house. This is the list of things they have to do today. Check the things on the list they've already done.*

   Judy and Paul haven't done the laundry. They have to wash the kitchen windows. They've paid the bills. They haven't given the dog a bath. They'll clean the garage later. They couldn't fix the bathroom sink or repair the fence, but they vacuumed the living room rug.

## Unit 5 – Page 60

*Listen to the conversation and choose the answer that is true.*

1. A. How long have you had a backache?
   B. For three days.
2. A. Has your father always been an engineer?
   B. No, he hasn't.
3. A. How long has your knee been swollen?
   B. For a week.
4. A. How long have you known how to ski?
   B. Since I was a teenager.
5. A. Did you live in Tokyo for a long time?
   B. Yes. Five years.
6. A. How long has Roger been interested in Egyptian history?
   B. Since he lived in Cairo.
7. A. Is Amy still in the hospital?
   B. Oh. I forgot to tell you. She's been home for two days.
8. A. Have you played hockey for a long time?
   B. Yes. I've played hockey since I moved to Toronto three years ago.

*Listen to the voice-mail messages between Gloria Rivera and her office assistant, Sam. Has Sam done the things on Ms. Rivera's list? Check Yes or No.*

You have one message. Tuesday, 8:15 A.M.

Hello, Sam? This is Ms. Rivera. I'll be out of the office all day today. I'm not feeling well. Here's a list of things you'll need to do while I'm not here. First, please write a note to Mrs. Wilson and tell her I'm sick. Then, please call Mr. Chen and change the time of our appointment. Also, send an e-mail to everybody in the office, and tell them about next week's meeting. Don't forget to speak to the custodian about my broken desk lamp. I hope he can fix it. Hmm. Let's see. I know there are a few more things. Oh, yes. Please make a list of all the employees and give it to Ms. Baxter. She asked me for the list last week. Okay, Sam. I think that's everything. Oh . . . one more thing. Please take the package on my desk to the post office if you have time. And that's it. Thanks, Sam. I'll see you tomorrow morning.

You have reached the voice mailbox of Gloria Rivera. Please leave a message after the tone.

Ms. Rivera? This is Sam. I'm sorry you aren't feeling well. I hope you feel better tomorrow. I'm calling to tell you what I've done today, and what I haven't done yet. It's been very busy here, so I haven't had time to do everything. I wrote a note to Mrs. Wilson. I called Mr. Chen and changed the time of your appointment. I also sent the e-mail about next week's meeting. I haven't spoken to the custodian. He's been sick all week. I made a list of all the employees, but I haven't given it to Ms. Baxter yet. I'll give it to her early tomorrow morning. Finally, I haven't taken the package to the post office yet. I haven't had time. I'm going to take it to the post office on my way home. Again, I hope you're feeling better. I'll see you in the morning.

## Unit 6 – Page 79

### WHICH WORD DO YOU HEAR?

*Listen and choose the correct answer.*

1. He's gone to the bank.
2. I've never written so many letters in one day before.
3. She's been seeing patients all day.
4. What courses have you taken this year?
5. Is Beverly giving blood?
6. Ben has driven all night.

### WHO IS SPEAKING?

*Listen and decide who is speaking.*

1. What a day! All the tenants have been complaining that nothing is working.
2. I'm very tired. I've given six lessons today.
3. Thank you! You've been a wonderful audience!
4. I'm really tired. I've been watching them all day.
5. I'm very tired. I've been looking at paychecks since early this morning.
6. It's been a long day. I've been selling tickets since ten A.M.

## Unit 7 – Page 93

*Listen and choose the correct answer.*

1. A. I avoid going to the mall whenever I can.
   B. Me, too.
2. A. I've decided to sell my car.
   B. Your beautiful car?
3. A. Please try to quit biting your nails.
   B. Okay. Mom.
4. A. Do you enjoy traveling by plane?
   B. Very much.
5. A. We're thinking about moving to Florida.
   B. Oh. That's interesting.
6. A. I've been considering getting married for a long time.
   B. Oh, really? I didn't know that.
7. A. Don't stop practicing.
   B. Okay.
8. A. Interrupting people is a habit I just can't break.
   B. That's too bad.

## Unit 8 – Page 103

*Listen and choose the correct answer.*

1. Did your parents enjoy eating at Joe's Restaurant last night?
2. Why don't you want to see the new James Bond movie with us next weekend?
3. Did you get to the play on time last night?
4. Michael, please go upstairs and do your homework.
5. Why did Carmen do so well on the history test?
6. We really enjoyed our vacation at the Ritz Hotel.

### **Side by Side** Gazette – Page 113

*Listen to the Olympic Game highlights. Match the highlight and the sport.*

And now, sports fans, let's finish today's program with highlights of the Olympic Games. Here are five of my favorite moments in the most recent summer and winter games:

There are three seconds left in the game. Number 38 gets ready to shoot again. His team needs this point to win the game. He shoots, and it's in the basket! [*Buzzer*] That's it! The game is over! And the United States wins 99 to 98. The U.S. gets the gold medal!

Kirshner is still in front. But wait! Look at Tanaka in the next lane! What speed! Look at him move through the water! Tanaka is even with Kirshner. Now Tanaka is ahead! And Tanaka wins the event! Japan wins the gold medal, Germany gets the silver, and Hungary gets the bronze.

Natasha knows she must do this floor routine perfectly to win the gold medal. She had problems today when she fell off the balance beam, and that's usually her best event. She's doing very well. What a strong and graceful athlete! And here's the most difficult part of her routine. Beautiful! But, oh . . . she falls! Natasha has fallen at the very end of her routine. What a shame! There will be no gold for Natasha this year.

What a race! Anderson is still in first place and Sanchez is right behind him in second place. Look at Sanchez run! He's moving ahead of Anderson. The lead has changed! Sanchez is now in front! He crosses the finish line! Sanchez wins with a time of two hours, ten minutes, and eleven seconds. So Mexico wins the gold, Canada gets the silver, and France gets the bronze.

And Tamara leaves the ice after a beautiful long program! I think that's one of the best programs I've ever seen at the Olympics. She moved so gracefully to the music. Let's see what the judges think. Look at these marks! Five-point-eight, five-point-nine, five-point-nine, five-point-eight, five-point-seven, five-point-nine, five-point-nine, six-point-oh, five-point-eight. Excellent scores! Tamara wins the gold medal! Look at all the flowers people are throwing on the ice! I'm sure this is the happiest day of Tamara's life!

## Unit 9 – Page 129

*Listen and choose what the people are talking about.*

1. A. Where can I try them on?
   B. The dressing room is over there.

2. A. Now remember, you can't bring them back!
   B. I understand.

3. A. Have you filled it out yet?
   B. No. I'm having some trouble. Can you help me?

4. A. Please drop them off at the school by eight o'clock.
   B. By eight o'clock? Okay.

5. A. Where should I hang them?
   B. What about over the fireplace?

6. A. Have you thought it over?
   B. Yes, I have.

7. A. It's cold in here.
   B. You're right. I'll turn it on.

8. A. Should we use it up?
   B. No. Let's throw it out.

9. A. What are you going to do?
   B. I'm going to turn it down.

## Unit 10 – Page 137

*Listen and choose what the people are talking about.*

1. A. To tell the truth, I'm a little shy.
   B. What a coincidence! I am, too.

2. A. I enjoy going to plays and concerts.
   B. We're very compatible. So do I.

3. A. I'm enjoying this course.
   B. I am, too.

4. A. I'm from Minnesota.
   B. That's interesting. So am I.

5. A. I go swimming three times a week.
   B. What a coincidence! I do, too.

6. A. I'm opposed to using animals in scientific experiments.
   B. I am, too.

## Side by Side Gazette – Page 148

*Listen to the messages on Mary and Jim's answering machines. Answer true or false.*

*[Monday, 6:15 P.M.]*

Hi, Mary. It's Jim. Are you by any chance interested in going to a jazz concert this Friday night? Please call me and let me know. Talk to you later.

*[Monday, 9:13 P.M.]*

Hi, Jim. It's Mary. I'm returning your call. Thanks for the invitation. I know you like jazz, and I do, too. And I'd really like to go to the concert with you, but I have to work this Friday night. Do you want to play tennis on Saturday afternoon? Let me know. 'Bye.

*[Tuesday, 3:40 P.M.]*

Hi, Mary. It's Jim. I'm sorry I missed your call last night. I was at the laundromat, and I got home very late. I'm free on Saturday, but unfortunately, I really don't like to play tennis. Actually, I'm a very bad tennis player. Do you want to go to the ballet with me on Saturday night? Let me know, and I'll order tickets. Talk to you soon.

*[Wednesday, 5:50 P.M.]*

Hi, Jim. It's Mary. I got your message. Believe it or not, I've already gone to the ballet this week. I went with my sister last night. I have an idea! Let's see the new Steven Steelberg movie. I hear that it's great. Call and let me know.

*[Thursday, 6:30 P.M.]*

Hi, Mary. It's Jim. Sorry I missed your call again. I guess we're playing "telephone tag!" The movie sounds great. I haven't seen it yet. Do you want to have dinner before the movie? There's a wonderful new Italian restaurant downtown. Let me know. 'Bye.

*[Friday, 5:17 P.M.]*

Hi, Jim. Guess who! You won't believe it! I just found out that I have to work this Saturday night. It's a shame because I really wanted to see that movie. I'm not busy on Sunday. Are you free on Sunday afternoon? Let me know. By the way, I don't really like Italian food very much. There's a very good Greek restaurant in my neighborhood. Maybe we can have dinner there after the movie. What do you think? Talk to you later.

# Vocabulary List

Numbers indicate the pages on which the words first appear.

## Actions and Activities

accept 119
accomplish 144b
act 4
add 94b
adjust 29
afford 110d
agree 144b
aim (v) 36b
allow 142
analyze 144d
answer (v) 35
apologize 144b
apply 20e
apply for 50a
appoint 10c
appreciate 78
approve 10c
argue 8
arrange 64b
arrive 10b
ask 29
ask for a raise 67
attend 26
avoid 80b
baby-sit 141
bake 2
balance (v) 144d
bark 70
be located 103
beat 144d
become 10c
begin 20c
behave 142
believe 50c
belong 10c
bite 91
born 33
borrow 28
box (v) 87
break 11
break down 20a
break into 10b
breathe 144d
bribe 10b
bring 32b
bring along 98
bring back 102
browse 26
bump into 102
buy 10b
calculate 144d
call 7
call on 124
call up 116
can 3
cancel 110a
can't stand 81
care about 144b
carry 10b
catch 145
catch a cold 107
change (v) 20e
chat online 3
check (v) 10b
check for 110c
chew 105
choose 110e
chop 14
circle 148
clean 2

clean up 123
close 10b
collect 114
come 19
come from 33
come home 66
come in 94b
come over 125
communicate 94c
commute 140
compare 144b
compete 111
complain 8
complete (v) 50a
compose 2
confirm 110a
consider 81
consist 110e
contact 80d
contain 32b
continue 81
cook (v) 2
copy (v) 94a
cost 127
count 57
cover (v) 13
crash 111
create 50c
cross 113
cross out 115
cry 13
cut (v) 10b
dance 4
date (v) 69
decide 20c
declare 10c
decline 148
deliver 12
depend 10c
deposit (v) 64e
describe 20c
deserve 109
develop 114b
die 10c
direct traffic 69
disagree 142
discover 80d
discuss 95
dislocate 105
do 3
do business 65
do card tricks 97
do homework 27
do over 119
do research 26
do sit-ups 69
do the tango 105
draw 38
dress (v) 144b
drink 13
drive 4
drop off 122
earn 109
eat 2
eat out 96
elect 10c
empty (v) 80d
end (v) 20c
enforce 10c
enjoy 31
enroll 92
enter 20b
envy 86

erase 119
evaluate 68b
examine 145
exchange 130c
excuse 83
exercise 3
exist 66
expect 140
expire 130d
explain 10c
express 68
fail 106
fall 11
fall asleep 13
fall for 147
fall off 113
fall through 108
feed 46
feel 17
feel better 104
feel like 120
fight 14
figure out 123
fill in 50a
fill out 26
find 30
find out 36b
finish 13
fire (v) 108
fit 127
fix 28
fly 30
follow 44
forget 13
form (v) 20d
free (v) 20d
get 15
get a promotion 109
get along 125
get around 19
get back 80d
get cold feet 108
get hurt 105
get into trouble 32d
get off 14
get on 30
get out 25
get over 124
get paid 64c
get ready 108
get rid of 44
get sick 107
get stuck 40
get there 18
get to know 148b
get together 122
get up 31
give 10c
give a party 97
give back 119
give blood 42
give up 111
go 6
go back 89
go by 100
go out with 23
go shopping 66
go to bed 46
go together 106
go with 128
gossip 85
graduate 56
grow 20d

grow up 5
growl 17
guess 88
hand in 115
handle (v) 64b
hang 80a
hang up 115
happen 17
harbor (v) 80a
hate 81
have 19
have to 35
hear 10c
hear from 124
help 32b
hide 131
hire 50c
hold 10c
hook up 115
hope 32b
hurt 11
identify 148b
imagine 30
immigrate 34
include 32b
infect 64c
injure 104
interest (v) 144d
interpret 10c
interrupt 85
interview 112
invite 108
involve 146
iron (v) 2
jump 17
keep 17
keep clear 80d
keep on 81
kid (v) 74
kill 20d
kiss 131
knit 2
know 34
know how 94b
last (v) 66
lay off 140
lead 20d
leak (v) 69
learn 32b
leave 30
leave on 119
lend 28
lift up 144a
light (v) 146
like 4
list (v) 50a
listen 9
live 9
look 16
look for 50c
look forward to 31
look through 50c
look up 119
look up to 125
lose 11
lost interest 144b
mail (v) 94b
major in 136
make 10c
make a list 67
make conversation 94c
make sure 110d
marry 33
may 68
mean 64a
meet 11
memorize 95

mend 69
miss 20a
move 30
move ahead 144b
move out 102
must 114
need 20c
notice (v) 128
occur 20e
offer 136
open 10b
operate 65
oppose 137
order 64b
organize 144d
own 53
pack 35
package (v) 64b
paint 2
participate 32b
pass 33
pass by 102
pass on 114c
pay (v) 10b
pay attention 113
peel 64b
perform 95
pick 69
pick on 124
pick out 115
pick up 66
pin (v) 146
place (v) 80a
plan 64b
plant 75
play 3
poke 14
practice (v) 3
prefer 140
prepare 14
prepare for 144b
present (v) 144d
press 144a
prevent 10b
promise 73
protect 110d
provide 80d
punch in 64c
punch out 64c
purchase (v) 95
put 80a
put away 115
put down 144a
put on 99
put to bed 66
put together 36c
quit 81
rain (v) 24
read 2
realize 16
receive 32b
recognize 10c
recommend 112
record (v) 64c
recycle 80d
refuse 80a
register 114c
rehearse 95
relax 31
remember 20d
rent (v) 48
repair (v) 49
report (v) 10b
represent 110e
require 144b
reschedule 110a
research (v) 144d
resemble 148

respect 143
respond 80d
rest (v) 44
result (v) 114b
retire 10c
return 10b
ride (v) 11
ring (v) 69
rinse out 50d
rip 14
run 20a
run away 99
run into 124
run out of 124
sail away 100
save 130c
save up 64c
say 20c
say good-bye 30
say hello 102
schedule (v) 94b
search 144d
see 17
seem 114
sell 20d
send 8
serve 10c
set up 94a
shake 17
share 94c
shave 14
shine 95
shoot 113
shop 26
shout 8
shovel 98
show 94b
shred 10b
sign (v) 10c
sign in 36b
sign up 36c
sing 4
sit 16
sleep 12
slice 64b
slip 117
smile 94c
snow 71
solve 144b
speak 11
speak up 144b
spend 34
sprain 105
stand 16
stand in line 69
stand up 147
start 58
state (v) 50a
stay 5
stay home 35
stay open 65
stay up 99
steal 10b
step up to 68b
stop 20b
store (v) 80d
study 2
submit 145
support 137
switch 65
take 13
take a shower 66
take a trip 102
take after 125
take back 116
take care 34
take down 115
take home 109

make conversation 94c

## Work Skills

# Irregular Verbs

| | | | | | |
|---|---|---|---|---|---|
| be | was/were | been | leave | left | left |
| become | became | become | lend | lent | lent |
| begin | began | begun | let | let | let |
| bite | bit | bitten | light | lit | lit |
| blow | blew | blown | lose | lost | lost |
| break | broke | broken | make | made | made |
| bring | brought | brought | mean | meant | meant |
| build | built | built | meet | met | met |
| buy | bought | bought | put | put | put |
| catch | caught | caught | quit | quit | quit |
| choose | chose | chosen | read | read | read |
| come | came | come | ride | rode | ridden |
| cost | cost | cost | ring | rang | rung |
| cut | cut | cut | run | ran | run |
| do | did | done | say | said | said |
| draw | drew | drawn | see | saw | seen |
| drink | drank | drunk | sell | sold | sold |
| drive | drove | driven | send | sent | sent |
| eat | ate | eaten | set | set | set |
| fall | fell | fallen | sew | sewed | sewed/sewn |
| feed | fed | fed | shake | shook | shaken |
| feel | felt | felt | shrink | shrank | shrunk |
| fight | fought | fought | sing | sang | sung |
| find | found | found | sit | sat | sat |
| fit | fit | fit | sleep | slept | slept |
| fly | flew | flown | speak | spoke | spoken |
| forget | forgot | forgotten | spend | spent | spent |
| forgive | forgave | forgiven | stand | stood | stood |
| freeze | froze | frozen | steal | stole | stolen |
| get | got | gotten | sweep | swept | swept |
| give | gave | given | swim | swam | swum |
| go | went | gone | take | took | taken |
| grow | grew | grown | teach | taught | taught |
| hang | hung | hung | tell | told | told |
| have | had | had | think | thought | thought |
| hear | heard | heard | throw | threw | thrown |
| hide | hid | hidden | understand | understood | understood |
| hit | hit | hit | wake | woke | woken |
| hold | held | held | wear | wore | worn |
| hurt | hurt | hurt | win | won | won |
| keep | kept | kept | wind | wound | wound |
| know | knew | known | write | wrote | written |
| lead | led | led | | | |

# Skill Index

# Grammar Index

# Topic Index

**162**